INDOMITABLE

Also by Guy Robin
Dysfunction

INDOMITABLE

GUY ROBIN

In memory of Karl Hermann Louis

Poole, Dorset
February 2014

It's as if she's already dead, he thought, as he sat straight-legged on the floor of the lounge, his back against the settee, surrounded by a myriad of black and white photographic prints. This was a little of what was left of his mother's possessions; the remnants of her life. Most of the larger objects and pieces of furniture were gone. Some, like the Noritaki Japanese dinner service, had been snapped up by a collector immediately it was placed on an internet auction site. A few other ornaments were to be kept and shared between the two of them. He wiped his eyes; he was more upset than he would have credited. His mother was not dead, she was suffering from ongoing vascular dementia and between them, Graham and his elder brother Ralph had organised a care home in Scotland, close to where Ralph lived.

His eyes settled on a couple of old cloisonné vases that he remembered from his childhood: a pair of blue china cats, both with chipped ears, and a pair of silver fighting cocks, that he had spent many an hour cleaning when he had still been living at home. In his memory, these silver birds had taken pride of place on top of the once state-of-the-art Sanyo stereo with the direct drive turntable and the reel-to-reel tape deck. The stereo was long gone, a casualty of one of the numerous trips to the municipal dump. He cast his eyes around the room, settling now on the small collection of Hummel figurines spread out on the mantlepiece. One figure of a small girl had

1

once been the object of his juvenile vandalism, when he had decided that she needed some better eyebrows and proceeded to draw some on in HB pencil. Despite being drawn in pencil, the new eyebrows – that gave the figure a distinctly oriental look – had taken enormous effort to remove. He got up from the floor and crossed to the figure for a closer look. *I can still see the bloody eyebrows*, he thought as he gazed at the small statue and smiled.

His mother Anne had lived in the top-floor, three-bedroom apartment since 1985. She owned it outright. When her condition was first diagnosed, Graham, her youngest son, had been able to organise some nursing care, someone to go in and assist her for a few hours every other day. He lived over a hundred miles away from the lovely spot his mother had found overlooking Poole Harbour, so he knew that he needed to find a more permanent arrangement for her. His elder brother, Ralph, was working in Australia, but was due to return within the next few months and they had worked out a plan to provide better and certainly more permanent care for their mother.

Initial discussions with Anne proved to be fruitless. She was in complete denial of any impairment of her faculties and would not entertain the need to move into a care or nursing home. Graham and Ralph had known this was likely to be the case and, having discussed and visited various English care homes, they had ultimately found a small, warm establishment in Scotland not far from Perth. They decided to invite Anne to spend Christmas at Ralph's house in Scotland, which was no more than a fifteen-minute drive to the care home they had selected. Graham and his wife came too, so that they had as large a family Christmas as they could muster. It had been decided that when Ralph's two grown-up children came home for New Year, this would be the perfect excuse to ask Anne if she wouldn't mind staying in a 'nearby' place, where they would look after her, as room at Graham's house would be limited. In reality, by the time it came to move Anne to the home, she had no real idea of where she was and very quickly settled in. She had a lovely bright lounge area, already furnished with one or two pieces that her sons had brought from her apartment in Poole. They had installed a new television and there were a number of her favourite pictures on the wall and other ornaments and memorabilia dotted around the space. She had a connecting en-suite bedroom, with a window overlooking the well-tended garden. One of the features that both Ralph and Graham had liked was the design of the home, being spread out at ground level, meaning that Anne would find it easy to get to the communal areas. The staff were very warm and welcoming and understood that these early days could be a struggle for Anne while she adjusted to her new surroundings.

Christmas came and went and before long February was upon them. Anne had seemingly settled into her new environment. Graham was still bothered by the slightly glazed look in her eyes when he would visit, not altogether sure Anne really knew who he was anymore. Both Graham and Ralph had found time in their respective diaries to visit Anne's apartment for a week at the end of February. The initial aim had been to clear and clean the property, with a view to selling it and using the invested capital to help pay for Anne's care. But after having listened to a selection of estate agents, the brothers had decided that a better option was to prepare the property for the rental market. A three-bedroom, two-bathroom top-floor apartment, commanding spectacular views of Poole Harbour was, in the opinion of every estate agent who visited, not going to be difficult to find a tenant for. The mathematics of the situation also provided an alternative way to fund Anne's care, all the while safeguarding the tangible asset of the apartment.

This was the reason Graham now found himself sitting on the floor of Anne's apartment in Poole, sorting through her residual belongings and working with Ralph to clear, clean and prepare the place for the tenants who would be moving in at the end of the week. Ralph had organised a new carpet in the main bedroom and they had used a carpet cleaner elsewhere in the flat. They had worked hard to clean the bathrooms, all the walls and skirting boards, the balcony and the kitchen, especially the oven and hob. They had installed a brand-new fridge freezer and replaced lights and lampshades, repainted some window frames and completely cleared the garage of thirty years' worth of accumulated 'stuff'. It was now just a case of going through these last few small boxes and wrapping and packing the small objects and ornaments that the brothers had decided to keep. They were just waiting on a man to arrive who had agreed to take the large, incredibly heavy, free-standing oak wardrobe from Anne's bedroom. It was the last piece of furniture, too heavy for Graham and Ralph to lift between them, and almost too large to remove from the apartment in one piece.

The man duly arrived with his van and two burly assistants and together they began to manoeuvre the wardrobe. Even with the three of them it was a major struggle, its bulk and weight causing the three men to strain as they approached the first flight of stairs. Ralph and Graham had continued with packing the last of the belongings to be removed from the apartment. Suddenly there was an almighty crash, followed by some colourful language. Graham and Ralph rushed out to the landing to see the three removal men staring both at each other and downwards. Graham followed their gaze and saw the splintered, shattered remains of the wardrobe, that had come to rest on its side at the foot of the stairs.

"Well, that's one way to get the thing downstairs," Ralph exclaimed.

"Are you all OK?" Graham asked as the three men looked sheepishly at each other. The leader glanced across to Graham and replied, "Errh! Sorry about that, once it started to go, we just couldn't hold onto it."

"We probably should have just broken it up before we removed it anyway," Graham said.

"It should be easier to remove now," Ralph commented.

They all slowly trooped down the stairs to survey the damage and remove the wreckage. Graham suddenly stopped as he saw the side of the wardrobe. The bottom panel now contained a large crack, that revealed a hollow space between the underneath of the wooden structure and the interior floor. The space looked to be about two inches wide.

"Has anyone got a crowbar or a screwdriver?" he asked.

The foreman of the removers went out to his van and returned a few minutes later with a crowbar which he handed to Graham.

Kneeling down to look inside the void between the two floors of the wardrobe, Graham found there was insufficient light to see inside. He gingerly levered the panel with the crowbar. There was a rending, cracking and splintering of the wood around the space, until Graham could put his hand inside the secret shelf. He cautiously felt around before slowly pulling out a large, bulky, dusty manila envelope, measuring about twenty inches by ten. He turned the package over. There was an obvious 'Top Secret' stamp, in a dull red, across the address, which was now very faint, but Graham could see that it was a Ministry of Defence envelope, addressed to The Next of Kin of Mr. H Louis Karl Luddolph, dated 30th September 1960.

H Louis Karl Luddolph was Graham and Ralph's grandfather on their father's side. One of Graham's middle names was Louis, in honour of his grandfather.

Ralph came over to where Graham was sat on the floor

and Graham showed him the envelope; the three wardrobe shifters also moved in for a closer look.

"I think that's all that was in there. Let me reach around and see if there's anything else." Graham put his arm back into the shelf, but all he brought out was a large wad of dust and fluff.

"All right, chaps! if we can leave you to get this thing out of here please?" Ralph asked the workmen. "Graham, let's go back upstairs and have a closer look at what you've found." Ralph helped his younger brother to his feet and the two of them slowly walked back up the stairs and into their mother's apartment.

There were two bar stools in the kitchen by one of the worktops. The two of them sat down next to each other at the breakfast counter and Graham gently placed the large envelope in front of them.

He turned it over to reveal old press stud fasteners closed with a length of thread. The end of the thread was covered in an old piece of sealing wax, imprinted with a crest unfamiliar to either of them.

"It's still sealed," Graham commented. "It's dated September 1963, before I was born, and it's still sealed. Have you any idea what it is?"

"Our grandfather died in 1962," Ralph said. "I was about eight or nine. I knew him, but not well. He was always known to us as Louis or Lou, but his real first name was the much more Germanic Karl. At that time, they lived down in Highcliffe-on-Sea, near Bournemouth. If memory serves, they had a really nice bungalow in Rothesay Drive, near to the golf course and the ruins of Highcliffe Castle. I used to go and spend holidays with them. He was a complicated, quite strict man. You knew he was from Germany originally? I know he came from somewhere near Leipzig and that after the First World War he became a successful engineering distributor somewhere in the Midlands. Our grandmother, Nanny, was his second wife and she was at least fifteen to eighteen years younger than he was, which must have been quite the scandal back then."

"Mum never used to mention him and Nanny never really talked much about him either," Graham recalled as they hunched over this ancient package.

"He married Grace – Nanny – and they just had the one child, our father, David. I think he had two children with his first wife, if memory serves. The daughter was called Freya and the son was called James."

"What do we do?" Graham wondered. "Shall we open it, take it to the Ministry of Defence?"

"I think we should open it, then we can decide." Ralph took the lead, as he always did when it was between the brothers. "Get me that carpet knife from the toolbox in the spare room please." Graham returned momentarily with a small silver-coloured blade.

"Thanks." Ralph examined the package. "I think I'll cut the thread and try and leave the wax seal as intact as possible," he decided.

"OK then, let's do it," Graham said encouragingly.

Ralph tried to lever the blade of the carpet knife under the taut ancient thread, but as he did so the dull red wax began to crack. As Ralph tried a second time to come at it from a different angle, the increase in pressure caused the friable wax seal to break, suddenly releasing the flap of the envelope and causing a mass of letters, loose papers and photographs to spill out onto the kitchen worktop. Ralph leaned forward and picked up a small, creased photograph.

"That's Louis with a young child and he's pushing a pram," Ralph exclaimed.

Ralph turned the picture over. Graham leaned in to see what was written on the back.

'Lou's 70th Birthday July 1955. Rothesay Drive; with Karl and Ralph'

"That's me in the pram then," said Ralph, smiling. "I wasn't even a year old and I don't know who the other child is. Amazing! I never knew anything about this."

Graham too reached forward and gently picked up a photograph from the pile. It was face down, but Graham could tell it was a photograph by the feel of the paper. There was also some faint writing across the back.

'Lou's funeral – 21st September 1962'

Ralph looked on as Graham slowly turned the photograph over to reveal a small gathering of people outside a church, captured in black and white.

"That's Grace, our grandma." Ralph pointed at the figure in the foreground, all dressed in black, shaking hands with several formally dressed men wearing dark suits and long dark coats.

"Is that our dad?" Graham asked, pointing to a uniformed figure further away from the camera towards the left of the picture behind Grace.

"Yep, that's him in his RAF uniform, shaking hands with…" Ralph never finished his sentence; he just stopped and stared at the photograph.

The figure just in shot on the left-hand edge of the 8x10-inch picture was shaking hands with their father David. He was roundly built, slightly hunched over, wearing a thick full-length coat. He was supported by a cane in his left hand. He wore an instantly recognisable tall black hat and as if there was any further doubt, he had a large cigar clamped in his mouth.

"My God, that's Winston Churchill!" Graham exclaimed.

Jade Bight, Wilhelmshaven
February 1903

He stood rigidly to attention within the squad of twenty men. He stood motionless, but his eyes watched everything, his other senses heightened, waiting to be called. His mind was figuring out the play, what was his best course of action when they called his name. He knew what was expected, they had all had the training and been instructed as to how the test would be conducted.

"Ackermann!" The first to be called stepped out of the line away to his left, brought his legs together with a smart thump and bawled at the top of his voice, "Sir!"

Two of the training staff affixed a thick rope belt like a girdle around his waist, then attached another rope to a metal ring woven into the strands of the thick hemp line around his waist. This other rope disappeared towards the rear of the ship, where it was threaded through a pulley system. Underneath it was a folding rope ladder with wooden rungs that had been lowered into the water. The cadre of recruits all stood firm, in spite of the fresh wind from the North Sea.

"JUMP!" Ackermann did so without the slightest hesitation from his position somewhere amidships on the port side of the ship. As he disappeared from view over the side, the other recruits were unable to see his plunge into the water; rather they heard a splash, followed by numerous bellowed commands for him to swim to the stern. A heavy-set instructor at the stern now took charge of the rope at the pulley and proceeded to haul on the line, keeping it taut. Out of sight, Ackermann was presumably either swimming to the stern of the ship or being dragged there by the instructor hauling on the rope.

Karl Hermann Louis Luddolph stood fast waiting his turn, allowing his mind to wander briefly over the circumstances that had led to him, as a young man of eighteen, standing on a training vessel in the Imperial German navy. He was at the start of week two of his recruit training course, with possibly three years of national service stretching away ahead of him. Even though born in Germany, Karl had a strange feeling around his fellow recruits. His family had emigrated to Great Britain four years previously and settled in Leicester. It had been his decision to return to Germany to fulfil his obligation of at least three years of national service required of all German men, once they had completed school. If he had not completed his service it would have become difficult for him to return to Germany, he figured, but this was not the motivation; rather it was Karl's willingness to serve and his devotion to and support for the country of his birth.

Ackermann reappeared at the rear of the ship having climbed up the rope ladder and now stood shivering on the rear deck, the thick dark trousers and white cotton smock clinging to his thin white body. The thick-set trainer who was in charge of the rope released Ackermann from his bondage and handed the rope girdle to another instructor who walked with it back to the squad of recruits. Ackermann was handed a grey blanket and directed to the starboard side of the vessel, where an urn of hot Bovril was waiting for him. Ackermann squelched over to the urn while wrapping the blanket around his shoulders, leaving wet footprints on the wooden deck.

"Armbruster!" The instructor called out the next recruit,

who immediately stepped forward and was shackled to the thick hemp ring and connected to the long line.

"JUMP!" And instantly Armbruster leapt over the side, to embark on his own swimming test.

Once again Karl watched and waited and returned to his musing. Born on 2nd July 1885, the second of three children to his parents Albert Franz and Charlotte. His elder brother Maximillian was now a qualified machine operator, working in the textile mills of Leicester. He had inherited the skill in part from his father, who was now a successful upholsterer in the same city thanks to an apprenticeship served in the textile mills of their town of birth, Apolda in Thuringia, southwest of Leipzig. Karl's younger brother Willy was still at school in Leicester.

The decision to emigrate had been a tough one for Karl's father. A sense of desperation set in as economic stability fell apart in Germany in the 1870s and they were plunged into recession. This was followed by a more sinister sense of foreboding as the gradual move towards empire and right-wing imperialism crept across the country.

"Baumgardner!" Karl was jolted from his memories as another candidate for the swimming test dove over the side of the ship into the frigid, still waters of the Jade Bight.

Of all his family Karl was the least inclined to emigrate. He had been successful at school and was already keen to be part of the military structure of Germany, only for his father to pluck them from his homeland and relocate to the Midlands of England. He had continued to do well with his studies and his command of English was very good after the four years he had been resident in Leicester. Despite this, Karl was still German to his core. He had a feeling of loyalty and belief in his country of birth and saw this time in England as just a temporary arrangement. His application to do his national service with the Imperial German navy would begin to change this.

"Dittmann!" The identified recruit shuffled forward, a little less confidently than those who had leapt over the side of the ship before him. As the order to jump was barked at him, he hesitated just long enough for the closest instructor to make a telling impact with his booted left foot on Dittmann's backside, launching him over the rail with a departing wail.

Karl smiled inwardly. He knew how to swim. He had been thrown into the school swimming pool by the physical training teacher at six years of age and was instantly confident in his ability to perform rudimentary strokes before the teacher saw his natural flair and taught him the front crawl and breaststroke. By eleven he was school champion, by fifteen he could swim several miles at a time, usually in open water and in all weathers.

Dittmann was dragged out of the water at the stern of the vessel, coughing up a fair quantity of the estuary, and he crept away to join the others who had completed the test at the urn.

"Freundlich!" The next in line stepped up to be attached to the rope. They were moving quickly through the complement of twenty recruits taking the Imperial German navy swimming test. Karl was trying to calculate how many before it was his turn to leap off the ship and drop thirty feet to the cold, dark surface of the saltwater estuary that lay to the south of Wilhelmshaven. Up to now none of the recruits had shown any inclination to attempt the test without the attachment of the safety rope. Karl was still deciding about this; the choice had been offered at the briefing for the test. Karl had some questions at that time, but decided to remain quiet and wait until his name was called. Freundlich reappeared a short time after his departure over the side at the stern of the boat and joined the other sodden candidates who had now completed the test.

"Goertzen!" A tall, fair-haired recruit stepped forward and in a clipped tone said, "Sir, may I attempt the test without the safety line?"

The instructors looked first at Goertzen and then at the chief instructor, who simply nodded.

"JUMP!" the supervising staff officer shouted and without time to blink, Goertzen fell over the side in a tangle of arms and legs and a loud splash was heard on the deck of the ship shortly afterwards. Three instructors rushed to the guard rail and looked over. After about twenty to thirty seconds, the instructor in the middle shrugged off his jacket and leapt over the side in a majestic swallow dive. The other instructors now shouted for their colleague in the water to move to the left and ahead of his position. After another pause in shouting, a voice from the water was heard. "Lower that rope." The other training staff lowered the rope, then with the help of the larger staff member from the stern they all hauled until the apparently lifeless body of Goertzen was dragged back onto the deck. The chief instructor pounced on him, put him on his back and ran his finger around the inside of his mouth. He tilted his head back and clasping the recruit's nose, breathed five large breaths into him, then immediately began pumping on his chest before repeating the breaths again. As he embarked on another set of chest pumping, Goertzen suddenly expelled a mixture of sea water and vomit and began to cough as he forced air back into his lungs. "Gentlemen, take him below please," the chief instructor ordered, as he nonchalantly returned to his seated position on a large deck locker near to the anchor chain housing.

"Hattendorf!" The next recruit readily agreed to be connected to the safety line and immediately launched himself over the side. Karl reckoned there were another two recruits before they got to him. In his application to join the navy for his service, he remembered that he had put down his swimming history, but also that he had been living in England for the past four years. He could only wonder how this was going to be regarded by the staff, the officers and his fellow recruits.

He refocused on Hattendorf as he clambered back onto the deck having completed his test and shuffled across to the warm Bovril and blankets.

"Jurgens!" The next trainee stepped forward and came to a proper attention. Karl had met Sigmund (Ziggy) Jurgens at the train station in Hamburg as they were waiting for the connecting train to take them up to Wilhelmshaven to begin their time in the navy. They had sat opposite each other on the train and after about ten to fifteen minutes of awkward staring at each other, Karl spoke. "Hello, my name is Karl and I presume we are both heading up to join the navy for national service? It's very nice to meet you," and Karl offered his right hand.

"I am Sigmund, but everyone always calls me Ziggy," Ziggy answered, and they shook hands.

That had been a little under two weeks ago and the two had become firm friends. Ziggy was from a small town in Bavaria near Munich called Jesenwang. He had listened as Karl explained that he had been living in England. Ziggy thought it both fascinating and adventurous to have been living in a foreign land at such a young age. They both seemed to have the same interests in outdoor pursuits, like cycling, swimming and hiking. Karl knew that Ziggy, with his superior size and weight and especially the breadth of his shoulders, would be a formidable competitor in any swimming tests.

"Sir, may I complete the test without the safety line?" Ziggy asked the instructor as he approached with the rope. The instructor stepped back, then picked up a metal board in the shape of an arrow.

"I heard you were one of our swimmers, Jurgens. Good! Once I give the command to jump, I want you to surface and swim away from the ship for one hundred yards. Then stop and tread water. I will then ask you to return and you must follow the direction I indicate from this arrow. Do you understand?"

"Yes, sir," Ziggy answered.

"Jump!" the instructor bawled in Ziggy's ear.

Ziggy leapt over the side and rose to the surface. He calmly and deliberately swam away from the ship in a slow, confident front crawl. When he estimated that he had travelled the required distance, he stopped and turned to face the side of the ship.

"Now swim back and follow the arrow," the instructor shouted, holding the metal arrow above his head.

Ziggy began to swim back to the ship, this time using a breaststroke. The instructor moved the arrow to the left and then to the right at random times. Ziggy reacted by swimming in the direction that the arrow pointed, returning to the ship in a zigzagging pattern, until he swam around to the stern and hauled himself out of the water, up the rope ladder onto the deck.

"Good, Jurgens! Get yourself a hot drink and a blanket." The chief instructor then addressed the recruits. "All of you listen. This test is designed to show us that you can still follow commands despite having either jumped or fallen into the water. It is how we would manage a man overboard situation. It is vitally important that you are able to still follow orders and instructions, in spite of the cold water and the additional stress falling overboard will cause you. Is that clear to you all?"

"Yes, sir!" the recruits responded as they all watched Ziggy Jurgens pad athletically up to the urn and pour himself some hot Bovril.

"Katz…En…Ell…En…Bog…En!" the instructor stumbled through the lengthy surname.

"Sir." The red-faced recruit stepped forward.

"Do you have a nickname perhaps?" the instructor asked.

"Yes, sir, I have always been known as 'Katz'."

"Then from now on you will be addressed as Katz, do you all understand?" The instructor cast his eyes around the other recruits, who all nodded.

"Sir, may I please be attached to the safety line?" Katz asked.

Once connected, the recruit was ordered to jump. Katz disappeared over the side and completed his test in good time, quickly moving along to the growing number of blanket-clad sailors who had been in the water.

"Luddolph!" Finally it was Karl's turn. He stepped forward and brought himself to attention in front of the instructor.

"Sir, may I complete the test without the rope?"

"Ah! Luddolph, the English swimmer!" the instructor offered, and his colleagues laughed. "Well, you watched Jurgens. Follow my instructions once you are in the water. Just do the same as Jurgens. After you dive in, come to the surface then swim one hundred yards or so away from the ship, then turn and follow my directional instructions from the arrow. Do you understand?

"Yes, sir," Karl answered calmly.

"JUMP!" the instructor screamed.

Karl catapulted himself over the side of the vessel into the dark water of the Jade Bight. Despite expecting the water to be cold, it still took Karl's breath away, as he fought his way back to the surface. Once he had regained his composure, he began a slow, economical front crawl away from the ship until he reached a point far enough away. He stopped, turned to face the ship and saw the instructor indicating with the arrow that he should swim back to the left; then the arrow went to the right. Karl followed the instructions until he found himself at the foot of the rope ladder at the stern of the ship. He climbed the ladder and was greeted by the burly instructor.

"Good test, Luddolph!"

"Excellent test, Luddolph," said the chief instructor. "Get some warm Bovril inside you and take a blanket."

Karl tried to supress the urge to smile, but failed as a grin crept across his face.

"Well done, Karl," Ziggy whispered as Karl poured himself a cup of the warm brown liquid from the urn.

"Meitinger!" The next in line was called forward. Karl now watched from his vantage point, closer to the side rail of the ship, as Meitinger flipped himself over the side of the small corvette.

The names were now called with what felt like increased regularity as the familiarity of the task became clearer to the recruits waiting at the end of the alphabetical list.

Nesselrode completed the test, with rope attached, in good time, then struggled to climb the ladder and was hauled aboard by the enormous instructor at the stern.

Oberhauser elected to try without the safety line and swam out to a position away from the ship, like both Karl and Ziggy had done. By the time he returned to the stern of the ship and hauled himself up the rope ladder, he was on his knees, wheezing with the effort.

"Good effort, Oberhauser. A case of too much too soon!" the instructor commented as he was assisted by the other recruits to get a blanket and a hot drink.

Peukert, like Oberhauser, attempted to complete the test without a safety line, but, as he returned to the ship, he didn't follow the direction indicated on the arrow despite shouts from the instructors, and had to have a rope thrown down the ladder to assist his climb out of the water.

"Peukert, there's no shame in completing the test with a safety line. This is week two; you will improve as the course continues. Now get warm and get some fluid in you." The chief instructor, albeit strict in his bearing, made a point of encouraging Peukert as he squelched past.

Karl watched the chief instructor, a man he now knew to be Oberstabsbootsmann (Chief Petty Officer 1st Class or Warrant Officer – equivalent) Otto Nadler. He was an enormous solidly built man, probably in his mid-thirties with a sharp blond crew cut and sporting a pair of extravagant waxed moustaches. His severe outward appearance gave way to glimpses of a benevolent spirit and a capacity to build up and encourage his charges, rather than break them down. At least that's what Karl surmised at this early stage of his training.

Next up, Raab took his cue from the chief instructor and had a safety line attached and completed his test without incident, in perhaps the slowest time of the squad so far.

"Come on, Raab, it'll be dark soon," one of the instructors shouted as Raab wearily climbed the rope ladder.

Rausch and Rinder, like two peas in a pod, completed the test attached to the safety line, with no incident and no comments from the instructing staff.

Three left to complete the test.

"Ackermann!"

"Sir," the recruit who had undertaken the test first replied, startled at hearing his name as he huddled with the other trainees at the Bovril urn.

"Ackermann, are you warm enough under that blanket?" Oberstabsbootsmann Nadler asked.

"Yes, sir," Ackermann replied.

"Good. It's important that we all learn resilience. Circumstances may present themselves where the effects of long exposure to cold wind and weather, when you are already soaked to the skin, have to be endured. With both fortitude and an understanding of the feelings associated with exposure to the cold and the frequent experience of it in our cosy training environment, we will prepare you for that eventuality. Do you all see that?"

"Yes, sir," Karl and the rest of the recruits answered in unison.

"Forgive me, Deckoffizier (Warrant Officer 2nd Class) Lowenstam, please continue," the chief instructor said to his colleague with the clip board, supervising the test.

"Thank you, Staff. Samter!"

Samter stepped forward, declined the offer of a safety line, and vaulted over the guard rail and into the water, all in the one movement. With guidance from the instructor with the arrow, he zigzagged his way back to the stern of the ship, deftly climbed the rope ladder, and marched past the chief instructor, who caught his eye and nodded sagely at him.

"Schwartz!"

The smaller of the two lonely figures still left to complete the test strode forward and brought his heels together in an impressive movement.

"Impressive, Schwartz. I almost saluted you then," the invigilating instructor said.

"Sir, may I have the safety line please?" Schwartz quietly asked.

"A polite recruit! Young man, you may." The instructor tied on the safety line.

"Jump!"

Schwartz hit the water with an almighty splash, surfaced, coughed up some sea water, then managed to propel himself around to the stern of the ship and return to the deck in reasonably good order.

"Final man then; you are Wunderlich?" The instructor addressed the last dry recruit on the deck.

"Yes, sir. May I try without the safety line?" the very thin, but very tall final recruit asked.

"Wunderlich, you may. JUMP!" The last word out of the mouth of the instructor almost blew Wunderlich over the side. Once on the surface he performed an impressive stroke out to a good distance from the ship. His return was textbook zigzagging all the way back to the vessel. He quickly joined the other recruits, now starting to visibly shiver in the wind that was now whipping across the estuary.

"All right, Wunderlich, get your hot drink, but all of you listen." Oberstabsbootsmann Nadler rose to his feet and addressed the blanket-clad gaggle of recruits.

"We are here to test you, yes, but not to break and dishearten you. We wish to build you into a strong, cohesive unit of independently-minded young professional German sailors. My staff and I will keep you busy, but we are here to guide and to listen as well. It is a good start today. We will do this test every two weeks and by the end of the training, I guarantee no one will need the safety line. Gentlemen, now go below, get dry and change into your day rig and report back here in one hour."

"Yes, sir," the recruits replied as one, and made their way into the superstructure of the ship.

Kiel

June 1903

The city of Kiel lies about fifty miles north of Hamburg, to the southeast of the Jutland peninsula, on the southern shore of the Baltic Sea. Along with Wilhelmshaven, Kiel was designated as an Imperial war harbour, or *Reichskriegshafen*, and regarded as Imperial Germany's main naval port. It has hosted an annual sailing regatta since 1882 and this was the reason that SMS *Kaiser Wilhelm II* was anchored in the bay alongside one of her sister ships, SMS *Kaiser Friedrich III*. They were there to be seen by the rest of the world as signs of the growing strength of the Imperial German navy, and also as prestigious viewing platforms for the various dignitaries and officials who had come to watch the sailing regatta.

Karl had joined the ship in early June and almost immediately they had set sail for Kiel from the training port of Wilhelmshaven. Four months of training had come to an end for the twenty sailors on Karl's course, and they had been equally distributed between five ships that made up I Squadron. When the postings had been affixed to the notice-board, the recruits had excitedly gathered around to discover which ship they had been posted to. Karl scanned the neatly typed piece of paper and smiled inwardly when he saw that Ziggy was also posted to SMS *Kaiser Wilhelm II*. A tap on his shoulder, followed by a bear hug, and he felt himself lifted off the ground.

"Karl, we're together, it's brilliant." Ziggy was beaming with delight to be allocated to the same ship as his friend.

"It's excellent, Ziggy. Who else is with us?" Whilst overjoyed to be on the same ship as his best friend, Karl was curious as to which other recruits would join them.

"Well, Henning Schwartz, just about the politest man I ever met. Konrad Hattendorf; I've hardly spoken to him. And then good old Katz! He's such a laugh. We have the most brilliant group. Now do you remember all those facts about the ship that we spent two entire rest days at the end of our training in the town library studying?" Ziggy asked.

"It's all in here," Karl smiled as he tapped the side of his head and they sauntered away from the melee of other recruits keen to find their future ships. Karl was confident he could answer most of the facts about his new ship.

SMS *Kaiser Wilhelm II* was 411 feet long with a beam of 66 feet. She was powered by three steam engines that drove three screw propellers. The power came from four coal-fired boilers providing an output of over 12,000 horsepower, which drove the ship along at a maximum speed of 17.5 knots. At the time Karl and Ziggy joined the ship it had a complement of forty officers and just over six hundred enlisted men. Karl had a memory for numbers and was aware of the tendency for officers to check a sailor's knowledge. Numbers were the most common way to do this. He therefore also knew that, as the flagship of the fleet, the ship was carrying an additional complement of twelve officers and sixty enlisted men, who were the Admiral's staff.

All five of the recently arrived recruits aboard the ship knew that questions would be fired at them at any time from anybody of senior rank to them, which was pretty much the entire ship's crew. So, when they had first arrived and been given a guided tour of the vessel, Karl was the one who was able to nail the numbers. This included the armaments of the ship and the defensive measures taken when constructing the hull and superstructure. Karl could be called upon to assist a fellow trainee, if he felt the answers were not immediately forthcoming from his colleague.

The ship's keel had been laid on 26th October 1896 at the Kaiserliche Werft in Wilhelmshaven. She was launched on 14th September 1897, at which time she was christened by Konteradmiral (Rear Admiral) Prince Heinrich, for his brother Kaiser Wilhelm II. The ship was formally commissioned on 13th February 1900 and after completing her sea trials in June of the same year, she was assigned to II Division of I Squadron as the flagship of the Active Battle Fleet. In July 1900, as a result of I Division of I Squadron being despatched to Asian waters to help suppress the Boxer rebellion, SMS *Kaiser Wilhelm II* was transferred to I Division to remain in German waters and be the flagship of the fleet at the start of the Kiel Regatta that June.

Karl and Ziggy and the other three new recruits all quickly joined in the daily tasks of a junior rating on a naval battleship. This seemed to involve an endless amount of cleaning and polishing. Then, there were the twice-daily drills and deck exercises to prepare for an unseen enemy which, from Karl's reckoning, seemed only ever likely to be the British navy. They were supervised by, and reported to, Deckoffizier Hartmann. He was a tall man in his early thirties, with a smart dark crew cut and an equally smart uniform including the most highly polished shoes Karl had ever seen. He had a strict demeanour and could be quite curt and brusque when delivering orders to his charges, but at this early stage of his service, Karl found him to be efficient and fair.

With the festivities of the Kiel Regatta week at an end, the ship posted that their next orders were to sail out through the complex myriad of islands that made up the east of Denmark, out into Swedish waters, where they were to rendezvous with the rest of I Squadron of the German fleet. This would give Karl another opportunity to see the waters of the Kattegat (between the Swedish and Danish coasts) and the Skagerrak (the sea between northern Denmark and southern Norway, before it forms the North Sea). One of the exercises was to perform a blockade around the Norwegian city of Kristiansand using the five battleships and six supporting vessels. The idea was to demonstrate how quickly such a manoeuvre could be accomplished. Once Admiral Hans von Koester, on board SMS *Kaiser Wilhelm II*, was satisfied that they had achieved their blockade, orders were given for the ships of I Squadron to disperse quickly. Some returned to the ports of Wilhelmshaven for annual maintenance and refits, some went to Kiel. SMS *Kaiser Wilhelm II* sailed back towards the Kattegat and, as a reward for the excellent standard of seamanship, the entire ship's company were gifted a week's shore leave at the port of Frederikshavn, in northeastern Denmark.

Ziggy took the lead in making sure that Karl saw all of the sights in the small Danish town. They made an impressive sight themselves in their smart Imperial German naval uniforms as they sat watching the people pass by doing their Christmas shopping. Ziggy's easy-going nature, good looks and charm made him a magnet for the various young ladies who caught his eye. Karl was much more reserved and found himself to be rather awkward and shy in the company of women. Ziggy was able to be charming enough for the two of them, and they were never short of company at the many restaurants and bars they frequented during that all too brief week's leave. Karl, although uneasy in the company they kept, always seemed to fall madly in love with every girl he was introduced to. Ziggy could see it in his eyes every time it happened.

"Once again, he's in love," Ziggy laughed as he watched his friend's eyes glaze over the moment whichever girl sat opposite them smiled in his direction. Karl blushed a deep crimson and took a sip of his schnapps.

"Your friend is so quiet and reserved. I think he has class," the girl giggled as she gave her appraisal of Karl's stoic demeanour.

"Class? Yes, I believe you're right, my dear, the boy has class. You hear that, my friend? You have class." And Ziggy punched Karl playfully on the shoulder.

Several hours later the two sailors stumbled slightly as they climbed up the gangplank to their ship. Karl was able to subtly help Ziggy stand straight as they approached the officer of the watch.

Karl was relieved to see that this officer was none other than Oberstabsbootsmann Otto Nadler, their former chief instructor and now the senior non-commissioned officer on board the vessel.

"Ah! Jurgens and young Luddolph. A pleasant evening ashore, gentlemen?"

"Sir, we have spent time in the company of some wonderful locals from the town, who showed us some of the sights that their Danish city is blessed with. We enjoyed a large meal and I suspect that Jurgens may have eaten something that didn't agree with him," Karl countered, hoping that Ziggy would remain upright.

"Well, I suspect that is entirely the reason for his inability to stand unaided. I suggest you take him below and I will see you two for an early morning swim at, shall we say, 6 a.m.?" And Oberstabsbootsmann Nadler walked forward to the bow of the ship, smiling as he passed the two recruits.

"Class, Luddolph! She was right, pure class," Ziggy whispered as his friend manhandled him through the deck hatch towards their sleeping quarters.

Aalesund, Norway
January 1904

In the early hours of Saturday 23rd January 1904, the small Norwegian town of Aalesund was quiet. A little after 2 a.m., one of the cows crammed into the barn of the Aalesund Preserving Company factory kicked a small oil lamp that was placed on a hook much lower than it should have been. The fallen torch quickly caught the straw and wooden barn alight. By the time two fire crews had been alerted to the blaze at the factory, the conflagration had spread to neighbouring buildings. Sparks and embers were being blown across the town by a strong gale coming from the southwest. Despite brave attempts at putting in fire breaks and pulling down some of the wooden buildings to create a gap, the fire simply jumped the gap and continued to spread across the entire town. Over ten thousand people were forced to flee their homes and seek shelter off the island where the town was situated. Some were able to flee by boat; the elderly and the sick were placed in carts and wagons and the majority fled on foot. It was reported that one elderly lady turned back to her house to retrieve her purse. She was the only known fatality of the night. The local governor, Alexander Kielland, stated that well over two hundred people had sheltered in the local Borgund church. By morning, it was clear that virtually all the buildings on the main island that makes up Aalesund, Aspoya, had been destroyed.

"Stand at ease, men," Oberstabsbootsmann Nadler commanded the company of other non-commissioned officers and men on the aft deck of the ship.

"We have new orders to sail at once to the small Norwegian town of Aalesund. A week ago, they were devastated by a serious fire in the town which destroyed most of the buildings, and the residents need our help. This news has just reached our high command. We have been ordered by the Kaiser himself. Aalesund is an area he knows well and he spent his holidays there as a boy. The place is precious to our Kaiser and we are to go and help the good people of Aalesund to recover from this disaster. You understand, men?"

"Yes, sir!" came back the loud cry from the entire company in unison.

"We must first go into Wilhelmshaven and collect timber, nails, tools, blankets, tents, clothing and anything else we feel may be of use to the people of Aalesund. You will divide into your squads and each squad leader has a list of what you are to collect from the town. We need to be thorough but fast – the ship will sail in four hours. Company!" Oberstabsbootmann Nadler bawled.

The company came smartly to attention.

"Now to your business, gentlemen. Dismissed."

The gathering of just under a hundred men all broke from their positions and rushed off in various directions under the leadership of their officers.

Karl and Ziggy's squad were responsible for acquiring tents and other canvas cloth to make temporary shelters. They gathered around Deckoffizier Hartmann who shared his orders.

"Katz, Hattendorf, you go and find as many tents as you can. Jurgens, Luddolph, you know the town now. You head to the sailing chandlers around the port and collect as much canvas cloth as you can. Go on, off you go."

Karl and Ziggy were quickly down the gangplank and

away into the port of Wilhelmshaven on their errand.

"Karl, do you know where Aalesund is?" Ziggy asked as they hurried towards the area where they knew there to be ships and sailing vessel suppliers.

"I do. Some of us were actually listening during our training! It's built on a few small islands off the west coast of Norway. I suppose it's about two hundred miles north of the city of Bergen. Does that help, my friend?"

"How am I never surprised that you know everything, Karl?" Ziggy laughed, as the two of them disappeared into the collection of shops around the port.

They returned in good time having secured the services of a local truck to transport the yards of canvas fabric they had obtained. With the help of some other sailors, the load was soon stored aboard the ship along with piles of timber, lashed down on the afterdeck, and a myriad of other equipment and supplies considered to be necessary for the mission. The SMS *Kaiser Wilhelm II* sailed with the tide that very afternoon. They were joined by SMS *Kaiser Wilhelm der Grosse*, SMS *Kaiser Friedrich III* and SMS *Kaiser Barbarossa*. The ships kept up an average speed of 15 knots and made it to Aalesund in a little under forty hours.

Upon arrival, there was a flurry of activity as the four ships anchored close to shore. Tenders, barges and other boats came out to greet the visitors and help transport the much-needed supplies and equipment to the other islands in the area where the evacuated people were waiting. Karl was despatched with his squad to assist all the ships' carpenters, who were already building wooden frames. Karl's squad was detailed to cover these with canvas to create temporary shelters for the displaced townsfolk.

Karl watched keenly as the carpenters worked. They also built raised platforms out of planks, to keep the bottom of the shelters off the cold frozen ground. Karl took it all in. He watched how they crafted the joints and put spars in to add strength to the structures. Within hours, there were between twenty and thirty of these makeshift shelters ready to be used by the Aalesund evacuees. By now the fleet's kitchen staff had a field canteen set up and were serving hot soup and stew with bread to as many of the Aalesund people as they could. Karl and Ziggy stood back and watched as some of the shelters they had created were filled with families, offering their thanks and shaking their hands.

"Makes you glad to be alive, eh Karl?" Ziggy nodded as they watched two young children look up and smile at a couple of ships' carpenters taking a break from their labours.

"Not what I expected to be doing as a naval seaman, but it does show how positive you can be as a collective, all of our fleet helping these poor people," Karl replied as he studied the burgeoning encampment they had helped create that afternoon.

"I thought I might find you two malingerers shirking the real work," came a familiar shout from behind the two of them and they both turned together to be faced by the towering figure of Oberstabsbootsmann Nadler. "Where is Deckoffizier Hartmann?"

"Sir, he's down amongst the shelters, allocating spaces," Ziggy said, pointing.

"Good, stay there you two. I have need of my two best swimmers!" And with that Nadler strode off in search of their Deckoffizier, leaving the two naval ratings wondering what he had in store for them.

Later, all became clear.

"We have a small problem with the rudder," Nadler explained. "According to the chief engineer, it won't respond fully when put hard to port. We can turn to the left, but something's stopping the rudder from moving right across its axis. Before we send a diving team down there, I want to see if you two can spot what the problem is and possibly remedy it, without the need for the dive team. Do you understand?"

"We can dive one after the other, Chief Nadler," Ziggy offered.

"Right, let's get you both in one of the boats and in position at the stern of the ship."

By the time they were in the small boat, they had a complement made up of Karl and Ziggy, Otto Nadler and two other naval ratings to help pull each of the swimmers out of the cold, dark water.

"The engineering team have rigged an electric floodlight, which they've lowered into the water, to see if you two can see anything when you go down there. So who's going first?" Nadler asked.

"I will," said Ziggy. "Let me see if I can assess the problem, then Karl can follow me and try and resolve the issue as he has a longer breath than me."

"Suit you, Luddolph?" Nadler asked Karl.

"Yes, sir. We may both need to take it in turns if the obstruction is hard to remove," Karl replied.

"Off you go then, Jurgens. Be careful, and don't stay down there too long," the NCO ordered.

Ziggy dove over the side of the small lifeboat they had taken from the ship. The eyes of the others followed him as he disappeared and Oberstabsbootsmann Nadler clicked a stopwatch. They all held their breath in time with Ziggy.

"Thirty seconds," Nadler called.

Karl kept his gaze on the frigid water.

"One minute."

Almost before the words were out of his mouth, Ziggy reappeared and grabbed the side of the lifeboat. The two ratings hauled him aboard, threw some thick towels to him and then a large grey blanket as he sat shivering in the centre of the boat.

"Well, did you see anything?" Nadler asked.

"Sir, it's still really dark down there, but there is something wrapped around the rudder shaft," Ziggy reported. "I could feel it rather than see it. It's a material of some kind We could try and cut it off but it will be too much for one dive. We will need to alternate, cutting the material away between us."

"Luddolph," Nadler ordered. "Take one of the knives and see if, as Jurgens says, it might be possible to cut this obstruction free."

"Yes, sir."

Karl picked up a 6-inch, slightly curved bladed knife from the bottom of the lifeboat, took some deep breaths, then promptly dove over the side and down into the sea off Aalesund. He felt the shock of the coldness of the water and the constriction in his chest as he descended towards the dim glow of the electric light. The view was shadowy at best, but Karl could make out the outline of the hull of the ship and the rudder at the stern. He could just make out something bulky around the vertical shaft upon which the rudder moved. He felt the roughness of the object and immediately began cutting into it with the knife. A small piece came free and Karl jammed it into the pocket of his trousers. He continued to cut as layers of the coarse rope-like material fell away from the rudder shaft. Karl continued as long as he could, then turned and ascended to the surface to be met by the arms of his colleagues, who hauled him back into the bobbing lifeboat.

Oberstabsbootsmann Nadler waited patiently for Karl to get his breath, then caught his eye as Karl looked up.

"Sir, I cut some of the obstruction free," and he pulled the piece from his sodden trouser pocket.

They all stared at the small ball of knotted rope and twine held in Karl's palm.

"It's part of a large fishing net!" Nadler stated. "Happens frequently when we spend time close to shore. I suspected that's what it was. Right, I'm sure you two can shift it. Your turn, Jurgens." And their chief supervisor sat back and pulled a large, intricately carved Meerschaum pipe from inside his tunic and set about cleaning, then loading it, before igniting the contents of the bowl.

In the meantime, Ziggy had swept up another knife and dived into the water. Nadler multi-tasked by commencing the stopwatch again as he gently sucked on his pipe. The sweet flavour of the tobacco smoke billowed around him, as he timed the disappearance of his two swimming recruits.

By the time their senior officer had inverted his pipe and was gently knocking out its contents against the side of the boat, both Karl and Ziggy had made about half a dozen dives each down to the rudder. As Karl reappeared again, his hand gripping the side of the boat, Nadler looked up and waited for the latest report.

Karl sat shivering under the blanket the ratings had draped over his shoulders, once they had pulled him aboard.

"Sir, the obstruction has been completely removed. I believe the rudder will now move freely in either direction and to the full limit of its range."

"Excellent work, the pair of you. Now we need to get you both warm and dry with some hot Bovril inside you. Back to the ship please, gentlemen." And the Oberstabsbootsmann indicated that the two other ratings should row the party back to their ship.

It was soon common knowledge amongst the fleet of vessels moored just off the island town of Aalesund that two new recruits had free-dived and removed the obstruction to the rudder of the *Kaiser Wilhelm*. The diving master on board jokingly threatened to retire, as he had clearly been made redundant by the actions of these two "young upstarts".

Word soon reached the fleet commander, Admiral Hans von Koester, that two serving recruits aboard his flagship had performed this feat. He hastily conferred with his fleet captains and together they devised a swimming competition between the four vessels. Work to create shelters for the displaced residents of Aalesund had now largely been completed, and the Norwegian authorities were at the scene to take over the relief operation. The Admiral thought that such a competition would engender a healthy spirit of competition amongst his sailors, and also provide something of a spectacle for the beleaguered people of Aalesund before the fleet weighed anchor and sailed south.

"Gentlemen, please listen carefully, I will explain the rules and route of this swimming race."

Otto Nadler was holding court on the packed afterdeck of the *Kaiser Wilhelm*. Officers and sailors had found vantage points amongst the superstructure of the ship, to best observe the race about to commence. The four ships were lined up parallel to each other about two hundred metres apart. The shoreline was packed with the townsfolk of Aalesund and the Norwegian emergency support teams, who had all rushed out to watch their German saviours and to thank them for their humanitarian efforts in providing shelter, food and support.

"Upon my signal, the swimmers are to enter the water and swim to the *Wilhelm der Grosse*, then swim under her hull and on to the *Kaiser Barbarossa*. Once again, they are to swim under her, then surface and finally swim to the *Kaiser Friedrich*. The winner will be the first swimmer to touch the side of the *Kaiser Friedrich*, do you all understand?"

"Yes, sir!" the eight swimmers lined up on the deck answered in unison. They were all liberally coated with a thick layer of goose fat to insulate them from the cold, and doing their last stretches before the command to start was given.

"For the benefit of all, our eight competitors are as follows." Otto Nadler cleared his throat and theatrically unrolled a piece of paper.

"Representing SMS *Kaiser Friedrich III*, Sepp Dalman and

young recruit, Rolf Wunderlich." A polite cheer from on deck for the first two swimmers to be announced.

"Representing SMS *Wilhelm der Grosse,* the experienced Martin Fellner and another new recruit, Johann Samter." A raucous cheer from across the water from the deck of the *Wilhelm der Grosse.*

"Representing the *Kaiser Barbarossa,* two veterans of our fleet, known to many of you from competitions past. I give you Ronald Bartels and Matthias Hirsch." A polite round of applause for the two men from the *Kaiser Barbarossa.*

"Finally, representing our flagship, the two recruits who have put our own master diver's career in jeopardy, Sigmund Jurgens and Karl Luddolph!" A roar of acclamation from around the deck and superstructure of the vessel as the 'home' sailors were announced.

"Remember Wunderlich, Karl? He was the best of us at recruit training," Ziggy whispered to his friend as they waited to begin.

"Yes, he was quick all right, but this is further than we've ever swum before. I think it's those two from the *Barbarossa* we need to watch," Karl answered, nodding towards the two physically imposing sailors down the line from them.

"Strategy, Karl?" Ziggy asked.

"Start slow, I think. Swimming under the hulls will cause the race to close up and whoever surfaces first after the *Barbarossa* will have it," Karl replied quietly.

Ziggy winked back in understanding.

"Gentlemen, to your starting positions please," Oberstabsbootsmann Nadler ordered.

The men all climbed over the guard rail at the side of the ship and held onto it behind them.

"Get ready." The eight swimmers all tensed ready to leap.

"Go!" the chief petty officer commanded at the top of his voice.

The competitors leapt into the water, surfaced as a unit and began to swim towards the *Wilhelm der Grosse*. Karl found the water to be cold, but he was now used to its sting and swam in a strong but economical crawl, watching as the fair-haired Wunderlich began to pull away, closely followed by the two from *Barbarossa*. They were soon close to the side of the first ship, the *Wilhelm der Grosse*. Karl, stopped and trod water, taking several deep breaths before diving under the hull of this first obstacle. He was soon able to see lighter water and surfaced on the other side. As he recommenced his front crawl, he looked up to see Wunderlich ahead of him, followed by Bartels and alongside him were Ziggy and Hirsch.

Wunderlich started to pull away from the group behind as they swam towards the next vessel, the *Kaiser Barbarossa*. Karl was aware of the loud cheering and shouting from the deck of the ship as they approached. He saw Wunderlich dive as he got to the side. Again, Karl trod water, took several deep breaths and dived down under the hull. The water was murkier here and Karl found himself almost at the limit of his reserves. He surfaced on the other side of the ship and could only see the darker, swarthier figure of Bartels next to him. They both recommenced their swimming. Bartels had a short quick stroke that looked powerful, but Karl was content to continue with his slow, almost languid front crawl, pulling powerfully through the water.

Initially Bartels began to create some distance between them, but the twin dives had taken their toll on the older swimmer and Karl began to reel him in. With less than one hundred metres to go, they were alongside each other. Karl let the finishing point get to about fifty metres, then upped his stroke rate and touched the side of the *Kaiser Friedrich III* three yards ahead of Bartels. Wunderlich, who had clearly got into difficulties under the *Barbarossa*, was still able to overhaul

Ziggy and finish third, with Ziggy fourth, then Hirsch, Samter, Fellner and finally Dalman.

The swimmers were hauled unceremoniously from the water and given blankets to warm themselves with. After some minutes, Admiral of the Fleet Hans von Koester appeared on the afterdeck of the *Kaiser Friedrich*. The bedraggled, blanket-shrouded swimmers all stood in a line and saluted their fleet commander as he addressed them.

"Men, a wonderful display of sporting prowess, you are a credit to the Imperial German navy. Captain Dietrich, you have the medals for our gallant winners?"

Captain Ludovic Dietrich, captain of the *Kaiser Friedrich III*, hastily brought forward three medals with Imperial German navy ribbons attached.

"Sir, in third place, may I present Sailor 1st Class Rolf Wunderlich of SMS *Kaiser Friedrich III*." Captain Dietrich ushered Wunderlich forward.

"Well done, Wunderlich. We thought you would catch the others," and placed the bronze medal around Wunderlich's neck.

"Sir, second, is Bootsmann Bartels of SMS *Kaiser Barbarossa*," and Captain Dietrich again indicated for Bartels to step forward.

"Ah! Bootsmann Bartels. Another excellent display, you put your peers to shame. Silver is proof of your enduring strength," the Admiral smiled.

"Thank you, sir! These recruits get younger every year," Bartels replied as the Admiral placed the silver medal around his neck.

"Now, sir, it gives me great pleasure to introduce to you the winner of this challenge; Sailor 1st Class Karl Luddolph of SMS *Kaiser Wilhelm II*," and Captain Dietrich ushered Karl to stand in front of the fleet commander.

"Young Luddolph, I understand from Obertsabsbootsmann

Nadler that you recently joined our flagship, along with Jurgens. That you were both responsible for freeing an obstruction from our rudder and now, today, you have bested the fleet's finest swimmers."

"Sir, I have swum all my life," was all Karl could manage to say as the Admiral placed a gold medal around his neck, stood back and saluted the line of blanketed swimmers.

The eight swimmers and a good few of the crew assembled there returned the salute, as the Admiral turned and disappeared back into the ship.

"Karl, let me see." Ziggy reached over and grabbed the medal from Karl's neck.

At the same time Ronald Bartels stood in front of Karl.

"Luddolph!"

Karl stood stiffly to attention.

"No need for that, young man, you had me there at the end, well done," and the Bootsmann saluted Karl, who returned the salute in silence.

"Karl, well done, I will get you the next time." Rolf Wunderlich punched his fellow recruit playfully on the arm as he walked past. Karl looked up at the tall, fair-haired Wunderlich and smiled.

"I look forward to it," he smiled back.

The North Sea
June 1904

The fleet sailed from the coast of Aalesund the following morning. A crowd of townsfolk had gathered on the shore to wave and cheer the gallant German sailors who had come to aid the Norwegian town in its hour of need. The four battleships then joined up with the rest of the fleet in the North Sea to conduct a series of training exercises. At the conclusion of these manoeuvres, the fleet had largely returned to ports at Bremerhaven, Wilhelmshaven and, in the case of SMS *Kaiser Wilhelm II*, Kiel for the annual regatta. Much anticipation amongst the crew ensued, once it was posted on the message boards that the Kaiser himself was to review the regatta from the deck of their very ship.

On the morning of the major review Karl was awake early in his cramped quarters, cleaning his dress boots so that they shone like polished anthracite. Ziggy on the bunk above was laying out his number one dress uniform.

"Karl, do you think he'll speak to us? Are you allowed to wear your swimming medal? He must want to be presented to the fleet's swimming champion."

"Ziggy, we are a couple of lowly naval ratings, I suspect our presence on deck will go completely unnoticed. I think we'll be lucky if we even catch sight of the Kaiser," Karl replied as he worked diligently on the buttons of his tunic. Ziggy left him to it.

Karl continued to prepare his dress uniform, thinking about the man who now ruled the country of his birth, as emperor of the newly created Imperial German Empire. This leader, who had been in charge since he had been a small boy. Karl's father, Albert, had spoken of him as Karl had grown up. Karl had been made aware of how it was Kaiser Wilhelm who had unseated the long-serving chancellor Otto von Bismarck, to take Germany into what was being termed as the 'New Direction' and to create Germany's status as a world power. Karl was feeling this directly, as part of the ever-expanding Imperial German navy, which his father had concluded was only being created to stand against the might of the British navy.

Karl's father had felt this was not a 'New Direction' he wanted to be taken in and at the turn of the century he had taken the opportunity to emigrate to Great Britain with his family, to build what he saw as a more stable future for himself and those around him. Karl recalled the heated exchanges between his father and himself, regarding the escalation of the military since Kaiser Wilhelm had come to power. Karl wanted to stay to be part of the expansion, but his father had forbidden it and it was with much reluctance (and a small amount of pride) that he gave his blessing for Karl to leave their home in Leicester to undertake his national service within the Imperial German navy.

Albert Luddolph was an intelligent man and had been one hundred per cent behind the massive changes to his country instigated under the leadership of Otto von Bismarck. He saw the pride in a more unified Germany, bringing diplomatic peace and prosperity to both Germany and her neighbours. Albert had only ever known Queen Victoria as the head of the British Empire. She ruled, as a sort of grand matriarch, for pretty much the entire planet. Her offspring had now become entwined within the great European powers. He had always been keen to ensure that his children understood the position that they found themselves in. Bismarck had been ushering in a new Germany, but with his forced resignation and the somewhat belligerent and capricious nature of the Kaiser, the country was now losing more allies than it had been gaining.

Karl respected his father and remembered his words regarding the Kaiser, but he was young and wanted to experience things as a young man. Now as a trained member of the Imperial German navy, he wanted to be part of the rise of the country of his birth. He smiled when he thought how his father had joked that they were all related to each other anyway. Here was the Kaiser, the son of Queen Victoria's eldest daughter Vicky. He was the nephew of King Edward VII and his cousin was Tsar Nicholas II of Russia.

Since his return to Germany to do his national service, Karl had become aware from conversations between his comrades about the obvious 'bad blood' and hostility that existed between their Kaiser and King Edward VII of Great Britain – a situation that existed from the moment Wilhelm became the Kaiser and removed Bismarck in 1890. Karl had heard his senior NCO, Oberstabsbootsmann Otto Nadler, speaking in an unguarded moment: "It feels like a royal family feud that has resulted in our Kaiser creating a navy to rival that of the British, in an effort to gain position over his uncle King Edward VII. To me it all seems rather pointless and petty!"

Karl found it strange that someone he respected as much as Oberstabsbootsmann Nadler would discuss their leader in such a disparaging fashion. But never having seen the Kaiser or heard any stories to the contrary about him, Karl now began to think more carefully, perhaps for the first time ever, about the direction the country was heading in under his leadership. He knew the Kaiser wanted the best for Germany, but began to wonder if the best was going to be the Kaiser trying to assemble a fleet of battleships intended to rival that of the British.

"The Kaiser's not coming!" Ziggy rushed into the small dimly lit sleeping compartment, bringing Karl hastily back to the present.

"How do you know?"

"I overheard Kapitänleutnant Schön talking with some of the senior enlisted men and he said that the Kaiser would not attend the regatta this year. Then he went on to say that King Edward VII of Great Britain was now attending and would be inspecting the men of the flagship *Kaiser Wilhelm II*. King Edward is coming on board; you get to see your king," Ziggy added jokingly.

"He is the king of Great Britain, the king of the country where I and my family currently reside," Karl snapped back, perhaps more vehemently than he had wished.

Ziggy held his council, then carried on: "In any case, we possibly get to meet a king, or at least be inspected by one, that's something to remember?"

Karl looked at his smiling friend and nodded back, adding, "I agree, it's going to be a memorable day."

It felt like they had been standing to attention for hours. In effect they had been ramrod-straight like this for about twenty minutes. The entire ship's company were dressed in their smart, immaculate dress uniforms, ready to receive the visiting dignitaries. The first visitor to climb aboard was rather disappointingly dressed in a dark suit of, admittedly, good cloth, with a white wing-collared shirt and a dark neck tie.

"Oh! He looks a bit drab," Ziggy whispered to Karl, standing next to him.

"I'll guess he'll be a politician," Karl answered.

The man shuffled forward to allow the next guest to ascend to the deck. Unbeknownst to Karl and Ziggy, this 'drab' man was indeed a politician: the Right Honourable William Waldegrave Palmer KG GCMG PC, 2nd Earl of Selborne, and at that time the First Lord of the Admiralty, that is to say, the political head of the British navy and the government's advisor on all naval matters and responsible for the direction and control of the Admiralty.

The next man to step onto the deck was much more impressive, in the full-dress naval uniform of a commodore of the British navy.

"That's more like it," Ziggy whispered.

This man was Prince Louis Alexander of Battenberg, a German prince within the British navy. He was at that time the head of British Naval Intelligence. Apparently described as 'the cleverest sailor I have ever met' by the man standing next to him, the Right Honourable William Waldegrave Palmer. Prince Louis was married to Queen Victoria's granddaughter Princess Victoria of Hesse and by Rhine. ★(see appendix)

Prince Louis held out his arm to assist the next person aboard. All movement amongst the officers on deck and everyone on parade visibly tensed as the King of Great Britain stepped onto the deck of the flagship of the German Imperial navy, SMS *Kaiser Wilhelm II*. The rather portly, grey-bearded King Edward VII strode onto the deck in the uniform of an Admiral of the Fleet of the British navy. He was greeted by Admiral Hans von Koester and the other senior officers of the ship. Out of Karl and Ziggy's earshot the contingent of senior German officers welcomed the King on board and invited him to inspect a selection of the assembled parade.

The King led the party towards the first line of sailors, with Admiral von Koester in close attendance, with both Prince Louis and Lord Palmer following behind. The King, used to these inspection duties, commenced his walk along the line of men. As was customary the King stopped on one occasion to study one of the enlisted men, commenting to the Admiral, "Very impressive."

Admiral von Koester must have had an idea, because he suddenly indicated for the King to inspect the third rank of the next squad of men, the line where Ziggy and Karl were standing rigidly to attention.

"Your Royal Highness, if I may direct your attention to one of our sailors, whose family currently reside in Great Britain." The Admiral had ushered the King to a point opposite Karl.

"Sir, this is Seaman 1st Class Luddolph, the recent winner of a Norwegian swimming challenge and currently completing his national service. Prior to this I am reliably informed that he resides in Great Britain and speaks very good English." The Admiral stepped back. Karl, without prompting, performed a perfect naval salute, returned immediately by the King.

"You speak English, young man?" the King enquired.

"Sir, I have studied the language for five years and have lived in Leicester since 1900."

"Excellent. And you have come back to join my nephew's navy. The question is, will you stay in Germany or return to Great Britain at the end of your service?" The King posed a question that had been weighing on Karl's mind too.

"Sir, I feel this decision, I have yet to make," was all Karl could muster as a reply.

The King smiled and moved on, continuing his inspection duties further down the line. Karl caught the eye of Prince Louis of Battenberg as he passed and watched as the Prince winked at him.

Much later, when the two young seamen were back in their small sleeping quarters, Karl was lying on his top bunk thinking about what the King had said to him.

"So, do you have an answer to the King's question, at least a better answer than the one you gave him?" Ziggy, with an almost sixth sense, posed exactly the question Karl was mulling over. He gave his honest appraisal of the situation:

"Ziggy, I thought this would be simple. I returned to Germany to do my national service and then it was going to be my intention to seek a regular position within the navy and see where that took me, but leaving my family behind in Great Britain is not easy."

"If I may, my friend, we have three more years of our service to complete. Many things can happen. Is it not too early to be making decisions of this magnitude?"

"You're right, we have these years ahead of us, but today has made me question the plan I had in my head, so we shall have to see what the future brings."

"Indeed we shall. Now our immediate future is to go up on deck and witness the firework display to celebrate the end of regatta week." Ziggy rose and waited for Karl to jump off his bunk, then the two disappeared into the labyrinth of corridors and gangways to watch the spectacle of the fireworks at the end of the Kiel Regatta.

Plymouth, England
July 1904

The room was decorated with ornate oak panelling on all the walls, with large stained-glass windows built into the impressive stonework above. The dominant feature was the large decorative pipe organ at the far end from where they had entered. This was the first civic reception that Karl or Ziggy had been invited to. There had been a selection of events for the senior officers to attend since their arrival, but this event had been organised by the local council to offer an official welcome to the NCOs and enlisted men of the Imperial German navy during their brief stay in Plymouth.

Once again, the two were resplendent in their number one dress uniforms as they were welcomed to the reception taking place in the Great Hall of the recently built Guildhall. Karl was a step behind his eager friend as they entered the room and were greeted by some local councillors and officials. They walked further into the room to see a number of their fellow sailors and in the corner a band was just setting up.

"Now I feel I will need you here, Karl, as your command of the language is going to pay dividends today. Look!" Ziggy perked up as he spotted an array of young, attractive and very smartly dressed women.

Karl was about to reply when he stopped dead in his tracks. There were two of them. One tall and slim, with a confident air to match her flowing blonde hair and beautifully made-up face. She held a wine glass in her hand and had the nonchalant look of someone who knew that all the male eyes in the room were upon her. Next to her, almost hidden by her statuesque frame, was a smaller dark-haired girl, with a shy demeanour and a porcelain-white face. She was dressed in a conservatively fashionable dark, plain dress and despite her heeled shoes she still only came up to the shoulder of her magnificent blonde friend. Karl was mesmerised. Ziggy watched with a grin and whispered, "Get in line, Luddolph, every man in here wants to dance with that!"

But Ziggy had not followed the gaze of his friend. Karl was staring all right, but he could only see the petite, dark-haired girl. Then her eyes rose from the floor and they met his in a fixed stare and after several seconds, her mouth formed the merest hint of a smile and Karl smiled back.

Ziggy watched in shock as Karl literally marched directly across the room and up to the two young English women. The small dark-haired one watched him come all the way across to their place at the edge of the dance floor. The blonde hardly noticed him until he was standing directly in front of them, with Ziggy, uncharacteristically, several steps behind.

"Madam, please permit me to introduce myself and my close friend." Karl stood stiffly to attention as he spoke directly to the petite lady. The blonde naturally assumed he was talking to her and was about to wave him away, when her friend replied, "I would be honoured, sir."

"This is Seaman 1st Class Sigmund Jurgens, who everyone calls Ziggy, and I am Karl Luddolph. It is our pleasure to make your acquaintance," Karl continued in a formal tone.

"May I introduce my friend Miss Stella Rice and I am Miss Lily Pope. Gosh! you speak such fine English," the girl, Lily, said with a quiet but warm and welcoming tone. Stella had not bothered to turn her head towards Karl and Ziggy, but on hearing her name she swivelled her head slightly, enough to appraise the two men. She dismissed Karl, but found herself staring at the dashingly handsome face of his friend.

"What did your friend say your name was?" Stella asked Ziggy.

"His name is Sigmund, but we all call him Ziggy. His English is not good, but I can tell you he is delighted to meet you." Karl stepped towards Stella and helped Ziggy to understand what was being said.

Stella smiled the most brilliant, radiant smile and offered her hand to Ziggy, who took it gently and bent forward and gave the gentlest kiss to the back of it.

Ziggy returned to type and whisked them all off to a table in the corner, and then organised some drinks as they sat down.

To Karl the three-hour reception passed in an instant. He was totally captivated by Lily and hung on her every word. He performed translation duties for Ziggy, but as the time passed, it was clear that there was very little language barrier between the two of them. Karl meanwhile listened as Lily explained that she had only attended the function to support her friend Stella and had only come to Plymouth the year before to perform the duties of a lady's maid to the wife of Vice Admiral William Henderson, the admiral superintendent of Devonport Dockyard. Karl was fascinated by her, captivated by her subtle beauty and her self-deprecating charm and reserved wit. Somehow Ziggy had managed to persuade Stella to meet them the next day, ostensibly to act as guides around the city of Plymouth, and Lily agreed to join them for the afternoon.

After they said their goodbyes to the two Englishwomen and were walking slowly back to the ship, Ziggy spoke: "So, my reserved friend, you're a dark horse. Usually struck dumb in the presence of women, tonight you even out-manoeuvred me in chasing down those two lovelies."

"Mr. Jurgens, we will have no more talk about 'love-lies' thank you. Miss Lily Pope is one in a million," Karl sternly replied, then burst into laughter as he sensed his friend's awkwardness.

"Oh! Very good, Karl, you got me there." Ziggy laughed with his friend as they reached the ship.

The next day after completing their duties, at 4 p.m. they were given a brief shore leave for the evening and walked up to Smeaton's Tower which was the most prominent landmark in Plymouth. The tower was the top portion of the Eddystone Lighthouse, which had been removed from the rock and rebuilt on the Hoe in the 1880's As the two sailors strode up the incline they were heartened by the many and various warm acknowledgements they received from the local English people as they passed. It was a warm and sunny summer's afternoon and a band were playing to a large appreciative crowd as they walked on up to the lighthouse. For a brief second, Karl had the most enormous sense of dread that the two women would not be there and he would never get to see the singular beauty of Lily again.

This melancholy feeling was swiftly lifted as he spied the two contrasting ladies and he quickened his stride to get to the lighthouse. Slightly unsure of himself, Karl bowed as he stopped in front of Lily. She giggled and stood on tiptoe to kiss his cheek, then she took his arm and they walked off together. Ziggy, in similar fashion, escorted Stella away from the lighthouse towards the Old Town of Plymouth.

"Stella is the housekeeper's assistant to the admiral. She looked after me when I started work with them last year. I suppose we have become close friends as she is not from this part of England either," Lily told Karl as they walked along the seafront in the late afternoon sun.

"Where shall we go? Would you care for a drink? Is that all right? I hope I'm not being too formal, too presumptuous?"

Karl stumbled to find the correct way to address this vision on his arm.

"Karl, you are so sweet and so proper," Lily giggled.

"There's a place I saw the last time we went through the Old Town. It's a small public house, looks very old and quaint." Ziggy and Stella had caught up and Ziggy led them all down the hill.

The public house was indeed tiny, but they were able to find a table in the corner of the dimly lit dark wooden bar area. Ziggy, as usual, ushered them to their seats and was swiftly back with some drinks for them.

"This place, according to legend, is where Sir Francis Drake used to come for refreshment. He used to live a little further along this very street," Ziggy said, passing on the information he had just been told by the jovial barman.

"Well, let's toast the memory of Sir Francis Drake." Karl, entering into the spirit of the establishment, raised his glass.

"Sir Francis Drake!" Ziggy and the two girls replied in unison. Ziggy looked towards the barman, who tapped his forehead with his finger in acknowledgement.

The company was excellent and the conversation flowed between the four young people. Ziggy and Karl talked of their short careers in the Imperial German navy and the two ladies followed suit by explaining the complicated structure below stairs of an English Edwardian household. But Karl wanted to ask Lily so much more and felt stifled by the company around him and too shy to say how he really felt about Lily. The opportunity arose when Ziggy stood and announced that Stella and he were going to see a little more of Old Plymouth. Karl stood as if to accompany them, but Ziggy cleverly halted his progress as he dropped a glove. As he bent down to pick it up, he whispered to Karl in German, "Stay here, my friend, tell her how you feel. Have the courage to be honest about your feelings. Remember, back to the ship by 10 p.m., we sail in the morning."

Karl nodded and sat back down as Ziggy and Stella left the bar.

"What happened there?" Lily asked.

"They wanted to see a little more of Plymouth and I suspect Ziggy wanted to talk privately with Stella," was about the best way that Karl could word what they both had possibly been thinking.

"What would you like to do, Karl?" Lily asked him.

"I want to talk to you, either here or outside in the fresh air. You know we sail tomorrow morning and are heading back to Germany by way of Amsterdam. We have a packed schedule of exercises and training ahead of us. My first opportunity to be released from my service is in September of 1906; that's over two years away." Karl suddenly felt the confidence to really talk to this beautiful girl.

"Let's leave and find somewhere to walk on this lovely evening," Lily suggested.

They stood to leave the bar. As he ushered Lily through the door, the barman looked up and said, "Good luck, young man!"

Karl smiled, brought his heels together and bowed as he left the premises. They walked back towards the Hoe. Lily again had her arm firmly in the crook of Karl's elbow. As they neared the top of the rise he saw an empty bench, facing out into the large bay.

"Would you like to sit?"

"That would be lovely," she replied quietly.

After what seemed like an eternity, but was probably no more than a minute, Karl spoke.

"You know how I ended up in the German navy, that I was born and brought up in a small town near Leipzig. My parents emigrated to England in 1900 and have settled in Leicester. It feels like fate, Lily. Here we are in a city on the south coast of Great Britain, both strangers to the area. We meet by chance at a reception and it transpires that your family are from Leicester too. I cannot believe in such coincidence. Is it too much to believe that we were meant to meet and by implication that we are meant to be together?" Karl suddenly stopped, fearing he had gone too far and said too much. "I'm sorry."

"No, Karl, please, I feel it too. I grew up in a quiet, poor neighbourhood, with many brothers and sisters. I knew I had to break out and make my own way in the world. I didn't know what I was looking for. The job is all right, but it's just a means to have money to live. When I first set eyes on you, I knew from that moment that whatever future I may have was going to be with you." Karl listened in silence as this wonderful, dark-haired English girl stole his heart.

"But I am gone tomorrow for at least two years, which could be longer," Karl groaned.

"You are a patient and honourable man. I fell in love with you the second you caught my eye. I can wait for you for as long as it takes." Lily's voice made the hairs on the back of Karl's neck stand up and he felt himself blush at her words.

"For me too, you are enchanting. I am young and perhaps immature in romance, but I find this feeling towards you is something I have never felt before. If this is love, then I love you too, Lily." Karl stumbled with his words. The pause in conversation was just enough for Lily to lean forward and kiss Karl fully on the lips. Karl returned the kiss, embracing Lily in his strong uniformed arms.

Norway
July 1906

"It's fitting that we should be returning to Norway and to the area close to where we had one of our first real adventures in Aalesund," Ziggy said as they watched the Norwegian coastline pass on the starboard side of the ship. "It's like we've come full circle."

"Do you know where Molde is?" Karl asked him.

"Hartmann showed me the map and it appears to be just to the north of Aalesund, on the mainland but surrounded by fjords. He also let slip that the Kaiser is returning to the region to join the newly crowned King of Norway to celebrate his birthday next week." Ziggy astounded Karl with the depth of information he had gleaned.

"These two years have really changed you, Ziggy," Karl joked.

"I don't see how, I just learned to maximise opportunities," Ziggy smiled back.

"It was always me that knew everything, now the tables appear to be turned."

"Karl, you still know everything. It's just that now I am able to keep up with your thirst for knowledge. Maybe you've changed too; two years of being in love can do that to a person!" He laughed at his friend.

"I'm sure I don't know what you mean." Karl put on his most pompous voice and smiled back.

"When did you get your last letter from Lily?" Ziggy asked quietly.

"She wrote it over a month ago, but it only got to us last week. She has handed in her notice to the admiral's wife. The printers where her father works have need of some secretarial staff and she's been offered a position there. It means she will be back living at home, but that home will be Leicester."

"Karl, that's wonderful news." Ziggy clapped Karl heartily on the back. "So, err, what exactly are you going to do when you get back to Great Britain?"

"Honestly I don't know. I'm good with my hands and like the way machines work, you know that. Maybe something in the engineering world. There must be jobs to be had in the area?" Karl sounded less than confident.

"One thing I've learnt since knowing you is that you have a stubborn will to succeed. You seem to be able to put your mind to almost anything and you can do it."

"Thank you, my friend. I'm not so sure about that."

"Well, take the zither; you picked that one up in that old shop in Kiel and have, after two years of repetitive tinkering, mastered it, so that you can hold a tune and even keep us entertained, albeit for short periods." Ziggy laughed out loud at his own joke.

"Bugger off!" Karl replied as he laughed too.

King Haakon VII of Norway had only been on the throne since November 1905. He was related through marriage to the British monarchy, his wife Princess Maud being the daughter of King Edward VII. After their investiture in June 1906, the new royal family were keen to meet their subjects and took a slow sailing trip down the coast of their new kingdom. They were due to arrive in the area of Molde where Kaiser Wilhelm II was to meet the new king in an area familiar to him and celebrate Haakon's birthday.

"Is every king and head of state we meet related to Queen

Victoria?" Ziggy asked as they once again found themselves standing to attention on the deck of the flagship of the fleet.

"It would certainly appear so. I wonder how the Kaiser will be today?" There had now been several occasions when the Kaiser had been on board the vessel that bore his name. Despite these being occasions of some celebration, it was clear that the Kaiser, certainly in Karl's eyes, was an angry man. He shouted at his staff in front of the ship's company; he was arrogant and surly to those attending to him. He found it difficult if attention was deferred away from him. *An arrogant spoilt brat*, Karl thought. *Would he even inspect the men this time?* Karl wondered as the rest of the crew waited for his arrival.

"Didn't even stop to look at us! All stood here for an hour, waiting for him to arrive. Didn't even address us as part of his navy. How is his haughty and arrogant behaviour going to endear him to his subjects?" Karl demanded of Ziggy in the privacy of their quarters.

"You see the way he walks, almost side on to conceal his withered left arm. It might be a bit uncharitable, but you do wonder if his general attitude is in some way trying to compensate for his physical disability?" Ziggy suggested.

"It's not just Lily entering my life that has changed my intentions," Karl continued. "I seriously worry about the direction we're heading in as a country. Everywhere we go, we're welcomed by the leaders of the countries we visit. We hear snippets and fractions of conversations and they all have the same disparaging opinion of our Kaiser. He seems to have an innate ability to antagonise people."

"I understand how you feel," Ziggy agreed. "You at least have the opportunity to return to your new life in Great Britain. For myself, I have to see where this man leads Germany in the next few years. I have made my own decision to leave the navy at the same time as you and pursue an engineering degree in Munich."

"You will be a success, Ziggy! How can you fail with your easy charm and sunny disposition?" Karl laughed as he reassured his friend.

"Enough of this seriousness, you have a twenty-first birthday coming up and I want to make sure we celebrate in spectacular fashion. Let's get ashore and see what the town of Molde has to offer."

Several hours later, but before the 10 p.m. deadline, Karl and Ziggy returned to the ship. As they began to make their way across the deck a familiar figure intercepted them.

"Jurgens, Luddolph, glad to see you back safe and sound," Oberstabsbootsmann Nadler greeted them. "Gentlemen, may I beg a moment of your time?"

"Sir," the two friends replied in unison.

"I have seen the requests you have both submitted to our captain. I'm so sorry to hear that you are to leave the service at the end of September. I had wondered and indeed hoped that you may both have been keen to sign on as regular sailors. You would be destined, I'm sure, for great things if you chose a career in the navy. That being said, I'm sure that whatever the future may hold for the two of you, it will be both long and prosperous."

"Thank you, sir!" Karl replied, just before Ziggy did the same.

"Sir, if I may ask, what of yourself? I had heard that you were considering retirement, if it's not too impertinent to say?" Karl nervously asked.

Otto Nadler looked at the two young boys who he had seen grow into fine young German men, and smiled with all the warmth and benevolence that the two had come to know over the years. "News of me ending my career is perhaps a little premature. The ever-growing navy that we seem to be a part of has need of me for a few years to come, I believe. I will continue for the moment. I have been offered a role on the new class of battleship currently undergoing sea trials, SMS *Deutschland*."

"We had no idea. Congratulations to you, sir." Karl stood to attention.

"Of course you didn't and it's not common knowledge, so I would appreciate it if you would keep it that way," the senior supervisor whispered conspiratorially, then continued. "What plans do the two of you have in place then?

"Sir, it is my intention to return to Munich and complete a degree in engineering and from there seek employment in that field," Ziggy replied.

"For myself, sir, I wish to return to Great Britain, where letters from home indicate that there are opportunities to be had in the industrial Midlands of the country," Karl explained. "I have my family already settled into prosperous employment in the textile industry around Leicester and I am confident that I can be successful there."

"Gentlemen, it has been my privilege and pleasure to know you. We may not get another chance to talk like this, so I wanted you both to know in what high esteem I hold you both. Never forget your time in the German navy. Whatever the future may bring I hope you will remember us fondly and value the time you gave."

"Sir, if I may speak on behalf of both of us," Karl said. "We have thrived here, due in no small part to your steadfast and solid support. Ziggy and I would never have met and become such good friends had we not embarked on our time here. Every challenge and exercise has been a learning curve and we have welcomed that. For my part I will be sorry to leave, but I have my memories and firmly believe you move forward in life. You have been our senior instructor and supervisor, we were fortunate to have coincided our service with you, for which I thank you." Karl stopped as Ziggy interrupted.

"I too wish to add my thanks and gratitude for your training and for the kindness you showed us all the way through our time. I wish to thank you on behalf of myself and Karl and we both wish you success in your future."

Both sailors stood to attention opposite the thick-set senior NCO. Otto Nadler held out his hand to Ziggy, who gripped it with his own. He repeated the handshake with Karl.

"Wherever you two may go and end up, you will always have my admiration and blessing," the rough-looking naval man whispered. "Now get yourselves below where you belong."

Karl and Ziggy took their leave of their talismanic former chief instructor and disappeared, so never saw the small tears form in Otto Nadler's eyes.

Leicester, England
December 1910

"What does it say?" Karl's father Albert asked as they sat around the table in the small dining room of their terraced house in the centre of the city. Karl ripped open the official manila envelope and pulled out a single sheet of folded white paper.

"They have rejected it. A great many words of no bearing or relevance, that then go on to say, and I quote: 'His Majesty's Government would not feel justified in allowing the provision of a certificate of naturalisation.' I mean, why would they, I've only lived here for the past ten years!" Karl spoke clearly and quietly, but his father could tell he was furious.

"I told you, Karl, they don't want us here, we're not good enough, in their eyes, to be 'British'," Karl's elder brother Maximillian (Max) interrupted. "I tell you, we need to get on the next available boat to America. For us to have any future, we need to get out of Great Britain."

Karl's elder brother was about an inch taller and much slimmer than Karl. He was three years older and had been a qualified textile mill supervisor for the past eighteen months. His responsibilities earned him a comparatively generous income and he was currently renting rooms in another part of Leicester. Apart from Karl's parents sitting round the table, a much smaller, fair-haired man, with a warm and calm air about him, watched the family debate. He was Wilhelm, but everyone called him Willy and he was three years younger than Karl. He had been an initial disappointment to his father, but had recently become employed as an assistant at a local barber's shop and had designs on a shop of his own one day.

"Boys, Albert, please let's eat! The food is ready and you know how I hate to see it spoiled." Karl's mother Charlotte (Lotte) was a tiny, dark-haired lady approaching fifty. Her stature did not diminish the power she wielded amongst the family and the men of the household immediately took their seats and murmured their apologies and grateful thanks for the meal in front of them. Max had remarked on their mother's general resemblance to Karl's fiancée Lily, adding, "There is a saying that men always marry their mothers and I have to say to you, Karl, that I believe you are about to do just that."

Karl smiled as he watched his mother distribute their traditional Friday night meal. He wished that Lily had been with him that day, but she was looking after her own sick mother. His reintroduction to Lily had been a wonderful reawakening of the love and special feeling he had in his heart for her. But, as so often in life, practicalities had interrupted this romantic dream. Lily's father, George, was a very strict and religious man and Karl had found himself having to conduct the most rigorously traditional courtship. In the four years since his return, he had finished a two-year engineering apprenticeship and was currently working for Nathanial Corah and Sons, makers of hosiery and textiles based in Leicester. The company was one of the largest in the region, employing over a thousand people, the majority of which were female. Karl had managed to acquire for himself a privileged position as one of the company's travelling salesmen.

Lily had been relieved to see Karl return from his time in the German navy and retained the same feeling she had for him from their first and only time together. The constant flow of letters back and forth between them had settled her concerns that she was waiting for a man she hardly knew. She

59

had to run the gauntlet of questions and observations from her father, who could see no future for his daughter with *'that German',* as he called Karl.

Lily confided in her mother that it was hard to stand up to her father when she had no real argument with which to defend her decision to devote herself to Karl. "All I can do is wait for the day when he comes back to me and then show you what a wonderful man he is," she had told her mother. Lily's father had a natural ability to push the male friends of Lily's other siblings in her direction at every opportunity. Lily was a polite and dutiful daughter and found herself being escorted out to dances and garden parties by a seemingly never-ending line of more than suitable young men. But they all, without exception, were not Karl.

When the time came for Karl to meet Lily's parents, he had already been home from Germany for about six months. He was as gracious and endearing as Lily could ever remember and spoke deferentially to her father and called him 'sir', which delighted him, although he did his best not to show it. Karl brought flowers for Lily, for Lily's mother Helen, and her younger sister Iris. He was quietly spoken but happy to regale them all with stories of his time in the German navy. He was most respectful and always brought Lily home at a considerate time. Gradually the strength of affection between the two young people was clear for all to see, even George Pope. After a little over a year of courtship, Karl proposed to Lily, who immediately said yes. Karl, of course, knew that in order for him to get Lily to actually wear the diamond ring he had bought for her he would have to seek permission from her father.

In his twenty-five years, Karl had been in one or two perilous and daunting situations, but nothing had quite prepared him for the nerves he felt as he prepared to meet George Pope and ask for his daughter's hand in marriage. On that day Karl was dressed in the finest grey suit he owned and had knocked at the Popes' house at a little after six in the evening. It was a cold October day and the light was fading fast.

"Come in, Karl. You look very grand this evening. Lily is still getting ready, would you like to join me in the front room?" George had taken on a much more affable demeanour these last six months, when he could see clearly how devoted his daughter was to this well-mannered, respectful German gentleman. Karl followed Mr. Pope through the small house into the front parlour. "Would you like a drink, young man?" George asked.

"No, sir. Please, I have something which I wish to ask you." Karl nervously began his prepared words. "As you know, I have been seeing your daughter since I returned to Leicester at the end of 1906. In that time, I have trained myself as an engineer's apprentice and found employment at one of Leicester's premier textile manufacturers. I believe I have sufficient funds to be able to find my own place to live now. I have always been conscious that I needed to show you my independence and become a success. It is therefore, sir, my great honour to humbly ask you for your daughter's hand in marriage." Karl took a half step backwards, to gauge the reaction from Lily's father.

"My dear boy, it is you who honour our family. If Lily is agreeable to your request, then I have no hesitation in giving you my blessing. Come here, young man," and with that George Pope held out his hand and Karl readily accepted a firm and favourable handshake from his future father-in-law.

"Have you set a date, my boy?" Karl's father Albert asked as he heard the news of his middle son's engagement to his long-term companion.

"Not yet, Father, I want to be able to afford and find somewhere for us to live. I also have the matter of our possible emigration to America along with Max to consider," Karl explained.

"What has made you decide on a future in America?" Albert asked.

"I believe Germany is on a collision course with various parts of Europe. The Kaiser seems hell-bent on alienating his immediate neighbours, Russia, Serbia and even Great Britain. I am concerned."

"But we're settled here, we all have reasonable and stable employment, I have this large house, now largely paid for, and we are welcome in the local community in which we live," Albert argued.

"I just don't know, I have this awful feeling, like a sixth sense. If things were to change between Great Britain and Germany, then you forget, we are all, in this family, still German citizens, with not a British passport amongst us. We may be married, or intending to be married to British ladies, but our applications for naturalisation have all been declined. I worry that we have no status here and that passage to America would afford, certainly Lily and me, opportunities unaffected by any worsening of the friendship between the country of my birth and Great Britain."

"So, do you have any idea of when you might consider applying to America for permission to settle?' Albert sighed.

"Max has been looking into the cost of the Atlantic crossing and I also need to ensure that I have sufficient funds for not only this, but also our wedding. Lily would like to wait about a year, while we save and find the right place to live. If during that time we apply for passage to America, then we may rent somewhere, until such time as we cross the Atlantic."

"Karl, I think you worry too much. I have lived here for over ten years. I have a respectable job, recently promoted to foreman at the knitting factory where I have been for the last five years. If there was any resentment to us as Germans, then I am sure my rapid rise through the hierarchy of the hosiery industry would have come to an abrupt halt. We have made great efforts to integrate with our town and all speak the language to a reasonable level." Albert paused then went on. "I have picked up a common phrase these past few years, that it is better the devil you know! How do you know that there will be such potential in America?"

"I don't, but Max has made some contacts over there already, within the textile business. I will also write to the American ambassador in London to seek permission to proceed to America, as I've been led to believe the application can take some time," Karl explained.

As time passed, the letters back and forth between Karl and the American authorities became more frequent as he sought permission to reside there. Additionally, he was now working with Lily to finalise the details of their wedding day. They were yet to set a date, but were working towards sometime in April 1912. Lily was initially a little dubious about emigrating to America, but after careful consideration and with the persuasion of both Karl and Max, she quickly saw that it was a logical step for the two German brothers to take. Her family were also not keen on the prospect, but everyone agreed that the love and devotion that these two young people had for each other would ensure that wherever they were, they would be successful together.

Max was delighted that his younger brother and fiancée would be coming to America with him. Several applications and documentation enquiries later, all three of them were accepted and given permission to enter the United States of America.

"Max, we have set the date for our wedding," Karl said as they sat down to Friday night dinner at their parents' house. Everyone was present around the table to celebrate the news of the wedding date. "It is to be on Saturday 6th April 1912 at Leicester Town Hall. When did you say we had our passage across the Atlantic booked?"

Max rose to his feet to toast his younger brother and his bride to be. "Little brother, you will be pleased to hear that after much research and some considerable effort I have booked us passage on what I have been led to believe is the greatest ship ever built. I apologise that I could only afford third-class tickets, but we have our passage booked."

"Yes, but when, Max?" Karl pleaded.

"Ladies and gentlemen, we are booked to set sail on the maiden voyage of the greatest feat of modern engineering in the history of man. We sail from Southampton on Wednesday 10th April 1912 at noon."

"What's the name of the ship, Max?" Karl asked.

Max, now warming to his role as the divulger of this momentous information, once again waited for quiet around the room and spoke. "We sail on the White Star Line's latest and may I say greatest vessel, the Royal Mail Ship *Titanic...*"

Leicester, England
6th April 1912

Karl stood ramrod-straight in Leicester Town Hall Registry Office. He had at first thought he might be allowed, or it would be suitable for him, to be dressed in his German naval uniform, but his parents and particularly Max decided it was not really appropriate. Karl was attended by his great friend Ziggy Jurgens, who had travelled all the way from Munich to act as his best man. They were both identically dressed in dark morning suits, with pristine wing-collared white shirts, both sporting dark bow ties. Their trousers were a matching grey, with white button-down spats above their burnished black shoes. Karl always felt slightly uncomfortable when dressed formally in Ziggy's company, on account of his good friend's ability to look so dashing and handsome.

They had been waiting in the small ornately decorated room, with Karl's direct family and the large collection of relatives that made up Lily's immediate family. The only people missing, due within the next few minutes if they were to be on time, were Lily, escorted by her father George and Lily's two sisters, Iris and young Evie, acting as her bridesmaids. Ziggy had been very quick to reacquaint himself with the statuesque Stella Rice, who had once again turned the heads of every male in the vicinity upon her arrival, dressed in the most eye-catching dark red velvet gown. "Just perfect, enough class and brilliance to be noticed, but subtle enough not to steal the day away from Lily, eh Karl?" Ziggy whispered as he patted his great friend on the back. Karl simply nodded nervously back.

"If you could all please stand!" the registrar asked as George Pope Sr. escorted his daughter Lily into the room, followed by the two bridesmaids. Lily was dressed in an off-white full-length dress of lace and silk, with a high waistline, as was the fashion at that time. She wore a wreath of little yellow flowers in her hair, with a veil over the top. The arms of the material of her dress were a little bunched at the top, tightening as they reached her wrists. She clutched a small bouquet of similar small yellow flowers in her tiny hands. She stopped next to Karl and turned her head ever so slightly towards him and smiled...

"What is it, my dear?' Karl spoke to his wife in their bridal suite bedroom. He had been awoken by his wife's cry of anguish in the dark. Karl turned on a bedside light and reached for Lily. She was cold and pale and her skin felt clammy to the touch.

"I feel so weak, Karl. I have no energy and this piercing pain in my stomach," Lily whispered to her husband. Karl quickly dressed and made his way to the reception of the hotel and asked for a doctor to be sent to their rooms. He then returned to his wife.

After about half an hour there was a quiet knock on the door. Karl opened it to be faced by a serious-looking man in his fifties wearing thick-rimmed glasses and carrying a small Gladstone bag.

"Good morning, I'm Dr. Moffat. I believe your wife has been taken ill?"

"Yes, sir, she's through here." Karl led the doctor through to the bedroom.

"Leave us please, young man, while I see to your wife." The doctor shut the door and Karl moved back into the lounge of the suite.

The doctor imparted his diagnosis a few minutes later.

"Well, she is very weak. I believe she has anaemia, caused by an imbalance of minerals in her body, mainly, I suspect, a lack of iron in the blood. I am going to have her taken into the local hospital just so they can monitor her for the next few days."

"Oh, I see. We are supposed to be travelling to America the day after tomorrow, will that still be possible do you think, Doctor?" Karl asked.

"Young man, your wife at the very least needs complete bed rest for the next few days, if not a week. I think you should seek to postpone your journey until we all consider your wife is in a condition to travel," the doctor explained.

Karl sat down and stared out of the window, considering his options, while they waited for an ambulance to convey Lily to the local Leicester Infirmary.

"Well, I ought to go." Max told him when he joined him in the waiting room. "I could see if I can sell your tickets at Southampton, but I can still travel and you can both join me when Lily has recovered."

"Why don't you postpone as well, Max, then we can all travel together, maybe in a few weeks' time?" Karl suggested.

"I think Karl is right, you ought to wait and all go at once," Albert Luddolph agreed.

"No, I'm going to go. I want to sail on this ship, on the maiden voyage, it sounds both wonderful and fascinating." Max had made his mind up.

"I have decided to rent rooms for Lily and me, local to where I work, so I can look after her," Karl stated.

"We will all look after her, Karl," Lily's sister Iris offered. She had been hovering near the men in the waiting area.

Karl looked at his brother. "Max, are you sure about this? We have time to postpone; if you can wait, we would be so grateful and then we can all travel together."

"I understand, Karl, but I just don't see the harm in me going tomorrow. I can get myself settled in America and it will make things easier for you when you come across later in the year."

Max left that very afternoon, travelling by train to London and then the following morning by boat train to Southampton, arriving at the railhead at about 9.30 in the morning. There was a very real buzz about the city, with throngs of people clambering over the rails to get a better view of the gargantuan ship moored in Southampton docks. Max alighted from the train and was guided by a smartly dressed White Star Line officer towards the ship. As Max approached he marvelled at the size and height of the vessel. As he got closer there were scores of people, he supposed waiting to board, but there were also spectators in amongst the travellers. There were many people without tickets, looking to find passage. Max saw an opportunity, with both Karl and Lily's tickets folded inside his wallet. He spied a young couple and approached them.

"Do you have tickets?" he enquired.

"No, mate, my wife and I just turned up on the off chance. You understand?" the male explained, speaking slowly when he heard Max's accent.

"I have some tickets if you wish, I can sell them to you for their face value price, if you have the cash?" Max offered.

"How much are they then?"

"I can sell them for what I paid, seven pounds five shillings"*

"How many do you have then?" the Englishman asked keenly.

"Two," Max said.

"Oh! I need three, my wife and I and my son Matthew." As Max watched, a boy of about twelve or thirteen ran up to the couple.

"Did you see all those people with their luggage arrive,

68

Dad, did you?" The boy pointed excitedly to the cars and carriages of the first-class passengers and their large amounts of luggage.

"I'm sorry, I just have two to get rid of, my brother and his wife are unable to travel today," Max explained.

The man reached into his coat and pulled out a battered brown leather wallet. He counted out five large white paper five-pound notes. "Here you are; why don't you wait in England for your brother? I can offer you twenty-five pounds for the three tickets you have, no questions asked," the man bartered.

Max looked at the pleading look in the man's eyes, the stillness on the face of his wife, and even their excitable young son stopped to watch the transaction. Max was in a quandary; he wanted to go, especially on this great ship, but he now felt the need and desperation in the eyes of the English family in front of him.

"I must give you your change." Max rummaged in his pockets trying to find some notes and coins to give the man.

"No, please, you must keep the twenty-five pounds, your generosity and kindness are worth every penny of it." The man handed the notes to Max, who in turn pulled out the three White Star Line third-class tickets and swopped them for the money. The man stood and offered his hand. Max took the hand and looked long and hard into the face of this stranger, now filled with renewed hope for his future, and Max saw the look of relief in the eyes of his wife and the bewilderment and excitement in the eyes of their young boy, Matthew. As Max told this story throughout his life, he always recalled how he never forgot the look of unbridled joy and contentment on the faces of that doomed English family.

Max bid them farewell and walked quickly away, concerned that he had just made a cataclysmic mistake. As noon approached he found a vantage point near to the bow of the huge ship. Suddenly the great mooring lines were slipped and RMS *Titanic* moved slowly forward. The sheer movement of such a vast object caused such a swell that the neighbouring vessel SS *City of New York* was first lifted, then dropped into a trough caused by its passing. This placed too much strain on its own mooring lines, which snapped, causing it to swing out from the stern towards *Titanic*. A tugboat managed to react and get the SS *City of New York* under tow, as the *Titanic* put itself full astern. It is believed that they missed each other by about four feet. Max watched the drama unfold and looked long and hard at this leviathan of the sea, as it made headway again out towards the English Channel. "There is something not quite right about that ship," he thought.

*Seven pounds five shillings equates to about £700 at today's prices.

Leicester, England
July 1914

"The doctor says I must rest, but I don't want to be an invalid, I want to be able to do things around the house and look after you when you come home from work." Lily lay recumbent on a sofa gently rubbing her expanding 'bump'.

"Lily, my love, we must listen to the advice. You are too weak to be able to continue with things as they were. We always knew that having a child was a risk and I can afford to pay for someone to care for you in the house while I'm away. Please, I want you to be careful," Karl answered, as he gently sat next to his wife in the small parlour of their two-bedroom terrace in Leicester.

"What about our postponed intention to go to America? Ever since the *Titanic* tragedy we've been waiting for the right time. Now I'm pregnant, what are we going to do?"

"You are my priority, my love. You must rest as much as you can through the remainder of the year and after we are a family, then we can think about emigrating again next year. Don't worry about anything else, you must concentrate on resting."

"And what about the general unrest in Europe? It concerns me that we need to be in America, in case this crisis in Europe between Germany and Russia escalates. I read yesterday that Germany is demanding France remain neutral and stay out of the crisis. Kaiser Wilhelm is beginning to look like he wants to do more than just support Austria-Hungary." Lily was thinking of the recent reports of unrest across Europe since the assassination of Franz Ferdinand by Serbs in Sarajevo.

"Lily, it's a complicated situation, but it shouldn't affect us here in Great Britain. I have lived here since 1899, and I'm now married to you, a British subject. I put great faith in the tolerance of the British government and people. I am now a senior salesman, earning good money here in Leicester, a city that I now call home. I have a large number of influential friends and colleagues, who I am sure would vouch for me if it came to it."

A knock at the door halted their conversation. Karl walked through to the narrow entrance hall and opened the door. It was Max and Willy.

"Look who's come to see us, Lily," he said.

"My darling Lily, don't get up." Max rushed forward to stop Lily rising from her chair and bent forward to kiss her on the cheek. Willy, always the shyest of the three brothers, shuffled forward and kissed her too.

"Hello, Lily," he whispered.

"So, what brings you two here?" Karl asked.

"Rumours and concern about us staying here in England," Max exclaimed.

"Lily mentioned the same, but I think you're wrong. We are fine here," Karl answered.

"I don't see it that way, Karl. Already the newspapers are talking about the German leadership as cold and brutal, wanting to start a war, being responsible for an arms race with the British navy, what…"

Karl held out his hand, stopping Max's words.

"But that's the German leadership. You forget I saw the Kaiser on many occasions in the navy. He is one man. He is blunt and foolish and the British can see that he is not the German people. They just happen to be saddled with a cantankerous and vain leader. I'm sure the generals will advise him to mediate with the forces massed against him."

"Sorry, Karl, you're wrong. I think we are in a most precarious state. None of us are naturalised British subjects. We are Germans, living in England. We need to get to America at the earliest opportunity. I have written to the American ambassador in London to resurrect our application to settle in the USA and have added Willy and his wife to it," Max said.

"But you know Lily's condition, her fragile state. I can't risk her travelling to America until the baby is born," Karl reasoned.

"My darling, I think Max knows that. He's talking about all of you going and then I can follow when I have had the baby." Lily smiled at Max.

"You see everything, Lily, you read my mind. Karl, we must get across the Atlantic in the next few months. I will make all the necessary arrangements," Max replied.

"But what about Lily? What about my pregnant wife? I can't leave her," Karl pleaded.

"Karl, I can go and live with my parents," Lily reasoned. "We are only renting this place anyway. I can be looked after at home with my mother and sisters still there to support me during the next six months. Once I've had the baby, we can arrange for me to travel to you. By then you'll be settled."

"It doesn't feel right, to leave you when you need me most," Karl moaned.

"Karl, please, make the arrangements, listen to your brothers. I want you to go with them." Lily took her husband's hand.

"What about you, Willy? You have a young wife too and young William is only three." Karl turned to his younger brother, who had been quietly listening to their conversation.

"We have moved to new rooms just to the north of here in a place called Mountsorrel," Willy said. "For the first time since being married, I feel settled. There's an opportunity for me to run my own barber's shop in that area. I'm not sure. It's a lot to give up, to then have to start again in America."

"You see, Max, there's so much to lose if we leave. We've built lives for ourselves, we are effectively British, even if we don't have a piece of paper to prove it," Karl said.

"But that's just it, you have no 'piece of paper', you are German and I don't believe the British government have either the time or the inclination to interview us all when deciding whether we are a threat to this country or not." Max almost shouted his response.

"How long before you hear back from the ambassador?" Karl asked.

"I suspect they're inundated with requests to emigrate at the moment. We will have to wait, but it might take a month at least," Max suggested.

"My boys, will you both stay to dinner?" Lily asked, as she levered herself out of the chair and stood in front of them.

"Lily, remember, you must rest," Karl interrupted.

"Oh, I think I can just about manage to cook a dinner for four. Now don't be rude and offer your brothers a drink." And Lily made her way through to the kitchen at the back of the property.

A little over three weeks after this family discussion at Karl's small house in suburban Leicester, the entire course of human history changed. Germany, fearful perhaps of fighting a war on two fronts, decided that they would declare war on Russia, after the Kaiser's cousin Tsar Nicholas refused to stop mobilising his troops in support of Serbia. After this refusal, Germany declared war on Russia on 1st August 1914. They simultaneously demanded that France remain neutral. The French commanders, always fearful of a German attack through Belgium, asked permission of their civilian leaders to move French troops into Belgium to counter a German offensive, but this was refused as it would be a breach of the 1839 Treaty of London, guaranteeing Belgium's neutrality. The French leadership said that their troops could not move into Belgium until the Germans had invaded it. On 2nd August German troops occupied Luxembourg and then the next day declared war on France. Simultaneously they demanded Belgium give right of way through any part of their country. The Belgians refused. On 4th August Germany invaded Belgium. Their king, Albert, ordered his army to resist and called for help from Great Britain under the Treaty of London. Great Britain demanded that Germany comply with the terms of the treaty and respect the neutrality of Belgium. The ultimatum expired at 11 p.m. GMT on 4th August 1914. No reply from Germany was received by then, meaning that the British Empire was now at war with Germany.

It is worth noting that at the time of the outbreak of war in 1914, there were some 75,000 nationals of 'enemy states' residing in Great Britain and Northern Ireland. It was felt in some quarters of government that these individuals could pose a threat or possibly engage in acts of espionage and sabotage. Therefore, a hastily prepared law was written. On 5th August 1914 the Aliens Restriction Act was passed. The first measure of the Act was to ensure that all foreign nationals were to register with their local police station. Other restrictions quickly followed. Areas deemed to be important to national security, such as military bases and power generating plants, were prohibited to the registered aliens and by November 1914, the entire south and east coasts of the country were also prohibited to them. If you lived in one of these areas, you had to obtain a permit to stay and if this was refused, you had four days to relocate. Additionally, a permit was required if you wanted to travel more than five miles from your home. 'Enemy aliens' were prohibited from possessing any communication equipment, including signalling devices or carrier pigeons, any photographic equipment, military maps or moto-rised transport. On 7th August the hastily convened War Office declared that all nationals from enemy states, between the ages of seventeen and forty-two, were to be interned. This was quickly rescinded, possibly because there was nowhere to put them...yet.

Leicester, England
Monday 2nd November 1914

A sharp loud knock at the door woke Karl. He picked up his pocket watch from the bedside table. *Six a.m. on the dot, this means trouble,* he thought.

"Lily, stay there, I'll go." He gently extricated himself from the bed, put on a dressing gown and made his way down the narrow staircase to the front door.

He was confronted by two burly uniformed police officers and a third man, who stood slightly behind them in a smart suit and long dark overcoat, finished off with a dark trilby hat.

"Are you either Karl Hermann Louis Luddolph or Maximillian Albert Luddolph?" the uniformed officer on the left asked sternly.

"I am Karl Luddolph and my brother Max is asleep upstairs," Karl declared.

The man in the suit stepped forward, between the uniformed officers and spoke.

"I am Mr. Archibald Sanders from the Home Office. We have here a warrant to detain both you and your brother as 'enemy aliens' under the Aliens Restriction Act. May I come in and we can discuss what happens next? I would appreciate your cooperation, sir." Sanders spoke quickly and efficiently, but he was at least polite and respectful.

"Yes, please come in. May I dress and wake my brother?" Karl asked. "May I also attend to my wife? She is heavily pregnant and due to give birth in just over a month."

"My men will wait outside. If I may see your papers and permits, issued by Leicester police when you registered there in August?" The man stepped into the hall.

Karl showed him through to the front room of the terrace and pulled some papers from the top drawer of a dark wooden cabinet. "Here are all my registration papers and permits to travel. May I please get dressed and attend to my wife now?"

"Yes, of course, I will wait here," Sanders replied.

Karl climbed the stairs and knocked on the door to the other bedroom. "Max, the police are here, please get dressed and go downstairs, I..." The door flew open and Max's head appeared.

"What's going on?" he asked.

"They have warrants to detain us. Look, just get dressed, get your things together and I suggest you wear something warm, while I speak to Lily," Karl whispered.

Max closed the door quietly, as Karl went back into his bedroom.

"Lily, the police have come to take us, I suspect to one of these new camps. Look, we have the application to America in place, once they sort that out I'm sure we'll be released." Lily started to weep as Karl dressed.

"Karl, did you tell them about the baby? What am I going to do here on my own, with no money? Most of our friends have deserted us too," she whimpered.

"Lily, it's very hard, I know, but I'm sure this will all be rectified soon. Maybe go to your parents for a few days? I'm sure I'll be back by next week."

Karl tried his best to placate Lily, but deep down he felt a sense of enormous disquiet. He dressed quickly, putting on some thick trousers and pulling a pair of old German navy boots from his wardrobe. He put on a vest, shirt, waistcoat, jacket and took a thick coat out of the cupboard. He opened a small leather overnight bag, that he used in his work as a sales representative. He quickly filled it with socks, underpants, three spare shirts and some vests. He found a woollen hat and gloves, which he added to the bag. Karl then went to an old chest in the corner of the bedroom. He opened it and lifted out a small dark wooden stringed instrument, a bit like an auto-harp; it was his zither. He levered the instrument into his bag.

Lily watched him pack and reached into a small drawer in her bedside table. "Karl, take this small bible, it was a Christening present. I want you to have it." She handed the small black leather-bound book to her husband.

Karl kissed the cover of the book and put it in the bag with his other things.

"Lily, don't get up. Rest here until a decent hour, then go to your parents. At least then I'll know you are safe. As soon as I know anything I will contact you there." With that Karl bent over the bed and hugged his pregnant wife and kissed her.

"I love you, Karl," she replied as he stood to leave.

"I love you too, my darling. Whatever happens I will always be in a better place if I know you are all right. Please look after yourself." Karl turned and walked out of the bed-room, then down the stairs, where his brother and Mr. Sanders were waiting.

"Is that everything?' Sanders asked, looking at the small bags each of the brothers were carrying.

"Yes, that's it," Karl answered.

As they walked out to join the uniformed officers and the waiting police van, a small gathering of neighbours had col-lected by the back of the transport – the same neighbours who less than three months ago had been into Karl's house, to share a meal or borrow some sugar, the sort of typical exchange between a small friendly terraced community. As Karl and Max climbed into the rear of the truck, a small cheer rang out, that got louder as the engine of the van started.

As they began to pull away, a few people shouted.

"Good riddance, bloody German scum!" Karl heard as he looked into the eyes of his brother opposite.

Max looked back and spoke: "Tolerant and understanding, welcome in our own community eh?"

Mr. Sanders had got into the front of the transport vehicle, leaving Max and Karl in the rear with the two uniformed officers.

"Excuse me, may I ask where we are to be taken please?" Karl asked the officers.

"To be honest, mate, I have no idea," the officer said. "There might be space for you at the new Handforth camp; do you know where that is?"

"We don't," Max replied for both of them.

"It's about ten miles south of Manchester. They've just converted a large print works into a camp for you people. In fact, have you got a relative called Wilhelm? We picked up a man of roughly your age whose surname was Luddolph in Leicester yesterday evening and took him to Handforth camp."

"He's our younger brother. Will it be possible to be taken to the same camp?" Karl asked the officer.

"There's no set place to put people. We'll take you to the police station and Mr. Sanders will contact the War Department and Home Office. They'll allocate spaces in whichever camps can accommodate you. It's not my place to say, but we've been picking up Germans from various camps and returning them to their homes as often as we've been taking them away. The Home Office and the War Department seem to have few ideas in common and the amount of spaces in the various camps is extremely limited. I say all this to reassure you, that you may well find yourself back home again in a matter of days."

The officer spoke candidly and honestly to Karl, who nodded his understanding and turned to look out of the rear window of the van as it drove through the quiet streets of Leicester back to the central police station. Karl clung to the officer's words and his own knowledge of the internment programme since August. He hoped that both Max and he would indeed be released after a few days and be allowed to depart for the USA, now that they had an application with the American authorities. All he could do was stay positive and hope.

They were not taken to Handforth camp. Once at the police station, which formed part of the town hall in Leicester, Karl and Max were placed in a large holding cell with several other German's living in Leicester. Karl recognised a local butcher and a couple of people he knew worked for one of the many textile factories in the area. After about two hours sitting in the cold, dark cell, the door swung open and Mr. Sanders walked in.

"We now have the spaces available to take you to one of the camps, where you will remain while we process each of you. It's possible the powers that be are minded to release some of you after this. But until a determination can be made you will remain at one of the camps we have in place. Now please gather your belongings and follow me to your transport." And with that two uniformed police officers entered and supervised the twenty or so German men as they gathered their things to follow Mr. Sanders outside. There were now a number of military guards outside the town hall in amongst the police officers. The soldiers were armed but looked relaxed enough with their rifles slung on their shoulders. Once all the men were in front of the town hall, Mr. Sanders spoke. "We will now march you to the train station, where you will embark on the train to a camp north of here. This journey should take roughly four hours, so please pick up your belongings".

Karl and Max, with a bag each, walked with the rest of the group the three quarters of a mile to the railway station, where they were herded onto a platform and told to get into

the carriages of a waiting train. There was no dissent from
the group of 'detained' men, who went compliantly onto the
train.

After about twenty minutes or so, the train suddenly
lurched forward and began to move slowly out of the railway
station. The men were all in one of the third-class carriages,
sitting in four compartments. The soldiers took up their station
in the connecting corridor and at each end of the carriage.
Karl noticed that the police were no longer part of this detail.

"Do you think we'll get to Handforth, perhaps be with
Willy?" Max asked his brother. Max might have been the elder
of the two, but he regarded Karl as more worldly-wise and
constantly sought his council when he was unsure of himself
or a situation.

"I think we'll be very lucky to see Willy. Judging by the
time we spent waiting to be allocated a camp, they clearly have
a number of different places where they could take us. To be
realistic, I think we're on our own."

The train trundled north, passing through Liverpool,
where more 'detained persons' boarded. As the train continued, the weather began to worsen, with a driving rain limiting
the view for those on board. The train slowed again and edged
though Lancaster station, then off the main line onto a siding
that curved around the town and into a large industrial development. Karl noticed a distinctive clock tower in the middle
of the building line. The train came to a halt and shouts rang
out, that were quickly repeated along the line of carriages:
"Everybody OUT!"

Karl climbed down from the train carriage and looked at
the buildings in front of him. It looked like an old disused
factory, with piles of discarded metal wheels outside one of the
entrances. There were other piles of assorted rubbish stacked
up in the areas outside the main building. The soldiers on the
train stood back as other men in uniform, clearly guarding this

establishment, shouted for the newly arrived men to proceed inside the building. As Karl began to walk he noticed several layers of barbed wire had been rolled along the top of the retaining wall around the factory compound.

Inside there had been an attempt to partition the huge space with some wooden panelling, but it was still a vast open area. It almost felt colder inside than it had out in the open. A young officer approached. Karl reckoned he could have been no more than twenty years of age.

"Good afternoon, gentlemen. My name is Lieutenant Graves* and I am in charge of the soldiers here, who are Royal Welch Fusiliers. They will be guarding you here. For your information, this used to be a railway carriage and wagon factory. You will shortly be allocated a bed space and three blankets. Settle in and we will then serve you some food at 6 p.m." The officer finished and shyly walked away.

Max and Karl found two spaces next to each other. Once they had established their territory, they went to explore the extent of the 'facility'.

In addition to the cold, there was a stale odour about the place. The whole interior had a dirty, squalid look to it, with very little light fighting its way through the small dusty windows. Some electric lights did create shadows amongst the throng of people, many of whom looked blankly back at Max and Karl as they passed by, no doubt shocked by the swiftness in their change of circumstances.

"How many are there here do you think?" Max asked Karl.

"I don't know, but this place is huge, there must be over two thousand I reckon," Karl said.

Most of the men were lying on their beds, reading books or newspapers, some were smoking pipes. Karl noticed a couple were sitting opposite each other playing chess.

A small man of no more than five feet six inches, wearing

tweed trousers and matching waistcoat with a heavy padded dark coloured jacket over the top, stepped in front of the two brothers.

"Good day. I'm George Ranke," he said.

"Hello," the brothers replied in unison.

"I am in charge of the prisoners committee, so I suppose I run things and deal with any complaints or incidents with the guards. I have been here since the middle of October, when there were only about five hundred of us. We have a register of in excess of three thousand here now. Before you say it, I know, the place is cold, damp, overcrowded and dirty. The guards are all untrained reservists, who are more concerned by their own situation than actually bothering us. The food we get is the same as theirs, which means it's the most basic military ration. You can write letters out to people, but they will be censored and anything coming in gets rifled through, so only ask your family for the most basic inexpensive supplies. Are you with me so far?" The man paused to allow the Max and Karl to take in his flurry of information.

"I don't know what either of you did before the outbreak of the war. I'm a merchant seaman, been working and living in Liverpool for over twenty years. I'm married to an English girl with two children. One day we're mooring the ship, the next thing, two police officers detain me at the docks. Two days later I wind up here. Didn't get to see my wife or kids before they transported me here. You will need plenty of spare socks, scarves, hats and gloves, as we have very limited heating. It's a cold, cold place."

"We both have applications to emigrate to America. When will they process us please?" Karl asked.

"Inform one of the officers. You saw Lt. Graves; he seems a fair chap and he's descended from Germans. He's probably your best bet. Applications like this are common here. They may take you to the Lancaster Assizes to hear your case in person, but it could take a while. I know one similar request has been outstanding since I've been here."

"Where can we get paper and stamps to send out our letters and applications?" Max asked.

"We have created a central stationary store at the far end of the building. There's not much, so we allocate each prisoner two sheets of paper a week. You can buy stamps and other small items from a camp shop, which again we run, that's up next to the stationary; we get supplies in from the guards. You can ask me for anything and as long as you have the money to pay for it, I can probably get a guard to bring it in. Like I said, the guards are all fairly young and new to this. From overheard conversations many of them come from remote parts of North Wales and seem to abscond back there on a regular basis. We're locked in here and at the moment it feels reasonably safe."

*Second Lieutenant Robert Graves went on to become a famous war poet and writer and briefly described the Lancaster camp in his book *Goodbye to All That*.

Lancaster Camp
8th May 1915

Karl was sitting on his bed in the left corner of one of the hastily assembled wooden compartments within the cavernous draughty old carriage and wagon works. He was staring at a small picture of his beloved Lily, which he had found tucked into the pages of the small bible she had given him the last time he had seen her in November 1914.

"Have you heard the news?" Max walked into the wooden room.

"No, Max, is it bad?" Karl could tell it was serious by the look on his elder brother's face.

"The guards have just told me a German submarine has sunk a passenger liner called the *Lusitania* off the coast of Ireland. Over a thousand people have died, including a number of American civilians."

"My God! Why would they do that? That's not good for us!"

"I suspect not. It may even bring America into the war now and I doubt we'll be given leave to go there now." Max looked very crestfallen.

"Did you hear anything else?"

"One of the guards has a brother in the Ministry of War, who stated that the decision to intern us will be expanded to include all men up to the age of fifty-five, which means Dad will probably be picked up. I have no idea what will happen to mother. How about Lily and Freya, Karl?"

Karl's daughter was now five months old.

"Lily is safe at her parents', I hope. Luckily, she has her mother and sisters at home to help her with little Freya. God, I wish I could hold her. I told Lily to apply for one of these grants that she is entitled to, something to help put food on the table while I'm stuck in here."

The general situation worsened for German subjects and those of her allies living in Great Britain. In the days following the sinking of the liner RMS *Lusitania* virtually every shop owned or operated by a German in the country had its windows put in. There were riots in the major cities and it was largely in response to this that the government expanded the internment strategy to include all males from 'enemy nations' between the ages of seventeen and fifty-five. A large number of German women, whose husbands were now detained, were forcibly repatriated to Germany and a number deemed to be a threat to the security of the nation were also interned. The newspapers of the day portrayed every alleged atrocity committed in Belgium by the Germans in bold banner headlines. The level of hatred and animosity towards those Germans living in Great Britain made it clear that locking them up was as much for their own safety as for the security of the nation.

About two months later Karl was tinkering with his zither, which he had brought with him all those months ago. He had become involved with a fledgling orchestra at the camp. Not that he was a keen musician, but it was something to offset the tedium of life in the camp. Max was lying on the bed opposite reading a week-old newspaper he had obtained from a guard. One of the soldiers, a happy-go-lucky youngster called Williams, came into their partitioned space.

"Got a letter for a Karl Hermann Luddolph, looks official?" He held aloft a brown envelope.

"That's me, thank you." Karl took the letter and Williams left.

"What is it, Karl? It must be about our current application," Max said, coming over.

Karl slit the envelope open with his finger and pulled out two sheets of paper.

"The top one is a copy of the letter from the American ambassador…"

"Read it, Karl."

Karl looked up at his brother and then back at the paper and began to read:

"'The American ambassador presents his compliments to His Majesty's Secretary of State for Foreign Affairs, and has the honour to transmit an enquiry received from the Department of State at Washington, relating to the detention in the camp at Lancaster of K H L Luddolph and M A Luddolph, both German subjects, and asking that if it is found that they come within any of the classifications of non-combatants to be released, as agreed between the British and German governments, they be rendered every necessary and proper assistance towards procuring their release and permission to depart for the United States.' And that's dated 11th June 1915."

"Is there anything else?" Max asked excitedly.

Karl pulled another sheet of paper from the envelope and opened it slowly.

"This one is from the Foreign Office about our enquiry," and he began to read again:

"'The Secretary of State for Foreign Affairs presents his compliments to the United States ambassador, and, with reference to His Excellency's note of the 11th June respecting the detention at Lancaster of the German subjects K.H.L. Luddolph and M.A. Luddolph, I have the honour to state that the cases of these men have already been more than once the subject of enquiry, and that His Majesty's Government would not feel justified in acceding to their request to be allowed to proceed to the Unted States'…and that's dated 3rd July 1915."

Karl finished reading and put the papers on his bed.

"That's it then. We've been refused passage to America, no reason given, we're stuck here for the foreseeable future," Max said heavily.

Karl stared at the official printed papers on his bed and considered this crushing news. His initial reaction was anger, mixed with sorrow that he would not get to see his baby daughter Freya anytime soon. That he would not be allowed to emigrate to America, as a way out of this forced imprisonment. But after a few moments, a more pragmatic and resourceful mindset overtook him.

"Max, if we are to be stuck here for any length of time, then it would be too easy to slip into a downward spiral of anger and depression. We are better than that, we have plenty to offer. My suggestion is that we use the opportunity afforded us to learn new skills and qualities from the people around us and enrich ourselves. I believe that if we don't rise above this, it will be the end of us."

"That's easy for you to say, you have a wife and child to live and fight for. I have nothing, I'm a single man in my early thirties, no wife, no children, now detained against my will, refused permission to go to America."

"Max, you are my brother. I will be with you throughout this period of our lives, however long or short it may be. We can use this time and make the best of things. The alternative does not really bear thinking about. You only have to look at the cold dead eyes of some of the prisoners to see that they have already given up, resigned to their fate. They are pretty much dead already. Well, that's not us, Max. Come on, we can survive and thrive."

About a week later the new lieutenant in charge appeared in the refectory space where Karl and Max were eating their breakfast. He was another young man, who had replaced Lt. Graves when he had been posted to the Western Front.

"If I may have your attention please?" the young officer started, causing a lowering of the volume in the eating area. "A number of you have had your applications heard and they are now considered to be at an end. In line with government policy, you are to be moved to a more permanent facility that has been constructed on the Isle of Man. A list of those persons to be transferred to the island will be posted on the main noticeboard. You will be escorted tomorrow morning at 9.30 a.m. to the ferry port at Heysham, where you will board the ferry to Douglas on the Isle of Man. Please use today to pack up all your belongings and I urge you to only take with you what you can carry as you will be marched the seven miles to the pier head." The lieutenant left the area, as the conversations quickly became loud and animated amongst the prisoners.

Lancaster
November 1915

The next day actually turned into almost two months. Karl and Max were on the list to be transferred with about another six hundred internees from the 'temporary' camp at Lancaster. There had been a good deal of adverse publicity surrounding the Lancaster camp. Some of the local women, whose husbands were fighting in the mud and filth of the trenches on the Western Front, had set themselves up to provide 'comfort' to the guards at the camp. Several brothels were closed down by police when soldiers were failing to report for duty. It was not uncommon for some of the girls to be smuggled into the camp over the walls and fences. This rather unsavoury image of the camp was kept out of the newspapers as much as possible but led to the premature closure of Lancaster as an internment camp.

Karl had managed to pack all he thought he would need into one bag, his zither now protected by a wooden box with a carrying handle he had built for it while at Lancaster. He had kept a close eye on Max since their application to go to America had been refused. His elder brother seemed quiet and withdrawn and Karl needed a way to raise his moral. While waiting for the day to travel, Karl had spoken with one or two friends he had made, pleased in a way that they would be going to the island too. One acquaintance, called Joseph, was a bundle of energy and ideas. Karl supposed they were about the same age. Joseph spoke almost no English; he had only been in Great Britain since 1912 and had been working in a variety of different roles. Karl smiled at the irony when he discovered that Joseph had been working as a boxing coach and trainer, which had led to him teaching bodybuilding to London policemen and self-defence to the detectives.

As the feelings towards Germans living in Great Britain had started to become hostile, Joseph had found work with a travelling circus as a tumbler and carried on some boxing training. He had been staying at a guest house in Blackpool when the police had arrived one morning in late August of 1914 and detained him as an 'enemy alien'. His journey since that date had been to a variety of camps as the authorities sought somewhere to house these internees. Joseph seemed in good spirits despite all the turmoil of the last twelve months.

Karl had found him to be a breath of fresh air, with his sunny disposition and highly energetic manner. Karl had spent the past months helping Joseph to learn English and in return Joseph taught Karl a series of stretches and exercises he had been working on. Joseph had been formulating these muscle stretches as a means to relax after a long day of physical exertion. Karl was impressed with the straightforward and easy-to-follow regime that Joseph suggested, and had remarked that he ought to commit his series of exercises to paper, so that others could benefit from them. This seemed to energise Joseph further and he began to make one or two notes, while they were still at Lancaster.

The guards woke the camp at 6 a.m. one September morning and breakfast was taken by the internees as normal. While they were eating, the young lieutenant once again called for everyone's attention.

"All those listed to be transferred to the island, please report to the main gate for 8 a.m. From there we will escort you to the ferry at Heysham." So the order had finally been given for transfer out of Lancaster.

Karl walked along the road with Max and Joseph next to him. There were in excess of six hundred men being marched to Heysham. It was thankfully a dry, warm autumn day, which made the seven-mile walk to the coast as bearable as it could be. The internees carried everything they possessed as they moved along. The guards were walking alongside the prisoners, but were relaxed, with rifles slung on their shoulders. The six hundred or so 'enemy aliens' walked with little or no dissent. Perhaps the lack of knowledge about what awaited them made them more compliant.

As the coast came into view, Karl spotted the smoke rising from a ship moored in the harbour. They boarded the SS *Duke of Connaught* by 1 p.m. Karl managed to find a space towards the rear of the vessel, deciding that he would rather be on the deck of this transport than trapped within the bowels of the ship, should anything untoward happen. Both Max and Joseph stayed close to Karl, aware of his years in the German navy and his obvious knowledge of nautical things.

The crossing on that Sunday afternoon was uneventful, the Irish Sea was calm and the weather was kind to the prisoners on board. They made it to the Douglas breakwater a little after 5 p.m. The guards ensured that all internees disembarked, but it still seemed an age before they reached the quayside. Karl reckoned that it would have been easy to stow away on board or, once on the quayside, to disappear amongst the throng of local people disembarking at the same time. But, as on the road to Heysham, there was little or no resistance to the orders being given. Karl, with Max next to him and Joseph just in front, marched along the South Quay to the waiting train that was to take them to this new and more permanent detention camp.

There had been a change of the guards. Karl noticed that these soldiers looked older than those at Lancaster and were wearing the insignia of the King's Liverpool Regiment. By the time they arrived at the railway station it was almost 7 p.m. and the daylight was beginning to fade. They boarded, the trio helping some of the more elderly prisoners with their luggage, and after another twenty minutes or so, the train pulled slowly out of the station. It trundled along, heading away from the sea. It was cold, uncomfortable and overcrowded. Again, Karl recognised how easy it would be to have slipped away, either at the station, or simply drop off the train which was travelling at times at no more than walking pace. Most of the guards were seated in a carriage at the front; no one would have noticed, especially as most daylight had now gone.

About an hour after having left the pier head at Douglas, they pulled into St. John's station. Whistles sounded and the order was given to alight from the train. By now it was completely dark and they heard from prisoners in front of them on the platform that they would march along the road to the camp. The progress they made was painfully slow, as suddenly the guards, perhaps aware of the ease with which prisoners might escape, began a series of counts to ensure that everyone was still there. It was a little after 9 p.m. that the column of men arrived at their destination. Karl heard someone ahead of him mutter, possibly an internee or even a guard, "Here we are, Knockaloe."

Knockaloe, Isle of Man
14th September 1915

Karl opened his eyes and stared hard at the timber ceiling, momentarily unsure of where he was. Then he remembered that this was a hut he had been allocated the previous evening in a compound of what he would come to know as Camp Four of the internment camp at Knockaloe. It had been dark when they arrived. There was another full search of both him and his meagre luggage, the allocation of a prisoner number (13888) and then finally Karl and the rest of the six hundred were taken to the entrance to Camp Four. An elderly British officer stood by the gate, with half a dozen soldiers of similar age lined up by the barbed wire-topped fences. Already Karl's boots were caked in a thick layer of mud and he was aware of several in the column struggling to keep their footing in the miserable conditions.

"Listen up, those of you who speak English can pass this on to those who don't!" came a shout from the officer in charge, Camp Four.

"We will count in the first one hundred and eighty. Those counted will make their way to the six huts in the allocated compound, thirty men per hut. Each of you select a bed space, where you will find three blankets and some bed boards to go under the mattress. Once the first hundred and eighty have been secured, we will count in the next one hundred and eighty."

Karl had watched the first group go through the gate, up a muddy avenue between yet more double barbed wire-topped fences. It was difficult to see more of the layout of the camp, as the electric lighting was poor and, in some areas, non-existent. Karl was standing in the line of men, with Max just ahead of him and Joseph behind. Suddenly Max was pulled forward as the last of the next batch.

"He's my brother, can we stay together please?" Karl pleaded with the guard at the gate.

"Look, it's nearly ten o'clock, we can sort it tomorrow," the guard replied in a surly and indifferent tone and pushed Max forward.

Max looked back at his brother as another guard grabbed him and pulled him up the slight incline towards the next compound.

Karl waved forlornly as his brother disappeared from view.

"Karl, I can swop with him tomorrow, so you can be together," Joseph whispered as they were counted in the next batch.

"Thank you, Joseph, hopefully we can remedy this," Karl replied.

Joseph and Karl were herded into the next compound of huts. It was too dark to see much, but they were at the front of this line of prisoners, so entered an empty hut first and immediately selected a corner bed space opposite each other. No food had been available since they had left Lancaster that morning and prisoners were calling out for any food that evening.

There was no response from the guards. Karl recalled that the officer had stated that breakfast would be brought to the huts between 6 and 8 a.m. the following morning.

Karl sat up on his bed that first morning and took in the spartan, cold and draughty wooden hut that was his new home. There were ten beds in the space he was in arranged around the edge of the hut, with a trestle table and ten chairs taking up the area in the centre. Karl would soon learn that each hut was split into three of these ten-man areas. There were three huts in a line, with three further built parallel, but with only a small gap between them. The gap was so tight that the windows of the huts that faced onto each other were soon covered over and in some cases boarded up by the occupants, to afford a better degree of privacy for themselves.

The huts were new but already showed signs of damp on some of the walls. They were not lined, just a single plank of timber between the prisoners and the elements. A small stove was at the edge of a panel that separated Karl and Joseph's section from the next one. Another internee was on his knees in front of the stove trying to get it lit.

All ten men in Karl's section of hut were now awake due to the metallic sound of food being distributed from large tureens and saucepans.

The door flew open and a man dressed in grimy chef's whites brought in a large pot, with the lid on.

"Got porridge this morning, lads," the distinctly Cockney-sounding orderly explained. "Lucky for some eh! Made half and half, milk and water. Now, you will find a box under your beds with a few bits, including something to put this porridge in and something to eat it with."

"Are you a guard or civilian cook?" Karl asked the man with the pot, as he hastily grabbed a bowl and a spoon from the box by his bed.

"Nah, mate. Prisoner, just like you. Been in London since I was five years of age. One day I'm happily minding my own business at Smithfield's, the next I'm detained at the market entrance and transported to this wonderful place. I mean, I aint no bloody hun, just me dad never did the paperwork when we came to England."

"What's it like here?'" one of the other men in the hut asked.

"It's a pigsty and no mistake. The huts are damp and cold and they let in water when it rains. They keep us in confinement in these smaller compounds to isolate and control us. The paths are always muddy and treacherous. They keep piling cinders onto them, but that just makes it worse. Be nice when it gets colder, at least then it'll be frozen mud and easier to negotiate. Look, lads, I know you have loads to ask, but I have loads to serve, so please, get some of this while it's still warm and get yourselves sorted." And with that the deliverer of the food was gone.

Munich

September 1915

At the time that Karl was just contemplating his situation at Knockaloe, Ziggy Jurgens was sitting in the kitchen of their small apartment in the suburbs of Munich with his pretty blonde wife, Petra, contemplating the choices facing him.

"I have received my notice of conscription and have to make a decision as to where I serve," Ziggy announced.

"I thought you were able to defer your service because of the job you've just been offered in Friedrichshafen? What about our move to that house we saw near to the lake?"

"I thought so too, but this letter states that although my work is considered important, it's not on the list of roles protected against conscription to fight in the war. The choice therefore is, do I enlist and be sent to serve in who knows where, or do I re-join the navy and have some determination of where I may end up?"

"If it comes down to a choice of those, then you must choose the navy and hope your previous service and experience will garner some degree of seniority." Petra had come to the same conclusion as Ziggy had already decided upon.

Several weeks later, after his letter to the Imperial German navy requesting to recommence his service had been accepted, Ziggy found himself travelling north through the German countryside by train. He had said an emotional goodbye to Petra and their five-month-old little boy Lothar at the station.

His orders were to report to the naval base at Kiel, to join the crew of one of the most recent additions to the German fleet, the newly commissioned SMS *Frankfurt*. Ziggy had been given a commission in the rank of Oberleutnant zur See (Senior Lieutenant at Sea). As he once again read his orders he wondered how much he remembered from his time in the navy during his national service. It had been eight years since Ziggy and his good friend Karl had left the service. In that time Ziggy had enrolled at the University of Munich and graduated with honours, obtaining a degree in mechanical engineering. During his last year at university he had met, finally, the girl that stopped him in his tracks and brought an element of stability and, perhaps, maturity to his life. He had found work as a supervisor in a machine tools factory in Munich. After nearly two years together, Petra and Ziggy were married in a small ceremony in late 1912. It had been such a small wedding that Ziggy had decided not to invite his closest friend Karl Luddolph. Petra had turned the small apartment they had into a comfortable home, just in time for the arrival of Lothar into their lives in the spring of 1915.

Things had been going well for them since Ziggy had successfully secured a job more suitable to his level of expertise at the new factory in Friedrichshafen, which was to provide gearing systems for the airships being built there for Ferdinand von Zeppelin. It was also, so Ziggy had believed, to be a protected occupation that would prevent him from having to join the military again.

Such was not to be and now here he was, once more dressed in the uniform of the Imperial German navy, about to take up the challenge of life on board a brand-new vessel. He found himself thinking about his last train journey to join the service; on that occasion he had been fortunate to meet Karl. He had not seen him since his wedding in April of 1912. They had been in regular contact by letter and he was aware that

Karl's wife Lily would by now have given birth to their first child. Since the end of 1914, there had been no further contact; Ziggy did have Karl's address, but had no idea whether any letter he might send would even reach his friend, now that Great Britain and Germany were at war.

Ziggy had joined the ship just after the SMS *Frankfurt* had completed a series of truncated sea trials so that she was ready for service more quickly. He looked at the crew, now assembled on the rear deck ready for inspection. His own detachment of sailors were all no more than teenagers, with a look of wide-eyed bewilderment on their faces as the ship's senior officers descended to the deck for the inspection. The new ship had been assigned to the I Scouting group, primarily as a reconnaissance vessel, acting as support to the battlecruisers of the group. This fleet of ships was under the command of Admiral Franz von Hipper, who was today on board the *Frankfurt* to inspect the crew of his newest ship.

Hipper already had a reputation for action since the outbreak of the war. In fact, Ziggy had heard rumours that Hipper was possibly due to be replaced as he had shown poor judgement at the Battle of Dogger Bank in the North Sea. Hipper had led the reconnaissance vessels close to shore and fired on Scarborough, Hartlepool and Whitby. Records show that over a hundred civilians lost their lives, with over five hundred casualties. The British were outraged that the German navy would sail close to their eastern shore and fire at these coastal towns with impunity. Hipper was actually branded a 'baby killer' in the British newspapers of the day.

The German communications had been intercepted and decoded by the British, who knew of the German plan to raid parts of Northern England. Criticism was levelled at the British navy who, despite knowing of the German plan, had failed to prevent the attacks upon the coastal towns. The smaller German fleet were eventually surprised by the larger, swifter, British fleet, and were forced to flee the area. After a long chase the British eventually caught up with the German ships. They engaged the enemy and managed to disable the German battlecruiser, *Blücher*. For their part, the Germans hit HMS *Lion*.

At this point the British broke off the pursuit of the rest of the German fleet. Hipper, decided to keep sailing, sacrificing the *Blücher* for the safety of the rest of his fleet. Due to poor signalling between elements of the British fleet and a fear of possible U-boats in the area, the British changed direction and this put them back on course with the *Blücher*. Despite overwhelming odds, *Blücher* was able to put HMS *Meteor* out of action and scored at least two hits on other British battlecruisers with its 8-inch guns. *Blücher* was hit by over seventy shells and wrecked. Finally, she was struck by two torpedoes causing her to capsize, and she sank shortly afterwards with the loss of nearly eight hundred crew. The British were hampered in their efforts to pick up German survivors by a German Zeppelin and seaplane that dropped small bombs on the fleet. The British had to leave some of the survivors behind to evade this aerial bombardment.

While no official criticism was levelled at Hipper, he also received no recognition either. He therefore now found himself back at Kiel awaiting a decision about his command.

Ziggy watched the Admiral walk along the line of sailors under his own command and stood rigidly to attention as the Admiral stopped opposite him.

"I understand you did your national service with our navy, young man?" the Admiral enquired.

"Yes, sir, three years ending in 1907; I served on SMS *Kaiser Wilhelm II*."

"We will have need of experienced officers like you as this war continues," the Admiral replied. "I wish you every success, young man. Your sailors will need a mature head to guide them in the months ahead."

"Yes, sir, thank you, sir."

The Admiral moved on with his inspection as Ziggy remained resolutely at attention. Once the senior officers of the inspection party had returned to their station, Ziggy and the other junior officers dismissed their men to return to their duties. Ziggy walked to the rear of the ship and found himself looking out over the city of Kiel, remembering another time, when as a young national service cadet he had been inspected by none other than King Edward VII of Great Britain. He smiled and was lost in thoughts of his great friend Karl and didn't therefore hear the approach of a heavy-set man, with a large bald head and an impressive handlebar moustache and greying goatee beard.

"Lt. Jurgens? May I present my compliments on your promotion and return to the service," the ferocious-looking warrant officer stated.

Ziggy recognised the voice and pivoted round quickly to see the smiling face of his former chief instructor and mentor, Otto Nadler.

"Chief Nadler, surely you're not still serving? I felt sure you would be enjoying a well-earned retirement by now." Ziggy smiled back at the formidable figure opposite him.

"I'm not finished yet, young man. I just happen to be important enough to this navy to be allowed an extra three years before I finish. I reckon looking at the crew, I may well have my work cut out." Otto smiled.

"Chief, it really is so good to see you. It may not be proper protocol, but it would be my honour to stand you a beer when we next finish duty." Ziggy smiled broadly as he spoke.

"I finish at 6 p.m. Let's meet on the shore by the companionway at 6.30. I have things we need to discuss." And with that the Oberstabsbootsmann walked back towards the rear 8-inch guns. Ziggy watched the hulking figure disappear from view, then he casually walked back to his men, who were busy cleaning the rear deck.

Knockaloe, Isle of Man
April 1916

"I think Joseph is onto something, you know. Especially in light of our currently confined situation." Karl spoke from his chair at the end of the trestle table in their hut.

"Well, I feel so much better now that I'm back with you. Who would have thought that a simple welfare request to put the two of us together would take almost six months!" Max responded.

"These simple techniques that he is getting us all to do each morning and evening are part of the reason you are feeling better, I'm sure of it."

At that moment Joseph came back into the cold, damp hut, his ever-present smile in place. He sat down at the table with the two brothers.

"So, my two good friends. How are you both today? I've been busy at the hospital. We have so many patients suffering with stiff backs, which is causing them to have poor posture and balance. I have an idea I wish to share, which maybe between us we can accomplish." Joseph's natural enthusiasm made Karl smile and Max perked up to listen to the latest of Joseph's thoughts.

"The hospital beds have a number of springs attached to the metal of the bedstead. With the cooperation of the doctors and the guards I have been able to acquire a bed, so that we can work on the springs to design something that can help patients to exercise, even when they are bedbound," Joseph explained.

"Where is the bed?" Max asked.

"I've been able to persuade the guards to allow you to spend tomorrow in the hospital with me. Between my duties I have an idea that we can adapt this bed, perhaps attach some of the springs to the headboard and footboard, thereby creating something that will give a little resistance to a patient wishing to do some mild exercise, while otherwise bedbound. What do you think?

"But surely these patients are too sick, they're laid up in hospital to recover, not to exercise?" Karl countered.

"That's my whole point. They are there to recover and part of that is to rehabilitate. Rather than just lie in bed, listlessly whiling the days away, they would be able to do a small and limited selection of exercises I will design, to at least get them to keep their muscles active. That in turn will help them regain strength, correct any imbalance and improve their posture. The exertion will make them breathe in a more controlled manner and with increased capacity. As with everything I have suggested, this will in turn help to focus their minds and lead to a better sense of well-being."

"You make it all sound so simple," Max suggested.

"I believe it is simple. Look how your own spirit has regained some of its zeal since you started the breathing and stretching exercises with the rest of us when you moved in here?"

"You have convinced me, Joseph," Karl declared. "I believe that your regime is part of the reason our section of this hut is in such a buoyant state, despite the dreariness of our situation. I feel focused and ready to use my time here to better myself. I have been to the compound library and have started a course in engineering. Without your 'Contrology' theory I think it would be far more challenging here."

"Thank you, Karl," Joseph replied, "that's kind of you. I am only the framework, there is so much we must continue to do in our efforts to survive our current imprisonment."

Some others from their section of the hut echoed Karl's sentiments as they all made their way outside for their daily exercise period. Despite it being early spring it was still cold and the sun had not been able to penetrate the thick grey clouds. The ground was a black sticky mess of dark mud that stuck to the bottom of their boots. As they laboured up the slight incline in the wired corridor between the compounds, the going got tougher as their boots got heavier.

Joseph was greeted on arrival by some internees who were already in the field. There were about thirty men now formed up into three ranks of ten, and Joseph stood at the front facing them.

"Now remember, gentlemen, just take these exercises at your own pace. Breathe deeply. In and out as you exert." Joseph began his class and demonstrated his breathing technique. The class ranged in age from eighteen-year-old fresh-faced teenagers to overweight, balding men in their fifties.

"That's good, lets smile as we breathe. Let your mind control the muscles as you stretch them," Joseph continued.

Joseph could see the front row laughing at something beyond his eyeline. He turned to be confronted with a line of ten or so British military guards, all following his exercise class and joining in with the routine, their rifles propped up against the perimeter fence.

"Would you care to join us here?" Joseph offered.

"Nah, mate," one of the senior NCOs answered. "We just thought we'd keep ourselves warm while we kept watch on you."

"Well, you're most welcome anytime," Joseph replied.

The exercises went on for another thirty minutes or so, with the guards keeping pace with their charges. The men separated from one another as they made their way back to their respective compounds.

When his turn came Karl sat on the step and removed his muddy boots, leaving them on a crafted covered wooden platform raised off the ground that one of the men in the hut had made. After the dreadful winter conditions, they had all agreed that they would always remove their boots before entering the hut. Only the boots of the guards would dirty the floor of the hut when they came to conduct monthly inspections and it just became a necessary chore to clear up after they had left. By now routines were well established with everyone in the hut.

"So tomorrow let's see if we can fashion some sort of exercise frame using the old bed and some of the spare springs from one of the bed frames?" Joseph suggested.

"That sounds good. Max, you've always been good with your hands, do you fancy helping Joseph with me?"

"Yes, absolutely! An exciting project and a change of scenery, of course I'm in," Max immediately answered.

"Thank you both," Joseph said smiling.

The time at Knockaloe passed perhaps more swiftly for those fortunate enough to have met and spent time with the effervescent and exuberant Joseph Pilatus (as he was recorded in the camp records), but whose real surname was Pilates. Karl and Max benefitted greatly from his friendship and favour, able to become willing students as Joseph developed the series of exercises and breathing techniques that years later would be the bedrock of a multi-million-dollar empire of exercise studios and literature.

But that was the future. For now, these three close friends simply sought to alleviate the crushing tedium and boredom of life as internees.

With better weather improving morale still further, the inmates of Camp Four found time to improve their lot. Additional tar paper was sought and supplied to keep the elements at bay. An additional library of books was established for the benefit of all at the camp, not just Camp Four. Committees were formed to be able to debate other improvements with the commandant of the camp. Entertainment was provided by the inmates themselves, creating concerts on a weekly basis. Karl joined a small orchestra with his zither and Max outshone his younger brother as a truly exceptional mimic and comedian, his exploits being recorded in one of the camp's own newspapers, which gave the inmates a rough idea of events beyond the barbed wire, as well as within.

After many months a trickle of letters were received by the inmates from their families and friends. Karl finally received a pack of letters from Lily in June 1916, most of them dated over a year previously. All were addressed to the internment camp at Lancaster. All were opened, and had clearly been read and censored by the authorities before being given to him. His feelings of anger and bitterness over this were tempered by the small passport-sized photograph of a smiling baby in her mother's arms: his beautiful wife Lily, holding their daughter, Freya. Max had been watching his younger brother closely and now sat down next to him and put an arm around him and spoke quietly. "They are both out there for you, Karl, both beautiful and devoted to you. I'm sure it won't be long before you are all reunited."

"Max, thank you for your words, but how can we know how long we must endure this imprisonment? I sometimes stop and think how we are caught between two sides. We could have so easily been fighting for the Germans, but equally we could have been citizens of Great Britain and been fighting for her. Instead we wait, neither on one side or the other. We wait while those in power deploy their forces against each other, in a futile gesture of nationalistic pride. Without Joseph and his exercise philosophy, I fear I would be lost to the despair of it all." Karl paused, then went on. "I'm so sorry, Max. Did you get anything today?"

"As a matter of fact, some news of our parents and Willy. It would appear Willy was moved around a great deal. From what Mother tells me, he went firstly to Alexandra Palace in London, and at one stage it was likely he would be deported back to Germany, before he was finally moved to the camp at Handforth. This is where he was on the date of Mother's letter, so, October 1915."

Karl nodded. "Is there anything else?"

"Sadly, yes. It would appear Father was detained shortly after we arrived here last year. After the *Lusitania* sinking, they extended the upper age of detainees to fifty-five and that included Father. From what I received, it would appear he has been seriously ill in Leeds Infirmary with acute appendicitis, then, after being moved to the camp at Wakefield, he was again taken to hospital with tuberculosis. That was also in October of last year. The last thing Mother says is that she fears for her own deportation back to Germany, now that Father has been detained. The address she writes from is a state-run centre near to Spalding." Max placed a supportive hand on Karl's shoulder.

"My God! Are our entire family to be swept away?" Karl's normal reserved demeanour gave way to real anger. "Lily was evicted from our little house by the landlord. In the eyes of the authorities she is a German, since she married one. She writes that she has moved back in with her parents and her two sisters are at home to help with Freya. She tells me she is healthy and well in her letters, but I know her handwriting of old and I can sense in the script that she is weak and suffering from the situation. Max, I'm so worried about her." Karl put his head on his brother's arm and wept.

Just then Joseph bounded into the hut, full of energy and good humour. But he sensed the atmosphere immediately and calmed himself and came and sat on the bed on Karl's other side. He also placed an arm over Karl's shoulder and simply said, "Breathe, Karl, like we practised. Breathe slowly in, and then slowly out."

The three men sat on that spartan, metal-framed bed in a hut in Camp Four of the Knockaloe internment camp, just calming their breathing, so they were in sync with each other and slowed the rate down. After twenty minutes or so Joseph stood. "Better, my friend?"

"Yes, Joseph, better, thank you," Karl replied.

"Good. We must not be affected in here by things we cannot control out there. Everything we hold dear demands that we emerge from this place, whenever that may be, in as fit and optimistic a condition as we can be."

"As hard as it continues to be, I agree with you, Joseph." Karl stood together with Max, and the three hugged each other.

The North Sea
31ˢᵗ May 1916

"Fire!" Ziggy gave the order to his gun crew and their 6-inch guns began firing. Above the cacophony of sound, Ziggy was receiving orders from the bridge to adjust his trajectory. "Keep firing, five shells, then re-calibrate for a thousand metres and a further five," Ziggy bellowed his order to the leading man. The noise and smoke from the propulsion charges was hard to bear as the second salvo of shells was shot off.

"Cease firing!"

Then another message was passed down from the bridge: "Stand down, men. The British are turning away." Raucous cheers broke out from his gunners in the forward turret.

Konteradmiral Friedrich Boedicker was aboard the *Frankfurt*, using her as his flagship for the battle. He was commanding II Scouting Group. His objective was to screen the I Scouting Group battlecruisers commanded by Vizeadmiral Hipper. This first salvo of ordnance fired from the 6-inch guns of *Frankfurt*, *Pillau* and *Elbing*, was aimed towards the corresponding cruiser screen of the British naval battle fleet. This took place shortly after 4 p.m., and firing stopped on the German side as the British ships turned away.

"Incoming!!" Suddenly shell fire exploded around them. The noise was terrifying, magnified inside the armoured gun turret. "Fire smoke!" Ziggy passed the order and his gunners put six smoke shells downrange. The incoming shells quickly subsided as Ziggy presumed they were hidden by the smoke. Ziggy took it upon himself to open the turret hatch to let in some North Sea air and told his men to drink water and to prepare the gun for further firing. This involved bringing the propulsion charges and explosive shells up from below. Ziggy checked on his men and then inspected the charges and shells. "Good work, men. Now you know how loud and chaotic this is going to be, you'll be prepared better for our next engagement," and he patted the closest gunner to him on the shoulder.

Just over an hour later (probably about 6 p.m.), two British destroyers, HMS *Onslow* and HMS *Moresby*, tried to break through the German cruiser screen and get to the German battlecruisers. "Fire," Ziggy shouted again and his forward turret began firing. "Keep firing, men, quick as you like, adjust to six hundred metres." The gun fired non-stop for a good five to six minutes. "Cease fire!" Ziggy ordered. "The British have turned away again," he relayed from command, receiving cheers and applause from his young men.

A short while later (records indicate just after 6.30 p.m.): "A British vessel dead ahead, range five hundred metres, load with high explosive rounds, men. Fire when ready, then continue firing." Ziggy looked through the range finder and observation slit in the turret. "A hit, boys! We've hit her! Cease firing." All was suddenly stillness after the frantic activity.

"Incoming! They've hit the *Wiesbaden* away to our port side. Hold tight, we're turning away. Put some smoke up again, lads." Again, there was a lull in the battle, as the respective sides regrouped and searched for each other.

Suddenly there was an almighty explosion midships, behind the forward turret, quickly followed by a second in the same part of the *Frankfurt*. There was a three-second pause then a smaller explosion forward of where Ziggy crouched. His men began screaming in terror. Ziggy swallowed the bile in his throat and forced himself to his feet. "Courage, men, we're almost out of range. Those last two felt smaller to me, that's lucky shooting, we're nearly out of this." His words belied his true feelings of fear, but he composed himself once more and strode amongst his men and reassured them individually.

Unbeknown to Ziggy the *Frankfurt* had been hit a total of four times. HMS *Canterbury* hit her with two 6-inch shells and two smaller shells. The last hit actually exploded in the water, but close enough to the stern of the vessel to cause damage. Crews were able to assess the situation quickly and SMS *Frankfurt* was still able to remain in the battle. Three men had been killed instantly in the forward area, but these were the only fatalities on the ship; a further eighteen wounded seamen were moved down to the rear quarters.

There was now a lull in proceedings, and as night fell it grew eerily quiet. The German fleet was heading back towards Danish waters. Still on high alert, *Frankfurt* spotted several British destroyers and fired a torpedo. Ziggy watched the torpedo leave his ship and then *Frankfurt* turned back to re-join the rest of the German fleet. Ziggy took a turn round the ship, talking to the seaman supping hot Bovril as he went, reassuring them and smiling as he saw a great hulk of a man carry a stricken sailor past some debris and lay him down and place a blanket gently over him.

"Chief Nadler, how are the men here?" Ziggy approached his former instructor, now confidant and friend.

"Sir, we are coping, only some cuts and bruises really and a fair deal of shock." The giant spoke quickly without turning his head.

Ziggy crouched down and came close to Nadler. "Otto, good to see you came through."

"Ah! Young Jurgens. I hear that the forward turret actually hit something tonight, congratulations, my friend." And he smiled back at the young lieutenant.

"We're heading home now," Nadler went on. "I think we've bloodied the nose of the enemy, but it's hard to see that we achieved anything more. We certainly didn't at any stage break through the blockade."

"I hear what you say, but what's to stop this happening again?" Ziggy replied.

"We must talk again when we are back in Wilhelmshaven. For the meantime, return to your station and be watchful. I bet there are still British ships in our area." Otto Nadler stood and saluted the young lieutenant.

The chief was right and SMS *Frankfurt* spotted two British destroyers at around 1 a.m. on the morning of 1st June. Ziggy's gun crew opened fire once again, then carried on their course further towards Danish waters. By roughly 4 a.m. the German fleet had reached Horns Reef and evaded the British fleet.

This naval engagement became known as the Battle of Jutland. It was the last major battle in world history fought primarily by battleships. In terms of total ships displaced, it was the largest surface naval battle in history. By the end of the engagement, fourteen British and eleven German ships had been sunk, with a total loss of 9,823 men. Both sides were quick to claim victory, but in the years since, debate continues over the performance of either fleet and the actual significance of the battle. For her part SMS *Frankfurt* had three fatalities and eighteen wounded. She had fired a total of 379 rounds of 6-inch ammunition, two 3.5-inch rounds and a single torpedo.

"What you're talking about is mutiny," Ziggy whispered to his erstwhile Instructor and now firm friend Otto Nadler. They were both dressed in civilian attire, drinking schnapps in a small dimly lit bar in the bowels of the old port of Kiel, well away from prying eyes and other naval personnel.

"Ziggy, I am fifteen years older than you and have seen so much of our world. I simply pass on the thoughts of the men and senior non-commissioned officers around me. There is a growing divide between the affluent and aristocracy and the rest of us. I understand this feeling of hopelessness coming from the ships in our fleet. Last month we fought a battle with the British navy that took over two thousand five hundred lives and wounded a further five hundred. Those figures have not been made public, as our great leaders seek to turn this farce into a propaganda victory." Nadler spat the words in his contempt for the German leadership.

"But we did sink so many of their ships and their losses must have been greater than ours," Ziggy replied, trying to defend the battle.

"Did we at any stage break through their blockade? Did we have any chance of breaking out of the Skagerrak and get even close to the Atlantic? How can we claim victory, when all we did was necessitate that the British fleet direct their activities in the North Sea? To keep an eye on us just because we sank a few of their ships? We are an inconvenience to the British navy, nothing more!" Nadler tried to keep his voice to a whisper, but the last outburst raised a few heads around the edges of the shadowy bar.

"What your colleagues are suggesting will end in arrest and most likely a firing squad. It is treason, Otto," Ziggy said, stating the obvious.

"I simply pass on what I've heard and felt that you would be in a better general position if such thoughts were to be brought to actual fruition." Otto resumed his calm deep whisper.

"You took a risk. I'm senior to you and by rights I should take this information directly to my senior supervisor," Ziggy explained.

"I know, but what would you say? While crouched over a table drinking schnapps with an enlisted man, you became aware of some rumours that the men below decks were not entirely happy with the way things were being conducted by the officers in charge. That sort of rumour has been around ever since a rank structure was introduced and I'm sure those in charge know full well how much the men despair of our situation. Have you heard about the latest battle in Belgium?" Otto asked.

"I know we kept our lines during a massive British offensive, but have not been able to read more," Ziggy replied.

"I think the British leadership are worse than ours in many ways. Their sheer ambivalence to human life, that they could squander so many men so needlessly. Did you know that there was an estimate that sixteen thousand British soldiers were killed in a single day at the River Somme? IN A SINGLE DAY! This whole war has to stop. Somehow Germany has to find a different path, perhaps a different style of leadership, even a removal of the monarchy and a chance at a republic perhaps?"

"Why are you telling me this, Otto?" Ziggy asked.

"I'm sick of fighting for something I no longer believe in. When the time comes, and come it will, I want you to understand and be ready. I'm not asking for your involvement, but simply wish you to know what is coming. You deserve to know, after all the time we've known each other."

"You should know for my part," Ziggy said, "that I basically agree with all you have said, but I will not be involved in any mutiny or action against our senior officers. You should also know that I was made aware that SMS *Frankfurt* and the majority of the fleet has been stood down and we are confined to port until further notice." These were the most recent orders Ziggy had received that very morning.

"Well, at least they see the futility in taking on the British, fleet to fleet. If we must continue in this campaign, we should try and use more of our U-boats, but the best course of action now would be to try and seek a diplomatic resolution to this conflict, as I see no way of us winning."

"Now there, my friend, I agree with you one hundred per cent," said Ziggy with a smile.

"Your round then, Jurgens!" Otto Nadler smiled back at the young man sitting opposite him, who he had come to regard as almost a son these past few months.

Knockaloe
September 1918

"Without your help I would never have been able to get the exercise frame to the finished article it is today," Joseph explained to the two brothers sitting opposite him.

"Well, having spent the last two years studying engineering again, I feel I have been able to better understand what it was you were trying to create and assemble it with you," Karl answered his fellow inmate.

"I can take this plan with me when we eventually get out of here," Joseph went on.

"When do you think that will be? Rumour is that the German forces are close to surrender." Max had heard this from a cook at breakfast that morning.

"Do you realise my daughter, Freya, will be four in December and I am yet to lay my eyes on her, let alone hold and cuddle her!" Karl bemoaned his situation.

"Look at us, Karl, we are strong and fit," Max said encouragingly, "unlike some of the walking corpses out there. Joseph and his ideas have kept us both physically fit and mentally strong. Remember how depressed I was when we got here? You both pulled me out of that pit of despair. Now is the time to put those thoughts of home to one side and remain steadfast in overcoming the next few months."

"I know, you're right and I understand. It's just hard, not knowing how much longer we are to be locked up here, while the world tears itself apart and my family becomes an ever more distant memory," Karl argued.

"Gentlemen, having been working at the camp hospital for so long, I feel it important that you know that there is another less visible risk to us all, that may prove to be as much of a challenge as anything we have faced thus far." Max and Karl turned to look at Joseph as he continued.

"We are getting a number of serious cases of influenza amongst the weak, elderly and other vulnerable patients. It's spreading amongst the camp and I suspect will kill quite a few. That is why it is now more important than ever to remain physically at our peak and to have the mental fortitude to overcome whatever this epidemic is."

"What can we do?" Max asked.

"We must maximise the time we spend training. Even as the weather here gets colder and damper, we must keep some of the windows open to keep the air in the hut fresh. I can see the dampness on the walls of our hut and the rot and mould on some of our clothes. We must dry our washing better, to only wear things that are completely dry and we must keep our heater going all day to try and dry out this damp hut of ours," Joseph concluded.

Some others in the hut had been listening to the conversation. They too, as hut mates of Joseph Pilates, had felt the benefit of his breathing philosophy and energetic physical training regime, so were supportive of any efforts to minimise the toll this influenza might take on them. Joseph proceeded to issue instructions to the occupants of the hut.

"Gentlemen, we are all strong now in mind and body. We eat poorly, but we must forage to improve our diet. I know some of you tend the vegetable patches grown in the compound. We must try to eat as much fresh food as we can. Any parcels from home need to include any citrus or other fruit. If you can, when out and about, cover your nose and mouth with something to slow the spread of this illness."

Over the next few weeks, Joseph was able to divulge just how many were now in hospital afflicted with influenza symptoms. At the same time parcels belatedly received from outside were packed with as much fresh fruit and vegetables as the loved ones outside could collect. As was the custom, all these parcels were censored and a certain 'levy' was appropriated from them by the guards before the packages got to the huts in Camp Four. As the autumn weather began to slip towards winter, the occupants of Joseph Pilates' hut had a generous supply of fruit to augment the meagre rations they were fed by the camp authorities.

Kiel
October 1918

By September 1918 the situation for the Kaiser was considered, by many, to be hopeless. Requests were being made from his war council to call for a ceasefire and try and create a more democratic government, in an attempt to secure more favourable peace terms. A new Chancellor, Prince Maximilian of Baden, included a number of Social Democrats in his Cabinet.

"Otto, we have been stuck in this port for over two years now. A good number of our colleagues transferred to submarines and smaller torpedo boats. Why didn't you go too?" Ziggy sat with his good friend in the same dingy Kiel bar that had become their regular haunt these past few years.

"I could ask the same of you, my young lieutenant. We both had the chance to carry on the fight, but we both decided to stay. You look thin, Ziggy," Otto remarked, taking in the gaunt features of his colleague. "Rations are becoming scarce, but you must eat, my friend."

"I thought more would happen after the abortive attempted protest by the sailors in Wilhelmshaven?" Ziggy said.

"I thought so too. I think it did its job though, there are war councils below decks and committees on virtually every ship of the fleet here in Kiel. I'm assured that the same is true in every German port. Everyone is just waiting for the right moment."

"Then I believe I have news that may well give these men the signal they need," Ziggy declared. "Admiral Hipper has devised a plan to once again take the fleet out, to meet the British fleet head-on for a final battle in the English Channel."

"My God! Is he mad? There'll be a full-scale riot. Apart from anything else, did he not see the futility of fighting the British fleet in this way? It's like they never learn from previous mistakes. When is this order to sail set to be issued?" Otto asked.

"As far as I know, the 24th October," Ziggy explained.

"Then here is what we'll do. I will let the war council operating below decks on our ship know this information, they will then quickly spread it to the rest of the fleet. We will then, you and I, watch for what happens next. You may, as an officer, find that you are considered to be the enemy by the councils formed below decks. There are a good number of Bolsheviks within these councils, who are not well disposed towards hierarchy and rank, so I will find you and we will stay together, as the situation develops. Do you understand?"

"I will watch for you, Otto, and thank you." Ziggy leant forward, they touched glasses and downed the schnapps in one.

The first noticeable action after the naval order to prepare to sail was issued on 24th October. Sailors on three ships of the fleet at Wilhelmshaven refused to obey orders and weigh anchor. Sailors aboard SMS *Thüringen* and SMS *Helgoland* committed more direct mutiny and sabotage. The squadron commander Vizeadmiral Hugo Kraft ordered torpedo boats the following day to point their weapons at the mutinous ships. The sailors quickly gave up and were removed but the orders to sail against the enemy had to be dropped. It was clear to the leadership that the crews of their ships were no longer reliable. Vizeadmiral Kraft ordered the fleet to return to Kiel by way of the Kiel Canal, that links to Wilhelmshaven. Kraft had about fifty of the identified ringleaders of the mutiny put ashore and imprisoned. As the fleet was nearing the open port of Kiel he had another one hundred and fifty mutineers put ashore at

Holtenau, and incarcerated in the military prison there.

"Ziggy, Ziggy!" Otto burst into the small ward room where Ziggy Jurgens was sitting quietly drinking a coffee.

"Coffee, my friend?" He offered a cup to the hulking figure of Otto Nadler crammed in the companionway door.

"We must go. Our stokers have opened the valves on the boilers. There is no pressure, we can't sail. This will be the beginning of it. I must get you to safety," Otto pleaded.

"Otto, you above all others have taught me to keep calm in a crisis," Ziggy said soothingly. "I have clothes I am going to change into while you, I see, have already done so. Have a coffee while I change and then we will depart the ship and see the lie of the land."

Otto's serious demeanour gave way to a large smile as he moved forward into the small seating area and took the offered cup of coffee from his young lieutenant. "I knew you were the right man to back. Ziggy, please take your time while I drink my coffee," and Otto Nadler sat down in the junior officers' wardroom of SMS *Frankfurt*, and drank a cup of fresh hot coffee as he waited for his friend to change into more suitable clothing than that of an officer of the line in the Imperial German navy.

After about ten minutes Ziggy returned to the wardroom. "Ready then?"

"I am, now stay close, but stay behind me. I know a good number of those in the war councils. They are suspicious men and do not know you. Let me do the talking OK?"

"Lead the way, Otto," Ziggy said, smiling at his friend.

"I understand that there's a meeting going to take place at the Union House in Legienstrasse, that's where we're going to go first," Otto said.

The two comrades left the ship after ten minutes or so of waiting for a lull in the pedestrian traffic coming and going. They made their way through the myriad of dark lanes and alleyways that led away from the naval dockyard and towards the rest of the city of Kiel. They kept to the shadows as the light of the day began to fade.

"When we get there," Otto whispered, "we will go inside, but keep to the back and make sure no one is behind you."

The lights of a large building on their right blazed, silhouetting a number of figures gathered outside. The two friends joined a group as they made their way inside. There were over two hundred sailors in attendance. Ziggy recognised one or two, so kept his head down as several others acknowledged the familiar bulk of Otto Nadler.

"We have sent a delegation to the senior officers of the fleet asking for our brothers to be freed from prison," said a man neither Ziggy nor Otto recognised, "but I've just been informed that they will not let them in to talk. The police are on their way to close us down, so the time has come to disband this meeting. I have called for a gathering with other political parties on the large drill ground tomorrow at 2 p.m. Tell everyone you can think of to join us there. Now disappear quickly before the police get here."

Everyone present took heed of the notice to leave and Otto and Ziggy made their way as covertly as possible back to the ship.

Another day, another meeting, and Otto was pointing out to Ziggy the figures on the raised platform at the front.

"His name is Karl Artelt, he works in one of the repair yards for the torpedo boats. The man stood next to him is Lothar Popp. He's another shipyard worker. They're both members of the Independent Social Democratic Party of Germany (USPD). Yesterday's meeting at the drill square was just a prelude to this."

Both he and Ziggy had attended the parade square the previous day and seen the crowd of protesters swell to around four hundred disgruntled sailors. By now, 3rd November, there were, by Ziggy's rough estimate, several thousand people crammed into the large square. The people were not just sailors now, but representatives of workers in the city. The cry from the crowd was for 'peace and bread'. The demands were succinct, but boiled down to the freeing of those imprisoned, the end to the war and better food provisions.

"There're moving towards the prison, seeking to free the sailors," Otto shouted as they both went with the surge.

Suddenly shots rang out and the crowd began to panic. Otto instinctively grabbed Ziggy by the collar and using his immense strength managed to drag him against the pull of the mob into a doorway, using the brick portico as cover from the shots. As the firing ceased Otto picked up his young friend and together they left the area through the back streets to once more, take refuge on their ship.

The governor of the naval station, Wilhelm Souchon, had only been in his post for a few days when the protests started. He immediately called for outside assistance, but was assured by his staff that the disorder was under control, so he cancelled his request. The breaking up of the protest on the 3rd November had resulted in the deaths of seven protesters and a further twenty-nine injured.

"They have brought in soldiers from outside," Ziggy remarked as he watched from the edge of the crowd of sailors and other workers, who had now joined the insurrection.

"Look, Ziggy, some are laying down their guns and joining the protesters. Some are retreating back up the street." Otto and Ziggy watched as the detachment of soldiers holding the line at the end of the street literally disintegrated, as some joined the protest and some fled.

This happened all across the town. Souchon did eventually ask for assistance and was sent six infantry companies. But upon their arrival these troops also refused to go out and those that did either joined with the demonstrators or were captured.

In the end Souchon had to negotiate with the leaders of the protesters to be able to withdraw his men. The original mutineers and stokers were freed from imprisonment. With Karl Artelt leading, the revolution had started and there were now sufficient numbers to take control of some public buildings and military institutions. Souchon once again decided to send in different troops to try and quell the rebellion. These forces were quickly intercepted by the sailors and workers and either joined the revolt, or were sent back from whence they came.

"I want to hear what they draft tonight." Otto grabbed Ziggy as he had made to leave the reopened Union House. Ziggy pivoted on his heels and quietly stood close to Otto Nadler in the shadows as the protesters declared their resolutions and demands.

"We, the first soldiers' and workers' council of Kiel, require the following..." Karl Artelt began to read his list. "The release of all inmates and political prisoners. Complete freedom of speech and the press. Next, the abolition of mail censorship. We expect appropriate treatment of naval crews by superior officers." Ziggy drifted closer to Otto.

"No punishment for crews returning to their ships and barracks. Most importantly, that the launching of the fleet is to be prevented under all circumstances. We wish to avoid any further bloodshed. All troops other than those from the Kiel garrison must be withdrawn." Artelt stopped to drink some water.

"What do you think?" Ziggy whispered.

"It all makes logical sense so far," Otto answered.

Artelt continued, "All measures to ensure the safety of private property will be determined by this council immediately. Superior officers will no longer be recognised outside of duty. Each man will have no limits placed upon his freedom at the end of his tour of duty until the beginning of his next. Officers who agree with our demands and resolutions are welcome here amongst us. Those that do not, must quit their post. Every member of the soldiers' council is hereby released from all duty. All future demands and resolutions can only be issued with the consent of this soldiers' council. All these demands are orders issued by this soldiers' council and are binding to every military person." Karl Artelt finished his list of resolutions to a loud and prolonged round of applause and cheering from the packed Union Hall.

"This will be the start of change," Otto exulted. "I would say that our service to the Imperial German navy is at an end, my young friend."

Ziggy moved from out of the shadow of the colossal senior NCO. "What should we do now?"

"Collect what personal belongings we can from the ship, then head out of here as quickly as we can," Otto suggested.

"What then?"

"My life has been in service to our country's navy. To see it torn apart these last few days has been difficult to witness. I'm at a loss. I have no family, no wife or children to return to. Unlike you my friend," Otto said with remorse.

"Otto, you are my great friend and mentor. In all the years I have known you, I never felt closer to you than I do now. It would be my honour if you would accompany me to Munich, where I will introduce you to my wife and child. Together we will start again," Ziggy offered.

"Then we must go now." Otto moved them into an aisle, as the applause still rang out.

The two figures ducked out of the Union Hall and crept back to their ship for the last time.

Knockaloe
April 1919

Armistice day came and went. The initial excitement and hope for release quickly dissipated as no visible change in conditions occurred. Representatives from the various compounds went to discuss the situation with the camp commandant. They returned somewhat crestfallen and posted notices of the 'resettlement' policy the British government had decided to implement.

```
To the Internees
Knockaloe Camp
Isle of Man

26th November 1918

With such numbers to be processed and assimilated
back into the communities from whence they
came, each case has to be examined individually
and this will take time. We will endeavour to
expedite your return to your families and loved
ones, or your repatriation to your countries
of origin as quickly as possible. It will
undoubtedly take several months to deal with
the entire camp population, so I would ask that
you continue to show the high level of patience
and fortitude that you have shown during your
time here.

Camp Commandant
```

"Nearly five months! We have sat and watched that notice on the wall curl, fade and turn yellow, while they claim to be processing us." Max stood up from the chair at the central table of their hut and pointed at the tired piece of paper on the hut wall.

"Max," Karl said soothingly, "I can't offer you an answer. There does not appear to be any system in place, clearly, it's not alphabetical or by our registration numbers. It would appear to be entirely random, but we're close now, I can feel it. There are less than five thousand of us still here."

Joseph burst into the hut. "They're sending me back to Germany. I've received word that a ship will take me and others to be repatriated off the island and back to England by the end of the week." As Joseph imparted his news he went over to the hut stove and warmed his hands.

"How do you know this?" Karl asked.

"The camp commandant was visiting the hospital to see how many of those there would be able to travel. He had a list of those that the British government have decided to immediately repatriate to Germany. He very generously allowed me to scan through the list of names..." Joseph was going to continue, but paused to look up at the two brothers who had become such good friends. "It gives me no pleasure to say this, but Max, your name was on the list. I could not find Karl's name anywhere."

"It's obvious, Joseph," Max explained, deducing the logic of it. "You and I are both single. Karl is married to Lily and has a young daughter, that must be why he is staying and we are being deported. It can be the only reason."

Karl stared at his elder brother and his friend Joseph. He was at a loss for comment on this news that these two pillars of his life at Knockaloe would soon be gone back to Germany. A wave of sadness crept over him as he sat and contemplated life without these two, with whom he had shared so much of his existence in this foetid, dank internment camp.

"Karl, my friend," Joseph said reasonably, "this is what I expected. I only came to England in 1912, with no family or friends. I didn't even speak the language, which, thanks to you these past four years, I have nearly mastered."

"But what about you, Max?" Karl demanded. "When we came here you were still a teenager. Where would you go in Germany? Is Mother back in Germany?"

"It will be fine." Joseph laughed as he patted Max on the shoulder. "I will take Max with me back to Germany and we will build a health and fitness regime to take over the world."

As it transpired, the authorities had clearly decided that the forced repatriation of internees back to their homelands would be the priority. Within a few days, several hundred of those still imprisoned at the camp were told to pack their belongings and were marched, still under guard, back to the entrance of the compound at Knockaloe. Here they boarded the purpose-built narrow-gauge railway back to Peel docks, where a ship returned them to the English mainland. A further rail journey across the country to the port of Hull delivered them to a ship which had been commandeered to take the deportees to Hamburg.

"Karl, I will write to Lily once I have settled and Joseph and I have found somewhere to live," Max explained to his younger brother.

"We will be in constant touch, Karl. I look forward to the day when I am able to meet your entire family." Joseph stepped forward and hugged his friend as the guards came to take them to the camp entrance.

Karl stood back and then hugged his elder brother. "Take care, Max. And remember to let Lily know where you are, so I can find you," Karl whispered as he embraced him.

And with that they were gone, leaving Karl sitting for-lornly on his bed in the cold damp hut that had been their home these past four years.

It was a further three weeks before Karl was given notice to pack his things. His journey was to be a similar armed escort to the docks at Peel. Karl stopped abruptly as he walked through the brick pillars of the entrance to the internment camp at Knockaloe and took one last look behind him. *Four years!* he thought. *What a waste.*

An uneventful journey from the Isle of Man back to the English mainland followed. Once there he was driven in an open-backed truck to Lancaster railway station. Here the guards effectively 'freed' the occupants and the group in Karl's truck climbed off the back and made their way into the station. Karl bid a couple of those that he knew farewell and made his way to the platform for trains south. He had been issued with a single rail warrant to take him to Leicester. His departure from the internment camp had happened so quickly, that he had not been able to let Lily know he was on his way back to her.

As he sat on the train heading south his head was filled with questions. How would Lily be? He had been so worried about her weakened condition. What would Freya be like? Would she be the spitting image of her mother? *I hope she hasn't inherited the enormous Luddolph nose*, he thought and smiled. What was he going to do for work? He had studied engineering in the camp library and while it wasn't ever going to be a recognised qualification, he felt he would be able to work in that industry if the chance arose. His friendship with Joseph Pilates had been a blessing and he knew that somehow, he and Joseph would remain friends for life.

The train journey afforded him time to sit and contemplate his lot. He was now nearly thirty-four years of age, with a wife he hadn't seen in over four years and a daughter he had never set eyes on. He was homeless with no form of income, who would, in the short term, have to accept the charity of his wife's parents while he sought to rebuild his life. He didn't know it at that time, but the First World War had changed Great Britain, not least for the huge numbers of young men who would not be returning from the trenches of Belgium.

The door to the house in the quiet residential street in Leicester was opened by Lily's sister Iris. She stared hard at the tall gaunt figure in a suit, that was clearly too large for him. She took in the pale complexion, the battered small suitcase and scuffed wooden box he was holding. For several seconds she just stared. Karl broke the spell.

"Hello, Iris. How are you?" he simply said.

"KARL!" Suddenly Iris burst into life as she recognised her sister's husband. She rushed forward and hugged him as a brother. "My God, Karl, you are so thin, that suit jacket looks at least two sizes too big for you. Let me take one of those." And she grabbed the wooden box from him as she ushered him into the narrow entrance hall.

"Lily, Lily, where are you? We have a guest!" Iris shouted down the corridor of the hall.

After a brief pause, an ever so slight woman came into the hall from the kitchen. She had clearly been working, wearing a white apron with the sleeves rolled up and her hair tied up at the back. Karl took it all in, the frail porcelain features of his wife Lily. Her face lifted and she stared squarely into her husband's eyes. They rushed towards each other, Iris moved deftly out of the way, and Karl lifted Lily off the ground as he embraced the woman he had not seen in so long. They kissed, then remembering where they were they let each other go, but continued to hold hands. As they stared into each other's eyes, Karl caught a glimpse of something behind the apron of his wife, clinging shyly to her legs.

"Karl, it's been far too long, but this is your daughter, Freya. Come out from behind me, Freya, and say hello to your father."

The girl, dressed in the prettiest white dress Karl had ever seen, was a tiny replica of his wife, with the smallest, pertest nose, Karl noticed with relief. Her hair was a blonde mass of curls. Karl crouched down on his haunches and looked upon his daughter as she slowly shuffled forward. He held out his arms for her. Freya sensing something about the tall thin man, who smelt of mothballs, ran up to him and put her arms around his shoulders and kissed his stubbly cheek. "Hello, Papa. I love you lots," Freya whispered in Karl's ear. As she stepped back she could see tears running down the man's face. "Why are you crying, Papa?"

Karl choked on his reply, completely overwhelmed by the reunion with his wife and meeting his daughter for the first time.

Friedrichshafen
June 1920

"Have you settled into your apartment then, Otto?" Ziggy quizzed his friend as they walked along the shop floor of the factory.

"It's the first time I have ever had somewhere that I can truly call my home," the genial giant confided to his young benefactor.

"New home, a new job here at this factory as a floor supervisor; it really feels like the fresh start we were both talking about when we left Kiel." Ziggy smiled at his close colleague.

"How are you finding the job? I know it's only on the shop floor, but I have every confidence in your ability to organise the work force and maximise our production." Ziggy's confidence in Otto was testament to years of watching the former senior NCO gently cajole and lead sailors of the German Imperial navy as they undertook their daily duties.

"And you, Ziggy? When are you going to move out of that apartment in Munich and find a place here in Friedrichshafen too? A bit more space for young Lothar to play, in a garden perhaps?" Otto wondered why his friend, now one of the chief designers at the factory, still spent so much time travelling the hundred miles between his home in Munich and this site close to the shores of Lake Constance.

"Petra is settled with her job at the university now that Lothar is at school. She loves lecturing there and I don't want to unsettle Lothar, he's happy at his school. Plus, this weekly commute means I can spend extended hours at the factory during the week, while I try and fathom the new design for the engine we're trying to develop. Now you're here and have your new place, we can reverse the order of things as they were in Munich and I can be a guest with you during the week!"

That initial time in Munich, which Otto had spent as a guest with Ziggy and his family, had been challenging, with opportunities for work limited as Germany recovered from the war and found herself in a seemingly interminable domestic fight for a system of governance. Both Ziggy and Otto had found work in one of the beer halls of the city, the Bürgerbräukeller, one of the largest in the city. In addition to the typical cellar it had a grand hall that could accommodate up to three thousand people. Ziggy rose to be a bar supervisor while Otto naturally found his niche as the head of security, responsible for keeping order in the raucous atmosphere of the beer hall. Ziggy and Otto quickly found themselves trying to keep strictly to their own business, when the beer hall became the favourite haunt of the German Workers' Party. During various heated debates among these patrons, a new, more insidious political party took shape in the form of the National Socialist German Workers' Party or to give it its more usual name, the Nazi Party.

One regular customer to the great hall was a slight, pale individual with the most unnerving appearance, with jet-black hair parted to the side and a small, truncated moustache. Ziggy would have paid no heed to the man except when he spoke. Those around him hushed their own conversation to listen in awe as this rather scruffy little man mesmerised them with his words. He had real flair as an orator to bring his sentences to a crescendo as he forced his argument on his followers and a fair few who listened from beyond. On one occasion while this man held the audience captive with his words, Ziggy ventured out from the serving area to listen to some of his rhetoric. He stood close to one of the man's followers.

"Excuse me, what is his name?" Ziggy pointed at the man doing all the talking.

"He is our Führer, our leader, and his name is Adolf Hitler…"

Both Ziggy and Otto had witnessed their fair share of turbulence in the country since their own flight from Kiel in 1918. The whole of Germany seemed to be lurching from the idea of communism one day, to the possibility of fascism the next. The Weimar Republic that had replaced the old monarchy was struggling to hold all these factions together and Ziggy felt that it was only a matter of time before Germany took a more radical turn. He had no real political persuasion one way or another, but it felt like in this new Germany, you were forced to take a side. The trouble was, Ziggy didn't know where he stood on so many issues. For him the priority was to secure proper employment to support his family.

The unsociable hours at least allowed one or other of them to look after Lothar when Petra announced that she wanted to recommence her teaching career at the university. Lothar very quickly warmed to 'Uncle Otto' and used him as a gargantuan climbing frame until Ziggy came to his rescue.

They both knew the work in the beer hall was simply a job, a means to put food on the table for them in the cramped apartment. Ziggy ceaselessly applied for work at every engineering factory in most of Bavaria and beyond. After many fruitless interviews and rejections, he eventually secured an interview with Wilhelm Maybach, who was now switching from Zeppelin engine production (banned under the Treaty of Versailles) to the creation of diesel engines for naval and railroad use. He had a facility at Friedrichshafen which he was looking to expand. Ziggy had applied for a role in the design section and after a very successful interview was rewarded with the offer of employment. Petra had been a little disappointed at the distance this was from Munich, but agreed it would be the right thing to do for Ziggy. He quickly sought permission from Maybach to commute on a weekly basis, staying at suitable accommodation in the town, which Maybach agreed to pay for, much to Ziggy's delight and relief.

Within a month of starting, Ziggy was already proving to be a skilled and thoughtful designer. When Maybach casually mentioned that he needed a reliable shop foreman, Ziggy immediately suggested Otto would be the very man. An interview was arranged, Maybach being at first a little doubtful due to Otto's head-turning size and appearance, but he quickly warmed to the affable character of the giant sitting opposite him. Ziggy had helped Otto find a more suitable apartment which Maybach had insisted he pay for during the first six months of Otto's employment while he adjusted to his new role.

With Ziggy's improved circumstances, he was keen for Petra and Lothar to join him and for the whole family to come and live in Friedrichshafen. But Petra was settled back into her role as a university lecturer and even after continuous persuasion from Ziggy, she put her foot down and refused to leave her work. To Ziggy's credit he respected her decision and did everything he could to ensure that, as a family, they spent quality time at the weekends together.

When Petra fell pregnant in late 1920, the situation changed for all of them. Petra very quickly realised that she would have to once again, give up her beloved lecturing and as a consequence the family would need to relocate to Friedrichshafen in a slightly larger house than their current apartment. Ziggy was thrilled with the news of the prospect of a second child, coupled with the fact that finally Petra and Lothar would be coming to live with him in what had become his new home.

After some searching Ziggy and Otto found a delightful

little detached house on the outskirts of the town, but quite close to the Maybach factory. The place was currently vacant so it became reasonably straightforward for Ziggy to purchase the house, albeit with a very favourable loan from Wilhelm Maybach.

With Otto's help, they packed up their possessions from the apartment in Munich and moved into their new house in March of 1921. Both Ziggy and Otto refused to allow Petra to lift a thing and made sure she was comfortable for the trip in one of the Maybach company trucks they had borrowed for the move. Lothar ran through the spacious new house and out into their new back garden to discover that 'Uncle Otto' had installed a swing prior to their arrival. Lothar was beside himself with excitement and immediately demanded that he be pushed and Otto duly obliged.

"Where did you find such a beautiful swing, Otto?" Petra asked as she witnessed her child being swung higher and higher by Otto's mighty arms.

"I found some wood at the back of the factory and used some of the lathes to fashion the pieces I needed to make it," Otto replied.

"It's beautiful and wonderfully kind of you, Otto." And she rose up on her toes to kiss Otto on the cheek.

"My pleasure, Petra. I don't think I've felt as content in my entire life since we returned from the navy. I would never have believed it possible to have found a fresh start so quickly, and so happily." Otto smiled down at Petra and continued to launch Lothar high into the air.

During the course of the next few months, Ziggy found himself busily splitting his time between designing the engine at the factory and helping Petra build a home for them. Sometime during a lull in the production at Maybach, Ziggy was approached by Wilhelm, the owner, and a suggestion was made.

Unbeknown to Ziggy, Maybach had been responsible for engine production and other systems for the Zeppelins, constructed up until the end of the war. One of the ancillary companies that supported the airship production was called Zahnradfabrik Friedrichshafen, or the ZF Group (Zahnradfabrik means cogwheel or gear factory). With Maybach concentrating on rail and naval engines at his factory, Ferdinand von Zeppelin wanted to become part of the growing automobile industry. One of the companies that he wanted to use to do this was the ZF Group. After some negotiation between the two owners, it was agreed that Ziggy would continue in an advisory capacity, kept on a substantial retainer at Maybach, but would primarily be employed by the ZF Group to design and create a new transmission system for various automobile companies and to look at other gearing ideas. In effect Ziggy was now earning two wages and had moved swiftly to a managerial level.

"It's a girl, Ziggy, we have a daughter." Petra's tired face smiled as she presented his daughter to him.

"My God! She's so beautiful, she is a tiny princess," Ziggy whispered.

"I can see that I'm perhaps no longer the number one girl in your life, eh Ziggy?" Petra joked; at least she thought she did.

"You will always be my number one girl." And Ziggy kissed his wife as he handed his daughter back to her.

"How is work?" Petra sensed something in Ziggy.

"You have no idea of the schemes Zeppelin and Maybach are cooking up. They want to be involved in the industry, but don't want to actually build a car. I'd actually quite like to design a car, but I'm confined to gears and differentials it would seem," Ziggy moaned.

"But designing these things for an incredibly generous salary," Petra reminded him.

A loud crash outside, followed by some laughing turned both their heads.

"Oh! That will be Otto and Lothar! I can't hold them back any longer. Prepare for the onslaught," Ziggy whispered.

A second later the double doors burst open and six-year-old Lothar strode into the room, closely followed by the enormous bulk of Uncle Otto, trying his best to shrink in size.

"Where is she then, where is my sister?" Lothar's shrill voice demanded.

"Quiet, Lothar. In your mother's arms," and Ziggy lifted him up so he could see this new addition to the family for the first time.

"Hmm! She looks all wrinkled, like an old man, like Uncle Otto," and he laughed as Ziggy put him down and steered him away from the beside.

"Ziggy, there was a letter at home for you. I picked it up before I got Lothar from school. It's been redirected, but it's from England, judging by the stamp." Otto passed the envelope to Ziggy.

"England you say?" Ziggy opened the envelope with his finger and drew out several folded sheets of paper. He suddenly shouted.

"Hah! It's from Karl, did you hear, Otto? Karl Luddolph. And he's coming to see us."

"That's lovely, dear, now can you all disappear, as you have woken your daughter and she needs feeding." And Petra ordered the men out of the maternity unit.

Aston, Birmingham
January 1921

"I'm sure the auditors will think favourably if you sell them an idea of a car for the masses," Karl interrupted his boss.

Herbert Austin looked up from his paperwork in the large office and peered at the confident man sitting opposite him. "Louis, I took you on, and against a good deal of criticism for the fact that you were, and still are, a German citizen, but nevertheless I took you on to work in the engineering department. Your success there, despite the bank breathing down our necks, has been a revelation, but do you really think that in our dire situation the banks and administrators will allow us to produce a completely new vehicle?"

"Sir, I believe they will. We can show them that we can advance our production line with superior engineering machines and drastically cut our production costs. We can pass on these savings to our customers and genuinely manufacture an automobile that is within the price range of people who would otherwise not be able to afford one." Karl stood to emphasise his point.

"But the directors and those we owe money to will never agree to this," Austin argued.

"If I may, sir." Karl left the office and soon returned pulling a very young, timid-looking youth by the arm.

"Sir, may I present Stanley Edge, who I found working as a draughtsman in an office close to mine at Longbridge. He has something that may be of interest to you."

Herbert Austin stared open-mouthed as the callow youth in front of him proceeded to lay out drawings on his desk and talk about a revolutionary small automobile powered by a small four-cylinder engine.

Austin watched as Edge, encouraged by his new engineer, sold the new concept to him.

"Gentlemen, I believe you may have something." Austin held up his arms in submission. "But walls have ears, so not here. Can the two of you make your way to my home at Lickey Grange next Monday at 9 a.m., where we will thrash this out?"

"Yes, sir, we'll be there." Karl helped Stanley pick up his drawings and notes and as he was ushering him out of the office Herbert Austin spoke.

"Not a word to anyone about this, you understand."

Both Karl and Stanley nodded as they left.

"How's my princess today?" Karl sat with Freya on his knee in the living room of their newly acquired house in Aston, one of the suburbs of Birmingham.

"A girl at school pulled my hair, she said she was trying to straighten my curls, but she said sorry when she saw that it hurt," replied the excited voice of the seven-year-old.

"Oh! Well at least she said she was sorry. Now shall we see if we can help your mother in the kitchen?"

Freya jumped off her father's knee and together they walked into the kitchen where Lily was busy draining vegetables at the counter sink.

"Freya, can you set the table please? Karl, can you get the joint out of the oven and put it on that platter to my right to rest? Just need to make the gravy and dinner will be ready."

"Is there somewhere amongst all of that where I get to give you a kiss, my love?" Karl came up behind the diminutive figure of his wife and gave her a hug and kissed her cheek.

The dinner, as ever, was a feast for all. Freya dutifully ate all her vegetables, keen to avoid another stand-off with her father, which she would never win. Once the plates were cleared and Karl had assisted Lily to clear up and put Freya to bed, they sat down in the comfortable living room. He even got away with just one bedtime story before his daughter's eyes closed.

Lily asked Karl about his visit to the office of his boss.

"We can get to that. How are you? Did you go to the doctor about these dizzy spells you keep having and how much weight you're losing?"

"Oh, I'm sure it's nothing, please don't fuss."

"But surely it won't do any harm to seek an opinion? Please will you go, just to put my mind at rest," Karl pleaded.

"I will, I promise. Now, we had some post from Germany today." Lily hastily changed the subject and offered an envelope to Karl.

"Well, well, well. I see it's addressed to your parents' house in Leicester, nice of them to forward it to us. I don't recognise the writing, do you? No sender's name on the back either."

"No, I don't recognise the writing either. Open it."

Karl lifted a silver letter opener from a side table and slit open the envelope and pulled out several sheets of paper with writing on both sides. He turned to the back to establish the sender.

"Good God! It's from Petra, Ziggy's wife Petra. We've never met her. Well, thank the Lord Ziggy has kept hold of someone for all this time." Karl was beaming with delight.

"Read it to me, dear?" Lily asked.

"All right, hang on." And Karl put the papers back in order. "It's addressed at the top from Friedrichshafen. I'm not even sure where that is. They have clearly moved from Munich." Karl scan-read the letter and précised the contents to his wife.

"Ziggy has become a designer for a very prestigious firm

on the shores of Lake Constance. They have all moved there including their own six-year-old son, Lothar. God, Ziggy has taken Otto Nadler out of the navy and he's working as a foreman in the factory."

"How did he do that?" Lily asked.

"Apparently after the war they both worked in the Bürgerbräukeller in Munich, one of the biggest beer halls in the whole city. Petra is pregnant and due to give birth later this year. Otto has become the number one babysitter for Lothar, not a role I would ever have imagined for Chief Instructor Nadler. Did I ever tell you about our leading instructor and senior NCO while I was in the navy?" Karl smiled.

"Frequently, dear. What else does she say?" Lily would have liked to read the letter in its entirety herself once Karl had finished, but realised that this would be impossible as it was written in German.

"Go on, Karl, please, what else does she say?"

"She states that Ziggy hates his job, but they love the money he earns. She is hoping they have a baby girl this time. Um! They would love us to come and see them."

"Oh, Karl, how wonderful, can we go, please?"

"I would love to, but it's whether I am allowed. More importantly, it's whether they let us return here, when we want to come home. Ziggy apologises for not writing himself, he has been busy at work, which has now become two jobs. Well, I always thought he would do well."

"So how can you find out if we can go to Germany to visit them?"

"I'm not sure, to be honest. I will speak to Mr. Austin on Monday, he might have an idea, or know someone I can talk to. Now, is there anything I can do for you?" Karl looked at his wife as he laid the papers on the side table.

"Can you just rub my neck, the way only you can, my dear?" Lily asked, then continued as Karl positioned himself behind his wife and began to gently massage her shoulders and neck. "How is the name change going?" Lily asked quietly, aware at how sensitive her husband was to this recent decision to make himself perhaps a little less 'German' by using one of his middle names, Louis, instead of the more Germanic 'Karl'. He wrote his title and signed his name as H Louis Luddolph now. He had done this officially, changing his name with the authorities. It had been at the same time that his latest application for naturalisation had been rejected.

"It's going to take some getting used to, people call me Louis and I just ignore them. Mr. Austin asked me about it when he interviewed me for the job and I just let him know our history, the time I spent interned during the war and my desire to become a British subject. In fact, this last week he has said that he would support my next application."

"Give it time, my love. I like the name Louis and looking at you now it does suit you. But you will always only ever be Karl to me." Lily half turned and kissed his hand as he continued to stroke her neck.

"This opportunity to see Ziggy and his family would be terrific, it's long overdue. I'm thinking that there may be a chance to work some business angle on this, what with Ziggy working as an engineering designer," Karl said, thinking out loud.

"Oh Karl! It's a chance to catch up with your best friend and meet his family, don't ruin it with business," Lily grumbled.

"But don't you see, the business angle may be the sole reason they let us all travel to Germany and then return." Karl was warming to the idea as he thought of it.

After a weekend that included buying new shoes for his very particular princess Freya, Karl was almost relieved to be heading off to work. He picked up Stanley from his lodgings in Central Birmingham, then drove the fifteen or so miles southwest out of the city to the 100-acre estate of the recently knighted Sir Herbert Austin, known as Lickey Grange. This great sprawling Victorian estate had a number of other buildings within its area, including a very handsome lodge house at the entrance.

"Nice house, Stanley?" Karl smiled as they drove in.

"Very nice, Mr. Luddolph," Stanley replied.

"Stanley, please. I think we've known each other long enough for you to call me Lou or Louis now."

"I don't know, Mr. Luddolph. I feel better with your age and such to keep it to Mr. Luddolph please."

"Understood. Well, if we end up working together, I'm sure that can change." Karl pulled up to the front of the large Victorian mansion.

"Tell me, young Stanley, what do you have in mind then?" Sir Herbert leant against the billiard table and scanned the two men sitting opposite him.

"Sir," Stanley started nervously, "I am convinced that the company needs to move away from the larger models that it has recently been making. I'm aware that you built a small 7-horsepower model in 1905." Stanley paused.

"Yes, we built that at the Swift factory in Coventry, but it was only really an experiment," Austin confirmed.

"Well, I believe that with the introduction of the new horsepower tax, we need to devise an engine with a very long stroke and a very low piston surface area. I think we should build a small four-cylinder engine, traditional side valves, with a capacity of no more than 700cc. The RAC, by my calculations, would give that a tax rating of 7.2 horsepower. That would keep the car within the price range of so many more potential customers, sir."

Sir Herbert stood up from the billiard table. "I am on board, lads, let's do this. I know the management board are going to go mad, so we will design it here and keep it away from prying eyes at Longbridge. Stanley, where do you live?"

"Sir, I have rooms in a building in the centre of Birmingham," Stanley replied.

"Well, I need you here, designing this car. The lodge house you passed on the way in is currently empty. You live there while we put this thing together, would that be OK? Oh! And you can eat your lunches in the library, next door!" Sir Herbert offered.

"Sir, that is most generous of you," Stanley accepted nervously.

"Good. I'm going to want you here morning, noon and night getting this thing done. Now, Louis, what can we do at Longbridge?" Sir Herbert turned to Karl.

"Sir, I think that we will need to improve the production line. I've been looking at the machinery on the shop floor and we could definitely be more efficient. There are some new ideas coming through and with your permission I would like to explore options while you design the car."

"That all makes sense. Do a full review of the plant while Stanley and I design this thing. Do it quietly?" Sir Herbert put his finger to his lips to reinforce the clandestine nature of the project.

"Sir, if I may? As you know, I am still a German despite several attempts to become a naturalised British subject. I have recently reacquainted myself with an old friend who coincidentally now works within one of the large German companies that manufacture components for the German automobile industry."

"Be very handy to see what those chaps are working on," Sir Herbert interrupted.

"You are ahead of me, sir. I agree it would be really useful to visit several factories in Germany to see what we may learn to improve our own production. As a German subject I will need a sponsor to help with my application to travel to Germany, but more importantly, be allowed to return. I am asking if you would endorse my proposed trip to Germany, sir," Karl said.

"Louis, my dear fellow, I feel I have sufficient friends within our Liberal government to influence whoever we need to in order to make this trip work. This is a serious undertaking. Most of the funding will be from me; I will not persuade the board, I'm sure. Louis, you will go to Germany to fact-find as well as review the plant at Longbridge, while Stanley and I will design our new model."

"When should I move into the lodge house, sir?" Stanley asked.

"No time like the present. Louis, would you help young Stanley collect his things from Birmingham and return him here? Once that's done, Louis, you book yourself passage to Germany. Where exactly does this friend of yours work?"

"He works for a subdivision of the Zeppelin factory in Friedrichshafen, on the shores of Lake Constance in Bavaria, Southern Germany, sir," Karl answered.

"Is there anywhere else you think you should visit?"

"As a matter of fact, I have a company in mind who are based in Berlin. I also have an elder brother who is working in Dortmund and another close friend who is now based back in Germany too. They were both interned with me on the Isle of Man and deported back to Germany at the end of the war."

"Not our finest hour," Sir Herbert answered quietly. "Now, gentlemen, I will detain you no further. Stanley, you get yourself set up in the lodge house. I will let the staff know you are going to be living there and they will open the place up, get some air in there, fresh bedding, get a fire going, make it comfortable for you," Sir Herbert said.

"Thank you, sir." Stanley stood with Karl as he thanked his boss and both men made their way out of the billiard room, where one of Sir Herbert's staff escorted them to the front door.

By the time the necessary permits to travel had been obtained and passage on the passenger ferry to Antwerp booked, Freya had worked herself into a frenzy of excitement over this trip across Europe. One evening, close to when they were due to travel, Karl took the time to sit her down next to him in his comfortable armchair in the living room. He opened a large atlas of the world at a page depicting Northern Europe, so that they both could gaze upon it.

"Now, you see this is a map of where we live, which also shows where we are going. If I say the names of the places we are going to visit, see if you can find them on the map," Karl encouraged.

"Karl, Freya is a seven-year-old, not one of your apprentices at work!" Lily smiled as she looked up from her sewing.

"I'm just showing her where we're going to be visiting." Karl rolled his eyes, but only so Freya could see. She giggled, delighted to have the attention of her father.

"Can you see Birmingham?" Karl asked. "That's where we live."

Freya bent her head forward to study the complex cartographical representation in front of her.

"Bedtime in half an hour, young lady," Lily said.

"Yes, Mother!" Karl and Freya replied simultaneously and laughed.

Friedrichshafen
August 1921

"Lily looks so tiny. I forgot just what a slight figure she was, thinking back to that first time we met her with Stella in Plymouth," Ziggy remarked to Karl as they sat on some comfortable chairs in the back garden of Ziggy's house.

"She worries me, Ziggy, if I'm honest. I think she's too thin and always so weak. Perhaps little Freya tires her, but I'm always pleading with her to visit the doctor."

"I understand, my friend. Perhaps I could say something to her quietly?" Ziggy offered.

"I don't know. You're always so sure of yourself, but I know Lily will be annoyed that I told you," Karl replied.

"I won't say anything then, let's leave it." Ziggy stood. "Come on, let's go and see if we can rescue Otto from the children." Ziggy pointed at their former chief instructor, now playfully being used as a climbing frame by both Lothar and Freya.

"Lothar, Freya!" he called. "May we please take Uncle Otto back to the house? It would be nice if Uncle Karl could spend some time with him too."

"Oh! Dad! Just five more minutes," Lothar pleaded.

"It's OK, Ziggy, I'll join you in a moment." Otto smiled as he picked Lothar up by his ankle and held him upside down, causing him to cry out and Freya to scream in delight.

"All right, my friend, we will see you inside." Ziggy

150

walked back up to the patio where Petra and Lily were deep in conversation.

"Ladies, forgive my intrusion, but can I get either of you another drink?"

"Still the most charming man who always gets the drinks, I see," Lily laughed.

Ziggy brought himself to an upright position and delivered a stiff-backed salute, "Your servant, as always."

"Darling, we are both fine, thank you. Take Karl inside if you're going to discuss business, but don't wake Emma please, I've only just got her off to sleep." Petra looked hard at her husband and made it clear she meant it.

"Tell me about the trip?" Ziggy asked his old naval comrade.

"It's been a whirlwind. I told you how difficult it was immediately after the internment. I basically had nothing, back living with Lily's parents. I applied for so many positions, many below where I had been before the war, but no one would hire a German. One of Lily's sisters happened to be stepping out with a man from Leicester who was doing business with some of the automobile manufacturers in Birmingham. To cut a long story short, he was able to get me some interviews within that industry. Again the 'German' factor caused a few problems, but seemingly not for Sir Herbert Austin." Karl paused.

"Yes, I've heard of Austin automobiles," Ziggy said.

"Well, he gave me a personal interview and offered me a job within his factory at Longbridge near Birmingham. Shortly after that I was able to buy a small house in a place called Aston, very close to the factory," Karl explained.

"And I understand you now go by the name, 'Louis'? Is this correct?"

"Lily told you," Karl said, as Ziggy held his arms wide and shrugged.

"Great Britain is, probably like Germany, a different place to what it was before the war. I just feel it will be easier for me if I have a slightly less German-sounding name and Louis is one of my middle names. It's not as though I made it up," Karl said reasonably.

"Well, I think it's splendid and it does suit you. What should we call you then?" Ziggy asked.

"To be honest, everyone who knew me before I changed it, continues to call me Karl, which is fine."

Otto suddenly ducked through the doorway into the cosy living room and took a seat.

"Otto, finally released from service. Can I get you something, my friend?"

"Some water please, they have worn me out," Otto replied smiling.

Ziggy disappeared into the kitchen.

"Mr. Luddolph, you look well and your daughter is the most wonderful, beautiful child," Otto said.

"Chief Nadler, if you had told me all those years ago that one day my daughter would be supervised by you I would never have believed it." Karl laughed at the false formality they used on each other.

"I'm so glad to see you've settled into such a peaceful existence, after all your years of service with the German navy," Karl remarked.

"It's all down to Ziggy and timing I suppose. After the breakdown of discipline in the last month of the war, we decided together to leave the service. Ziggy suggested I join him here and having nowhere else to go, I was happy to come."

Ziggy returned with a glass of water and handed it to Otto.

"So, what now for you, Karl?" Ziggy asked as he retook his seat.

"Well, Sir Herbert has asked me to do an efficiency report

on his factory production line. In addition, he asked me to inspect your factory, which you very kindly allowed me to do yesterday, and I have been able to make some useful contacts in Berlin. I caught up with my brother Max, who now lives in Dortmund since his repatriation to Germany after his internment with me. I was also able to catch up with a man called Joseph Pilates, who was also interned with me. He is actually in Hamburg, training their police officers in physical fitness. You would both love his physical drive and motivational exercises. It is without doubt Joseph who, more than anyone, helped me survive four years of internment," Karl explained.

"Was it tough?" Ziggy asked.

"Very! The not knowing, the boredom and endless monotony of the existence was hard to deal with. Like I say, without Joseph Pilates and his unique set of breathing and physical exercises, I would have descended into a deep depression, of that I am sure. But, gentlemen," he added candidly, "you both served and I understand from Petra that you saw action against the British navy in the North Sea. So, I am not the only one here who has suffered. We all, it would seem, lost a little something of ourselves during the war."

"But we all came through it," Ziggy concluded. "For me, Germany is a mess! We have a newly formed republic, but they seem to have upset as many people as the system under the Kaiser. People are still fighting for control of things politically. We need stability, but with so many factions arguing about the nature of our defeat and the severity of the conditions imposed by the Treaty of Versailles, most people just feel angry and it's like there is an inability for us, as a nation, to move forward."

"What about England, Karl?" Otto asked.

"There is a good deal of change happening. A war like we have all just endured takes some getting over. I think England is very nervous of its position in the world as the

United States and Russia begin to assume more power. For my part, I don't know where I am really. I should feel less sympathetic to England than I do, but I don't. They may well have imprisoned me for four years, but I feel no animosity toward them. I want to be British, I still strive to become a citizen of that Island. I am married to the most wonderful English girl, with a beautiful English daughter. I have secured permanent employment in an expanding industry, earning comparatively good money."

"For my own self," Ziggy said, "I agree with you that it is a war that will take some recovering from. I try and stay away from the political mess we have created for ourselves. I too have a good job, earning good money, with a settled family life. We three have seen so much between us, that I feel the time is right for us to become rich and enjoy the fruit of our labours." He held up his glass. "Gentlemen, let us drink to our prosperous future."

Ziggy lent forward and the three men touched glasses and drank to their onward journey to prosperity.

"You know, Petra is so intelligent," Lily said, sitting up in bed while Karl undressed. "She was a lecturer at Munich University, in fact she is only on maternity leave. I sometimes wish I had spent more time studying. Lothar is such a handsome boy and little Emma is just adorable."

"What would you study, my love?" Karl asked as he folded his suit trousers over a hanger.

"Oh! I don't know, history perhaps, have a greater understanding of what went before, something like that," Lily laughed.

"Well, as long as it's not politics! Seems to me those in power create far more problems than they solve," Karl stated.

"But that is the very reason why understanding history is vital, so that we can argue with those in power when they make mistakes, or take us down the wrong path," Lily argued.

"Hmmm! You make a reasonable point, but I think I'll just leave them all to get on with it, while I spend my time making us as wealthy as possible."

Lily, sensing her husband's irritation, deftly changed the subject. "Otto is a powerhouse, I see now that all your stories about him were not in your imagination. He's so kind and patient with the children."

"He is a remarkable man and a true friend. I will make sure that we keep in touch more closely from now on with all of them. This trip has been such a success. I'm so glad we got to meet with Max. I wasn't sure how he would be, but clearly, he has rebuilt his life in Dortmund. It would be nice if he could find a nice girl to settle down with," Karl mused.

"I'm sure he will. He too has done so well finding such a good job at that brewery."

"We'll stay in touch with Joseph too. I feel that his ever-expanding ideas and exercises will become so important in the years to come." Karl leant forward and kissed his wife's cheek. "And you, my darling wife. How have you enjoyed our trip?"

"I feel better than I have in a long time. Perhaps this fresh German air agrees with me. I do have one more piece of news to share with you." Lily paused.

"Oh, yes?" Karl replied.

"I'm pregnant!"

Aston, Birmingham
March 1922

However distracted Karl may have been by the delicate condition of his pregnant wife, he still threw himself into the work with Sir Herbert and the creation of a brand-new 'compact' automobile. Lily's sister, Iris, had come to stay with them and helped with getting Freya ready for school and ensured Lily got as much rest as the doctors had recommended.

The new compact vehicle being designed had moved on and three prototypes were in production in a quiet part of the Longbridge plant. Stanley, working closely with Sir Herbert, had managed to reduce the length. The vehicle now had a wheelbase of only six feet three inches and was considerably lighter than the equivalent American Model T Ford at 794 pounds.

While work continued on the prototype, Karl had been making strides to increase the efficiency of the production line that would be required for the new model, when it hopefully went into full production later that year.

With Sir Herbert's approval, Karl had been in contact with Jerwag milling machines, based in Berlin. They were one of a host of companies he had visited briefly on his recent trip to see Ziggy. He had placed an order for some of their new machines to replace those currently at Longbridge. Karl could see the superiority of these machines and it was this deal that gave him the confidence he needed to suggest his ambition to Sir Herbert.

"You want to leave us and set up on your own then?" Sir Herbert said, summarising the stumbling words that came from his employee.

"Sir, please. I want to stay and assist you, as I have been. But this is an opportunity for me to make my own mark. I want to be able to bring these machines and other products I saw in Germany to this country and to distribute them to the wider industrial community."

"Well, I need you, Louis! Can you at least oversee the changes to the plant, while you also set up your new company?" Sir Herbert wasn't pleading, but almost.

"I would be happy to undertake whatever you need from me. My goal is to stay with you, but as I move forward, I want to be an independent supplier and distributor right across the country," Karl explained.

"I make no bones about it, I am sorry that you want to go your own way. But I suppose I fully understand. I wanted to make my mark when I came here too, so I do understand. If you can just help me and Stanley get the new car into production, I would be most grateful," Sir Herbert said magnanimously.

"Sir, it would be my honour to continue the project at this time and I will only devote myself to my own initiative when you are happy for me to do so. I will, if acceptable to you, begin setting up my own premises, but always be available to you, as the new automobile continues to progress."

"That's more than acceptable, Louis. Now please, enough business. I understand that Lily is pregnant which calls for a celebration." Sir Herbert went to a drinks cabinet in the corner of the room and poured two generous measures of brandy from a crystal decanter. He brought the glasses over to Karl and handed one to him. They stood opposite each other in the large office.

"To the future and the health of your growing family,

Louis." Sir Herbert held his glass towards Karl. They touched glasses and took a healthy sip of the fiery liquid.

Sir Herbert didn't see the flash of concern deep in the eyes of the man opposite him as they stood together.

About six or seven weeks later Karl had found and obtained the premises he was looking for in Solihull, which was only about ten miles from his home in Aston. Although not strictly by design, he was now reassuringly close to home, and to Lily. Karl had been initially overjoyed at the news of a second child. But as the weeks passed, he could see the toll it was taking on his wife. Her fragile constitution kept her confined to their home and she spent most of her time resting in bed. Without Iris to cope with the effervescent Freya and to provide the round-the-clock care Lily needed, Karl would never have manged to set himself up as an independent businessman. Lily, for her part, was devoted to Karl's plan and listened with as much strength as she could muster when he returned home each evening with tales of new deals done and the burgeoning order book that he had created.

As Sir Herbert drew close to announcing his new automobile to the public and with the changes to the Longbridge plant all but complete, Karl was finally able to devote himself to more time at his own new premises, H Louis Luddolph Ltd.

With Lily's approval, Karl had asked her elder brother, John, to leave his Leicester textile salesman's job and come and work for him. He was to supervise the importation of the new products whose supply and distribution rights Karl had negotiated for the whole of Great Britain. Karl had known John since his return from his time in the German navy, and had come to respect his relaxed but discerning demeanour, trusting him implicitly. When Iris called Karl's office to announce Lily had gone into labour, he was able to be home in fifteen minutes and between Iris and himself they got Lily safely to hospital in good time.

Lily fought hard to be strong, but there was a limit to what her body could cope with. It was as if she knew it would be a fight to bring her new baby into the world, a fight she knew they could not both survive. Lily fought for her baby, rather than for herself. The midwives called for a consultant when they could do no more. Lily was too weak, and had lost too much blood to fight on. The consultant tried everything he could to stabilise the patient. Seeing the look in her eyes he asked a nurse to fetch Karl.

Lily looked up and saw the man she had devoted herself to. "Hello, Karl. I'm so sorry," she whispered.

Karl leant forward, gripping her right hand. "You can do this, please stay with me," was all he could say.

"Don't cry, my love. I have loved you in my life, that's enough. I would have been so proud to see you become successful, as I know you will be." Lily stopped to regain her strength.

Tears were now streaming down Karl's face as he watched the centre of his world weaken and begin to crumble. "I love you, my beautiful Lily."

"I have loved you since that first time in Plymouth, my love." Lily's voice faltered.

Karl stroked his wife's hair and leant forward to kiss her forehead.

"Be kind to Freya, she dotes on you. Help her, Karl." Lily was finding it difficult to talk now.

"My love, please…I love you…" Karl stopped, seeing his wife's body go limp and her eyes lose that sheen and become distant.

Karl knew the worst and didn't hear the nurses and consultant rush to Lily's side. One of them ushered him out of the room and placed him into the arms of the waiting tearful Iris.

Karl sat in a chair in a corridor of the hospital. "She's gone," he whispered to his wife's sister and he just sat staring straight ahead as he tried to block out the terrible anger and sense of desolation that threatened to overcome him. He wiped the tears away and determined that there would be no more. And that was where he was when the nurses came through that door, where he had lost his wife, carrying a small bundle. "You have a son, Mr. Luddolph," the nurse announced, and she went to place it in Karl's lap.

Karl stood and backed away, ashen-faced.

Iris quickly stepped forward. "Here, let me take him." And she took the newborn child from the nurse and sat back down gently rocking him.

Karl stared at Iris, then at the nurses. "May I please see my wife?" he asked in a quiet controlled voice.

"Of course, sir. Please give us a few minutes," and she disappeared. A short while later she reappeared and held out her arm, indicating for Karl to follow her back into that room.

Inside was now calm, and nothing stirred as Karl walked slowly over to the table in the centre of the room. A pristine white sheet now covered Lily's body, leaving just her head exposed. Karl looked down at the still beautiful face of his wife. She looked so serene, her beautiful, tiny, elfin features somehow even more striking in death than they had been in life. Karl felt the smoothness of her cheek and brushed a stray wisp of hair from her brow.

"You were my world, my love. Everything I did was for you. I love you, my dear, sweet, beautiful Lily." Karl then once more bent forward and kissed his wife's cold lips. He stood back and took one last look at her face. He then very swiftly turned his back on the body of his wife and without a backward glance marched purposefully from the room.

Karl stood at the end of the pew, closest to the aisle. He stared straight ahead at the pair of golden candle holders and a large golden cross atop the high altar of the church. In the row of pews on the other side of the aisle were Lily's parents, clinging to each other as the church organ played some loud, mournful Bach. On the same side, but further back, was an assortment of more distant relatives and friends. There was an empty pew behind Karl and then behind that was a formidable line of smartly dressed men. They were as close to Karl's family as could be in attendance. Max had not made the trip and Willy had not been in touch for some years. Karl's father Albert was too sick to travel down from Leicester and his mother Charlotte had not wanted to come on her own. They sent flowers.

This line of men knew more about Karl than the rest of his family put together. Ziggy Jurgens, his closest friend since their days in the navy, and Otto Nadler, their former chief instructor, stood by him. The third man to travel from Germany, standing on the other side of the imposing Otto Nadler, was Karl's friend, through internment, Joseph Pilates. These three men stood a respectful distance behind Karl as he watched the priest walk to his pulpit. Karl sat, and the rest of the congregation followed his lead.

Karl was aware that the priest was speaking, but didn't hear the words. His eyes had fallen onto the highly polished oak coffin that contained the remains of his wife. There were no tears today. Karl had been teetering on the edge of despair before something pulled him back from the brink. In the dark recesses of his mind he had heard a voice calling him. He could just make out the words, in the shrill high-pitched voice of a child. It was his daughter Freya and she was calling "Daddy, Daddy, help me, Daddy, please."

Karl came back from his daydreaming as the priest gave the congregation a blessing, *At last, it's over,* Karl thought. He stood again and the rest of the people in the church followed suit. There would be no burial, Karl had chosen to cremate his wife's body and the coffin was slowly hidden by a deep burgundy velvet curtain.

There was a pause amongst the people at the end of the last organ voluntary. He stepped out from his pew and turned to Lily's parents and bowed deeply; then he turned his back to the altar and walked stiffly from the building. Outside, he stoically soaked up all the anticipated grief of the rest of the people. He shook hands with those that offered theirs and spoke quietly in reply to the host of inane questions fired at him. His three close confidants did their best to shield him and the ordeal was soon over. They were driven to Karl's home where Iris had now taken up residence, ostensibly to look after Freya and Karl's newborn son, James.

As the wake began to break up, Karl thanked Lily's parents for coming and wished them well. He promised that he would see them soon and bring their grandchildren with him, all things he knew would never happen. Freya had gone to spend a few days with Lily's brother John and his family. Iris had gone there too, taking baby James with her. Since starting work for Karl, he had relocated to the area and now only lived ten minutes away by car.

The four men now sat around the dining room table, a bottle of whisky in the centre, a glass in front of each of them. They all variously stared at Karl, at each other, into the depths of their whisky glasses.

"Enough, gentlemen!" Ziggy suddenly exclaimed. "Karl, I know you don't want to talk about it, but we are your closest friends, I want to know what happens now."

Karl, who had been rubbing at a scratch on the edge of the table, looked up when he heard his name.

"Karl, did you hear what I said?"

"Ziggy, yes, you asked what I'm going to do now."

"And?"

"I…" Karl paused to reach for the bottle of whisky and pour himself a generous measure "…am going to finish the rest of this whisky." He smiled as he raised the glass to his lips.

The three other men just stared, and Otto fidgeted in his chair, causing it to creak alarmingly under the burden.

"My esteemed friends," Karl continued, "I have lost the person I loved more than any other in the world. I have shed tears and despaired at the thought of continuing without her. But you all know me, you know what sort of man I am. The loss I have suffered should finish me. The anguish I feel may never go away, but I will not let this define me. I have a daughter and a son who need me now. Joseph, you taught me on the Isle of Man that we must show mental fortitude and move on through adversity."

"Yes but, Karl, in these circumstances, no one would expect you to."

Karl interrupted, "Ah! Joseph, please! Enough! I am breathing as you showed me and I have locked the heartache and anguish away. No more, all right?"

"The man has spoken," Otto murmured, as he too reached for the bottle to recharge his glass, he then did the same for the others around the table. "Karl, it is good to see you again. Yes, under such terrible circumstances, I admit, but it is still damn good to see you. I say that we should make a toast here tonight, then draw a line under this tragedy. Are we agreed?" Otto stood.

The three others stood, glasses in hand.

"Gentlemen. To Lily, the sweetest, most perfect woman and the true love of our favoured friend, Karl." The four downed their glasses and re-took their seats.

"I am going to move." Karl was the first to speak. "I am going to relocate to London. I will keep the office and warehouse up here. Lily's brother John has proved himself to be a reliable and trustworthy partner, he can continue here. I will find new office premises close to London and a new home, where I can make a fresh start with Freya and James."

"When will you go?" Ziggy asked.

"I have already found somewhere suitable to live in Edgware on the outskirts of London. I believe that there are some suitable business premises close by, but in the short term I can run the office from my home and the warehouse space can be expanded in due course. Sir Herbert has detailed a very generous severance package for me now that his new Austin 7 is close to mass production. I have several existing contracts with German businesses to supply to British factories. I intend to split my time between building a successful business and bringing up my two children."

"Then we must toast to this new venture." Ziggy stood and began to wander away.

"Where are you going?" Karl asked.

"To find another bottle of this very pleasant whisky," Ziggy shouted as he disappeared.

Munich
November 1923

"Why are we going to this meeting?" Karl queried.

"Because, my friend, there is a chance that someone will talk some sense about trying to get Germany back on its feet and lower inflation," Ziggy replied, as they walked through the busy streets of the Bavarian capital Munich.

"Can't we just find somewhere to have a quiet drink and talk about the latest deals I am trying to strike with some of your competitors?" Karl smiled back.

"Luddolph, Jurgens, we are going to the meeting, all right?" Otto Nadler entered the conversation, using the two surnames to less than subtly indicate that he was still in charge, despite the enormous grin on his face.

They walked through a large brick archway and into a huge beer hall filled with men seated at tables and drinking from huge steins of beer.

"What is this place?" Karl asked.

"This is the Bürgerbräukeller. Otto and I used to work here when we first returned from our navel service at the end of the war. Always lively and they serve good beer," Ziggy explained.

The three of them found some space at one of the tables, made easier by the intimidating presence of Otto. Ziggy nodded at one of the many waitresses and three large pitchers of the finest German pilsner lager appeared in front of them several minutes later.

"How many people are here?" Karl shouted across the table at Ziggy, struggling to be heard in the vast beer hall.

"Must be a couple of thousand at least. That's Gustav Kahr on the stage. Do you know who he is, Karl?" Ziggy shouted back.

"Is he another of your right-wing agitators, looking to bring down the government in Berlin?" Karl suggested.

Ziggy laughed. "Something like that. There's such a void in the country right now, it feels like Germany is just treading water, we're not making any progress as a nation."

The man on the stage could hardly be heard within the huge space. As Karl watched, he noticed a group of twenty or so men enter the hall and fight their way through the throng of people in the auditorium to the stage area. At once, a lone figure jumped onto a chair and fired a shot into the ceiling, quietening the crowd.

"The national revolution has broken out," he cried. "The hall is surrounded by six hundred men, nobody is allowed to leave. The Bavarian government has been deposed and I wish to declare a new leadership with Erich Ludendorff." He stopped, receiving loud cheers from all sides of the room.

"Who is this joker?" Karl quietly whispered to his friends, as he looked at the small, rather awkward man standing on the chair, dressed in an ill-fitting crumpled overcoat, with his dark hair plastered to one side and a stupid-looking little moustache.

"That, Karl, is one Adolf Hitler," Ziggy replied. "We saw him speak when we worked here, didn't we, Otto?"

"He might look a bit foolish, but I will say this for him, he knows how to speak, how to control a crowd, even a mob in a beer hall like this," Otto conceded.

After a brief flurry around the stage the man Kahr was hustled away by the men surrounding Hitler, along with others on the stage, and they walked out of the main hall.

"Are we safe here, Ziggy?" Karl asked as the crowded

room of men returned to their beer and their conversations.
"Let's just keep our heads down, see what happens next,"
Otto suggested.

They didn't have to wait long. Hitler returned to the stage
of the beer hall, to rapturous acclaim from the crowd. He was
flanked by two of his loyal lieutenants. He used his arms to
quieten the crowd once more.

"Our actions this night are not directed against the police
and Reichswehr. We stand against the Berlin Jew government
and the November criminals of 1918." Hitler's words were
received with more loud roars and cheering; he already had
the crowd in the palm of his hand.

"Outside this hall, in a small room, are Gustav Kahr, Hans
von Seisser and Otto von Lossow. The three of them are struggling to make a decision. May I say to them that you will stand
behind them?" Hitler paused, as the crowd raised the level of
noise to new heights as they yelled their approval of his words.

"You can see that what motivates us is neither self-conceit
nor self-interest, but only a burning desire to join the battle
in this grave eleventh hour for our German Fatherland. One
last thing I can tell you: either the German revolution begins
tonight or we will all be dead by dawn!" The hall went noisily
berserk, standing to applaud Hitler, banging their beer glasses
on the tables as they showed their support.

Hitler once again left the main hall and the level of noise
dropped so that they were able to hear each other speak.

"Have you two managed to invite me to the next German
revolution?" Karl remarked to his oldest friends.

"I'm as surprised as you are," Ziggy confessed. "There
has been unrest for such a long time. I suppose we should
have seen the warning signs, but we are quite isolated down
in Friedrichshafen. We've been buried in the development of
new products at the factory. We are one of the few industries
still offering good employment for skilled workers."

By now it was a little after 9 p.m. After twenty minutes or so, the volume ramped up once more as Hitler returned to the stage. This time he was accompanied on his left by the aforementioned three right-wing leaders, Kahr, Seisser and Lossow, and on the other side by Erich Ludendorff, the heroic war general, who had once been regarded as a viable leader after the departure of the Kaiser. To tumultuous applause and roars of approval, the men all shook hands and agreed to begin the revolution. Hitler closed the evening's address by allowing the crowd to leave the beer hall if they so wished.

"Time to leave, gentlemen." Otto literally picked up his two colleagues and ushered them through the throng of people out of the beer hall.

"What's going to happen now?" Karl asked.

"This feels like a more serious attempt than those that I've read about before. I think we should head back to our hotel and keep out of the way," Ziggy said.

"Down this street then." Otto steered the three of them down a side street and away from the melée of people streaming from the beer hall.

It was about 2 a.m. by the time they got back to their hotel and tried to get some rest.

They were woken early by shouts from a large crowd close to their hotel. They all quickly dressed and met in the foyer.

"Let's follow," Otto suggested. "I'm keen to see where this goes. And remember, keep your heads down. I noticed most of the people surrounding the leaders are armed."

And he led them out onto the busy streets of Munich.

"They seem to have stopped," Ziggy shouted above the noise.

The mob had indeed stopped and the leadership were arguing about what to do next. Unbeknown to Karl, Ziggy and Otto, Ludendorff was now at the head of the mass, accompanying Hitler and his cohorts.

"Hang on, we're on the move again, let's keep up with them." Otto saw the crowd surge forward and took hold of Karl and Ziggy to keep them together.

"There must be hundreds of men in this crowd," Karl said as they marched along.

"More like thousands," Ziggy replied.

The crowd got larger and despite efforts to keep their own space, Otto, Ziggy and Karl were soon hemmed in amongst the vast number of protesters.

"Where are we?" Karl shouted.

"This is Odeonsplatz, near to the Defence Ministry. We seem to have stopped again," Ziggy said.

Suddenly, from across the square, shots rang out and people in front and to the left of them cried out. Shots were now being returned from within the crowd.

Otto took control of the situation and screamed to his two friends, "Ziggy, grab my jacket. Karl, you grab Ziggy's and both of you do not let go and do not stop for anything or anyone. I'm going to force our way through and out of here."

Otto then proceeded to use his considerable size and strength to force his way through the panicked mob. Otto literally knocked people flat as he made progress. He recognised one of the leaders of the march, the diminutive man with the dark hair and pale complexion. The man stood facing those shooting at the crowd. He didn't see the charging Otto Nadler coming towards him at pace. Otto dropped his shoulder and struck him in the ribs. The man went down, unable to regain his feet, and both Ziggy and Karl trampled over him as the three of them strove to leave the crowd. None of them even looked back as they heard the man cry out.

"Was that Hitler you just knocked over, Otto?" Ziggy asked as they reached the building line.

"Err! I think so, yes, it might well have been," Otto replied, a sheepish grin on his face.

"Thank you for getting us out of there, Otto." Karl patted his friend on his enormous shoulders as they all caught their breath. "Can we head back to Friedrichshafen now please?"

"You should know better!" Petra berated them. "Three grown men, at your age, behaving in such a fashion. You are all successful businessmen, not student revolutionaries!"

The three of them all stood in a line inside the entrance hall of Ziggy's house like three naughty school children, variously looking at the interior decor of the hall, their feet, each other, anywhere but at the very angry Petra.

"It failed anyway, like all of these anti-government protests," she went on, as they had missed the outcome travelling back to the shores of Lake Constance. "This morning's newspaper has declared that the leaders, Ludendorff, Hitler and his followers, have fled from Munich and warrants have been issued for their arrest. So, let's hope that will be an end to this talk of nationalist fervour and revolution. It also said that as little as a hundred and thirty soldiers held back the crowd of over two thousand and during an exchange of gunfire, four police officers and sixteen of those Nazi people were killed. It says Hitler was injured, but it doesn't say how." Petra stopped and looked up at the three men opposite her. Both Karl and Ziggy were looking at Otto.

"Well?" Petra continued to look.

"Um! I may have… Well, he may have been one of the men I knocked over as we forced our way through the crowd to the safety of the buildings. It was him or me to be honest," Otto admitted.

"So, you were in the thick of it then? I thought you said you were just following events, not involved in them?" Petra began to build to yet another verbal assault.

"Listen, my darling! We just got too close to the front when the march stopped, could have happened to anyone. We…." Ziggy never finished.

170

"Enough! And don't you 'darling' me, Ziggy Jurgens! Well, I hope you're satisfied, the three of you. Somehow you manged to injure the leader of the Nazi Party. Let's hope we don't live to regret it." Petra finished her lecture and walked through to the kitchen.

"She'll be fine, honestly. Now shall we get some sleep?" Ziggy tried to make light of his wife's anger as his two friends smiled back at him.

Upon Karl's return to England he threw himself into setting up his new premises and new home in Edgeware, North London. Lily's brother, John, was as capable as Karl had expected him to be in managing his existing premises in the Midlands. In a very short period of time Karl had made numerous reliable contacts with German businesses to supply British industry with their superior machinery. Karl had been able to persuade Iris to move into the new house he had purchased in Edgware and act as nurse, babysitter and housekeeper for both Karl and the two children. Freya had become wilfully independent as she grew and adapted to her new school.

With Karl so frequently away in Germany and other European countries developing yet more contracts, he quickly realised he needed to appoint an office manager and his own personal assistant to manage the increased workload and organise his diary. Karl was able to easily fill the managerial position, plucking Charles Ebden away from a nearby engineering plant and promoting him to run his business in his frequent absences. The provision of a personal secretary was proving to be more difficult, as each of the candidates interviewed so far were not quite what Karl was looking for. Not that he really knew what that was; he simply didn't feel any of those that had applied were suitable.

Edgware
May 1924

"How long are you here for this time, Louis?" Charles asked his boss as he sat opposite him in Karl's very comfortable office.

"Probably a couple of weeks. I have to arrange a trip to Sweden. I've been invited to view some of their innovative new machines and related products which may have a market here in England. Why do you ask?"

"I have another candidate coming in this afternoon applying for the personal assistant role." Charles had a nervous smile on his face as he brought up the notorious subject.

"Oh, yes, another lamb to the slaughter, eh!" Karl chuckled as he ripped open another envelope from the pile in his in tray.

"Well, she's due at two o'clock. Would you care to meet her?"

"Two o'clock, you say? Yes, that should be fine." Karl was now reading one of the letters he had opened and not really paying attention to Charles.

"Do you want to know her name, or anything about her?" Charles tried to regain Karl's attention, but his boss was totally engrossed in the letter he was reading and didn't reply.

"See you at two then?" And not receiving any reply or acknowledgement, Charles rose from his chair and quietly left the office and Karl, with his mail.

"Louis, she's here, shall I show here straight in?" Charles had opened the door and stood in the doorway as he spoke. Karl looked up from his desk. "Who is here, Charles?"

"I told you, the lady applying to be your secretary and personal assistant," Charles smiled.

"Ah! Yes, of course, I recall now. Well, please show her in." Karl cleared some papers from his desk and stood ready to greet the visitor as Charles showed her into the office.

The young lady was certainly striking, as she strode confidently into the room. Karl put her in her early twenties. She had her hair pinned up neatly, and presented a beautiful smile with clean pristine white teeth below her deep blue eyes. Karl reckoned her to be about five foot five or five foot six. She wore a very well-tailored dark grey, two-piece suit that emphasized her sleek, athletic physique. Karl was seldom lost for words, but found himself momentarily just staring at this vision as she approached his desk and held out her slender hand with exquisitely manicured nails. "Good afternoon, sir, my name is Grace Ball, I'm delighted to meet you." She spoke in a very polite, clipped Home Counties accent.

Karl recovered his composure and shook the lady's hand. "Louis Luddolph, and it is my pleasure to meet you. Please do take a seat and make yourself comfortable." Karl offered Grace the seat opposite him, waiting for her to settle herself before retaking his own chair. "Can I offer you something to drink, tea or coffee perhaps?"

"I suspect that should be something that I should say, if I'm fortunate enough to gain the position I'm applying for here," Grace replied, a playful smile creeping across her face as she spoke.

Karl laughed. "Indeed yes, but there are so many other things required, not least to keep control of my diary and appointments as I build the business. I cannot continue with little scraps of paper everywhere with schedules and meetings on them. Is that something that you feel you could organise?"

"I feel sure I can manage that, sir," Grace replied confidently.

"Please call me Louis. If you don't mind my saying, you seem too young to be an experienced secretary or personal assistant." Karl looked challengingly at the spirited lady opposite him as he spoke.

"Sir, I'm nearly twenty-two. What I lack in experience I make up for in my drive and determination to succeed. It would seem my age is proving to be a real impediment to my securing employment anywhere. It seems that anyone younger than thirty is not taken seriously. If it is to be the same here, then I will take my leave." And with that Grace rose to her feet, as if to leave the office.

Karl quickly stood. "Please, please, sit. I am intrigued by your situation and keen to know more." Karl indicated for Grace to once more, sit in the chair opposite him. He didn't know why, but he knew that he wanted this very vivacious young lady to stay in his office a while longer.

Grace once more sat. "Thank you, sir," she said quietly.

"So, please do tell me about yourself?" Karl resumed.

"As I said, I am almost twenty-two years old. I recently completed a secretarial course including Pitman shorthand, but I have not had an opportunity, as yet, to employ my skills properly. I live at home with my parents, local to this area. I regard myself as both punctual and polite. I am reliable and efficient in all I do. I just seek a position where I am able to prove my worth."

"Do you know what we do here?" Karl asked. "We are, after all, a very new company. I have not been based here for even a year yet."

"I have discovered that you began in the Midlands, working with Sir Herbert Austin, the car manufacturer. You started your own machinery and associated products distribution and supply company near Birmingham and have brought many products into Great Britain from Germany. You have recently relocated to this area. I know that as a German subject you were imprisoned during the war."

"You are very well informed. How did you acquire all this information?" Karl was staggered by Grace's knowledge of his company and him.

"I took the liberty of contacting your manager in Birmingham, a Mr. Pope," Grace explained politely, "and he was kind enough to explain how you began. He also mentioned about your time during the war. I hope he, or I, did not overstep?"

Karl smiled, then broke into a laugh. "You are certainly thorough and direct, I admire that. How would you like to come and work for me then?"

Grace was initially silent, then quickly responded, "When would you like me to start?"

"I just need to check with Charles, but that will be a formality. How would next Monday be?" Karl felt he wanted to secure the employment of this vibrant young woman as quickly as possible. "Do you have any questions for me?" he added.

"Will my hours be along the lines of a traditional nine to five, or do you, as I suspect, actually keep much longer hours of business?" Grace queried.

"You read me very well. I do keep quite unsocial hours, yes. Will this be a problem for you?"

"Not at all, sir. I will be available as you require me to be," Grace replied confidently.

Karl stood, indicating that the interview was at an end. Grace stood also and once again offered her hand. "Thank you, sir, for this opportunity," she said.

"I have every confidence in your abilities. I will see you on Monday." And Karl shook Grace's hand again and stayed standing as she turned towards the door and left his office. He was still standing a short while later when Charles knocked and entered.

"So, Louis! Do we have a new secretary?" Charles asked.

"We do indeed. She certainly is a formidable young lady." Karl laughed again as he responded.

Charles smiled as he closed the office door, once more leaving Karl on his own, to think about the woman he had just employed. He felt strangely bereft after her departure from his office. He experienced a sudden emptiness and a desire to see her again. He also felt a little confused. He was still mourning the loss of his beautiful, exquisite Lily and yet he was oddly elated by his encounter with Grace Ball.

Friedrichshafen
May 1924

"Unbelievable! They have somehow managed to turn him into some sort of folk hero, battling to save Germany from the communists. The judges all sided with him from the outset. They gave him a daily platform to espouse his views and as a result he has gained enormous popularity amongst the public and workers." Ziggy paused and looked over the top of his newspaper to see if Petra was listening. She was busy darning some socks in the armchair opposite. Ziggy was not sure if he had her attention or not. He returned to his newspaper.

"Interesting that he never once mentioned or blamed the Jews for the state of Germany or in fact said anything remotely anti-Semitic. He both flattered and frightened our business and industrial leaders, making them fear the spectre of communism is around the corner. Which I'm sure it isn't." Ziggy paused and glanced once more at his silent wife.

This time she looked up at him. "That is quite enough thank you, Ziggy. You will wake the children." And instantly Petra had defused her husband's rant, or so she thought.

"Five years he got, five years for treason! And then they send him to Landsberg, talk about soft punishment. No hard labour. Unlimited visitors. Mark my words, we've not heard the last of Herr Hitler!" Ziggy folded his newspaper, anxious not to antagonise Petra any further.

177

Petra, for her part, subtly changed the subject. "Have you heard from Karl since he's been back in England?" Petra asked.

"Quite a few business calls from him at the office. I understand he has secured sole distributor rights for several of our products at the ZF Group. I was talking to two of our competitors at a conference last month and they too have contract deals with him. He's becoming very successful over there."

"Any other news, my dear?" Petra asked.

"Do you remember Karl talking about his close friend Joseph Pilates, who is currently instructing in Hamburg? Karl reckons he's about to emigrate to America and make a fresh start with his revolutionary exercise routines. You remember I said that Joseph and Karl had been interned together during the war?"

"Yes, I remember. Do you think Karl might get involved in this fitness venture in America, maybe invest in it?' Petra asked.

"It would not surprise me, my love," Ziggy replied. After a pause for thought he went on: "Did I tell you that Karl and his elder brother Max tried to get to America just at the start of the war? That would have been before the *Lusitania* was sunk. After that they had no chance and the British government refused to let them leave, instead imprisoning them for the whole war. It was just poor timing, they were so close to being able to make a fresh start in America, instead spending four dreadful years in a prison camp."

"That is so sad and such a waste," Petra said quietly.

"He's settled into his new office premises and as I have to say, he is certainly doing very well."

"Did he mention Freya or little James?'

"Not really, you know how driven he's become since the loss of Lily. It's hard to get him to talk of anything but business. But he did mention something else." Ziggy smiled at Petra.

"Oh yes!" Petra listened more intently.

"He managed to find the time to mention a new secretary he's just employed at his London office. For Karl he was quite upbeat and positive about her. He even described her to me in great detail." Ziggy was almost laughing now.

"And does this new lady have a name?" Petra asked perceptively, smiling broadly back at her husband.

"He said her name was Grace," and Ziggy laughed as he watched his wife's eyes widen in delight.

Cork
April 1926

Grace watched from the car as her boss, H Louis Luddolph, negotiated with the security guard at the docks entrance. She watched how he confidently shook hands with the burly guard and casually passed him a folded note. Grace continued to watch as Louis returned to the car.

"That didn't take you long, is he going to let us through?" Grace asked as her boss clambered back into the vehicle.

"Once the language barrier was overcome and he understood that we just wanted to say goodbye to one of the passengers, he was fine. Coupled with the five-pound note I gave him of course," Karl replied smiling.

Grace accepted the fact that her boss would routinely offer people monetary incentives to get his way, or to afford both him and his guests or colleagues favourable or preferential treatment. He was never subtle about it. He just saw it as a necessary part of keeping all parties he encountered affable and receptive to his requests and needs. Take, for example, the loan of the office manager's car from one of the facilities that Karl now ran from Dublin. Karl had travelled to Ireland to ensure that his machinery distribution network was established and thriving there. He recalled a letter received from his great friend and former comrade at Knockaloe internment camp, Joseph Pilates. A quick check from his most efficient personal assistant, Grace, had indeed found that Joseph would be travelling to America that same week and was due to stop in Queenstown, before the trans-Atlantic crossing.

On the spur of the moment and with considerable help from Grace it was established that the ship, SS *Westphalia*, would be taking on additional passengers at Queenstown, having left from its port of origin, Hamburg. Courtesy of a very helpful travel clerk there, Grace had been able to discover Joseph Pilates amongst the list of passengers.

Karl had been delighted and another quick handshake with the young Dublin office manager had delivered the use of the new, very compact, Austin 7 that Karl was now steering through the docks at Queenstown.

"Did I tell you I was part of the team that helped produce this car?" The moment Karl mentioned his involvement with the production of the Austin 7 he regretted it. It made him sound so boastful, so pompous.

"I didn't, and it's a lovely little car. But don't you find it a little cramped?" Grace had an ability to keep Karl's feet firmly on the ground with her gentle and informed comments.

"Well, of course, the idea was to provide a car for the masses. I shall look for something more suitable for myself once we return to London," Karl declared.

He had been delighted when Grace had agreed to accompany him on his trip to Ireland. The business was expanding and he now had two other people to help Charles with the sales and marketing side, while Grace concentrated on managing Karl's hectic appointments schedule. He had marvelled at the way Grace took each day in her stride from the moment she started working for him. She was behind her desk each day before 8 a.m., immaculately presented, and it was rare for her to depart before seven in the evening. As an idea to give her a change of scenery, Karl had invited her to join him on his tour to the Ireland office. Everything arranged for them was meticulously planned by Grace, with separate rooms booked at the various accommodations for the week-long trip.

Grace was devoted to her boss. She knew so much about this stern-looking, smartly dressed man in his early forties. He ruled his offices and business with an iron determination and there was seldom any chance to see his private side. But on occasion the guard would slip, and Grace would discover what a truly generous and polite gentleman Lou was. She knew he was really called Karl, but she had decided and settled upon Lou, once she had agreed to dispense with the initial address of "sir" she used for the first few months of her employment.

Her devotion had begun on a very professional level, and she didn't have any other feelings towards him. But as the time passed and the closeness of their working environment brought them into such immediate daily contact, a very natural affection began to overtake her. Grace was young and had had a few short-term boyfriends – all, in her opinion, drippy young men with no idea about life. No ambition and no conversation. As she regarded her boss over time, she saw glimpses of the pain behind his eyes amid the drive to succeed that dominated his personality. She knew of his history, of his internment during the war at the very moment his first child was born. The loss of his wife as she gave birth to his son, only four years previously. She found herself often staring at the framed picture of Louis' wife Lily that took pride of place on his desk. She knew his two children were cared for mainly by Lily's younger sister Iris at Louis' home in Fairview Way, Edgware. She knew Freya was a remarkable but feisty eleven-year-old, going on eighteen, mentioned by Louis on more than one occasion, and that his son James was a healthy and well cared-for toddler. She knew of his brothers, one elder, Max in Dortmund, and a younger, Willy, still close to where Karl's parents, Albert and Charlotte, lived in Leicester. She didn't feel she was prying, she was just genuinely interested to know all she could about the remarkable force of nature her boss was.

This trip had been an opportunity too good to miss. To spend an extended amount of time with him exclusively. She had found hotels of distinction, where the custom was still to dress for dinner. She had expanded her wardrobe to include a selection of 'head-turning' gowns, that she now wore each evening when sharing a sumptuous meal in decadently expensive surroundings with her dinner-jacketed boss.

He was, as she had predicted, the most wonderful host, the perfect gentleman companion. The right word to everyone they encountered, from the cloakroom attendants to the maitre d' at the Liverpool Adelphi. She felt a rush of pride when he would take her arm in his and escort her into the dining rooms of these prestigious establishments. He would be attentive and regale her with stories of his life in the German navy as a teenager and the friendships he had forged with his naval colleague Ziggy and their former chief instructor Otto. He had promised that he would one day take her to Germany to meet these two great characters and also his brother Max.

"I can see the ship, Lou." Grace pointed over to their left as they drove past the wharves and other dockyard buildings. Karl continued to drive slowly onwards and came to a halt by a wall. He got out and immediately went around to assist Grace. They then walked towards the trans-Atlantic vessel, SS *Westphalia*, already docked. Once again Karl's charm and deep pockets allowed them to climb the gangway and to board the ship.

"Good afternoon, sir." Karl addressed himself to the senior-looking man at the centre of three uniformed officers. "My name is Louis Luddolph. My assistant and I are not passengers for this journey, we have travelled to wish a close friend bon voyage. Is there any way that you could locate him for us?"

"Sir, if you give me his name I should be able to determine his cabin number for you and then direct you to where that might be." The man smiled genially at Karl and spent rather too long for his liking appraising Grace. He then reached for a clipboard of papers and after a quick survey of his notes, he looked up at Karl.

"His name is Joseph Pilates," Karl told him.

"Peel, Pike, yes here we are, Pilates. He is in cabin 317. Now if you follow this passageway and go down two flights of stairs amidships, you will find his cabin aft of the stairs on the left-hand side, if memory serves."

"My good man, you are most kind. May I finally ask at what time you sail please?" Karl thought it prudent to check.

"You have just under five hours before we depart, sir," the man said, and beamed as Karl placed a five-pound note in his hand.

"My God, Karl, it is so good to see you," Joseph said from the very comfortable lounge chairs found in one of the upper deck areas of the ship. "What a splendid surprise. My dear, this is so unlike the man you work for. Spontaneity is not an adjective I would use to describe him."

Grace laughed as the waiter brought an ornate tray of bone china tea, with a tiered cake stand of mini sponges and pastries.

"Let me pour the tea while the two of you catch up." Grace instinctively went into assistant mode while Karl and Joseph chatted about their lives.

She could have found the conversation boring, not being involved in it, but she was hooked on every word that both her boss Louis and the exuberant Joseph Pilates spoke.

After a while she excused herself to find the ladies' room.

"My God, Karl, you are a dark horse. That vision is really your secretary?" Joseph whispered to his friend.

"Indeed she is, my personal assistant and nothing more. Just so you know, she is incredibly efficient at what she does."

Karl was a little taken aback by Joseph's thoughts.

"I didn't mean to offend you, my dear friend, but I just had to comment after seeing the way she looks at you," Joseph pointed out.

"And how does she look at me?" Karl was puzzled.

"It's with utter devotion. Please do not get upset about this, but in my opinion that girl is besotted with you, she never takes her eyes off you. I should know because I haven't taken my eyes off her since we met."

"Rubbish!" And Karl laughed.

"Well, when you come and see me in New York, I will wager that you will be accompanied by the next Mrs. Luddolph."

On the journey back to Dublin Karl found himself repeating in his mind the statement that his friend Joseph had made about the way Grace had looked at him. It had never entered his head in the time that Grace had been in his employ that there was anything more than a professional working relationship between the two of them. He was more than satisfied with her work and he had no complaints about the way she behaved both in the office and on this trip across to Ireland. He stole a glance across at her in the passenger seat of the small car; and found himself thinking what a truly beautiful woman she was, with poise and confidence in abundance. She suddenly looked back at him and he jolted his head back to the road in front of them, feeling guilty that she had caught him looking at her. But he felt so relaxed, so comfortable in her company.

He continued to weigh up the situation. He was now forty-one years old, had built up a successful business these past few years and was making good money. His two children were growing up fast, with Freya now nearly a teenager and his son James a handful for Iris at just four. Grace was what, twenty-three! *My God! Put away these ideas*, he thought.

But the attraction for Grace would not go away. Her

ceaseless devotion at work to support his business was surely more than just a professional pride in her occupation. He had wondered if she had a boyfriend. She certainly never mentioned anyone and was still living at home with her parents. Karl was still confused by his feelings. He ached with the loss of his dear wife Lily, but the attraction to Grace felt acceptable and not least because he had now been given to understand this attraction was reciprocated on her part. *What to do about this?* he pondered.

Finally, after several months of indecision on his part, Karl finally brought the subject to a head.

"Grace, would you come and sit down please?" And he offered Grace the chair opposite his desk once more. The same chair where he had interviewed her for the position within his company.

Grace sat. "Oh! Do I need my notepad?" and she went to get up. But Karl lifted his arm.

"No, Grace, that's fine, I just need to talk to you." Grace lowered herself back into the chair as Karl's arm indicated for her to do so.

"My dear Grace, this is suddenly really difficult," and Karl paused.

Grace, sensing the nature of Karl's unease, helped him out. "You want to ask me out to dinner and you just don't know how?" She smiled sweetly at him.

Karl was stunned by the perception of his secretary.

"You are worried that it would be considered awkward and unseemly for a man in his forties to ask a lady in her early twenties out for dinner; perhaps more so as this man is the boss and the lady in question is his secretary?"

"Well, there is a considerable age gap between us. There's no getting away from it. It could cause quite the scandal," Karl offered.

"Louis Luddolph, you do not strike me as the kind of man

easily swayed by public opinion or in any way concerned by gossip." Grace looked directly at Karl as she spoke.

"Well, obviously I also must consider your feelings towards this situation. We have never really spoken like this. I am keen to know your thoughts on us perhaps becoming something more than secretary and employer?"

"Finally, you actually talk to me! Louis, I have been transfixed by you from the moment of our first meeting. I have felt the adoration from a host of men of my own age, but they are mere boys and adolescents compared to you."

"And the age gap between us does not bother you?" Karl said tentatively.

"You are young for your age and I have always regarded myself as older than my years. The age thing is just numbers. I know how I feel about you, Lou. Let me show you how to be cared for again."

"You understand my love for Lily? I'm not sure I can ever love anyone in that way again."

"I do understand. I want to be your devoted companion, but I realise the limits of what you can give. I would take any piece of you, however small. You deserve to have someone in your life to help lessen the void you feel since the loss of Lily," Grace said sincerely.

"And my two children? Freya can be very difficult and John is still only a baby really."

"Freya is wonderful and so beautiful, but I concede she can be quite wilful. That may be a challenge in the years to come, but that's why you brought it up." Grace once again saw the doubt in Karl's mind.

"Perhaps, then, we should continue this very frank conversation over dinner?" Karl said, suddenly deciding to take the plunge.

"That would be delightful." Grace rose from her chair. "Now I'm going to return to my desk and I will be ready for you to pick me up tonight at 7.30 this evening from my parents' house." And with that Grace smiled at Karl and left his office.

Well, that was easier than I thought it was going to be. Karl scratched his head and picked up the phone.

Edgware
February 1928

"You will not speak to me like that, young lady, do you hear?" Karl found himself in the awkward and perplexing situation of having to admonish his daughter Freya.

"She is your secretary and young enough to be your daughter!" Freya did nothing to moderate her anger and astonishment at her father's behaviour.

"Age has no bearing here. I have been seeing Grace for well over a year now and our relationship has reached a stage where I felt it appropriate to ask her to marry me."

"I don't trust her, she must be a gold digger. What does a girl in her twenties see in a stiff, middle-aged man like you? Apart from your money of course!"

"Now look, Freya, money does not come into it. We are both extremely fond of each other and your brother likes her. So what, please, is your problem?"

"I mean it's not as if Mother has been dead that long and you ignore her and her memory to take up with this other woman."

"ENOUGH! I will not have you speaking about your mother like that. You are my daughter and I love you, but you do not have the right at thirteen to speak to me in this manner. Now you will go to your room, I do not wish to be in your company anymore."

Karl's tone quietened Freya and immediately she knew she

had gone too far. She looked at her father and was about to speak again, but saw the look in his eyes and thought better of it. She very slowly bowed her head and walked from the lounge and made her way upstairs to her bedroom, where she closed the door quietly behind her.

Karl sat down in an armchair and tried to calm himself. He had known that Freya had not warmed to Grace in the same way as his much younger son James had. He considered that it was just Freya being at a difficult age; hopefully! Grace had tried, on numerous occasions in the last fourteen months, to interact and engage with her, but Freya could be frosty with almost everyone. He wondered as he sat there whether he had spoilt his daughter. He thought about sending her away to boarding school, but dismissed it on the advice of Lily's sister Iris, who still lived with them as a full-time nanny for James.

He realised that marriage to Grace was a serious step and perhaps Freya's mentioning of the age gap between them was going to be echoed by a good many of his friends and other family members. Karl didn't know what to think. He knew he wanted to be with Grace. He was devoted to her, welcomed her company and felt complete when she was with him; but it was a devotion different to that which he had enjoyed with Lily. To Grace's credit she recognised this and had spoken to him about it not affecting how she felt about him.

Karl had decided to keep the marriage as low-key as possible. A very small registry office ceremony, with Charles Ebden, his office manager, and Iris the only witnesses. Grace had not been bothered by the small scale of the occasion, understanding the need for the official status, and her husband not wishing to broadcast the news. He had asked Freya to be in attendance, but she had declined, excusing herself by saying she had a migraine. *The first migraine I can recall her ever having*, Karl thought.

He had decided to take Grace on an extended tour of Germany. It may have started with the best of intentions on his part to show her the beauty of the country of his birth, but it very quickly became a tour of the various factories with which Karl did business. He did, though, find time to visit Ziggy and Petra and introduce his new bride to them. Grace, while nervous, immediately fell in love with Petra and the handsome Lothar and his delicately beautiful sister Emma. Ziggy had spent much of the time candidly remarking on Grace's youthfulness, until he received a sharp clip around the ear from Otto, who found himself captivated by his friend's young British wife.

Karl was relieved to see that Germany was actually doing rather well and its economy was starting to rebuild. People genuinely seemed to feel optimistic about the future. But there were still factions that were determined to try and effect change. The revolutionary firebrand, Hitler, was vainly striving to gain seats in the German parliament, no longer trying to achieve power by overthrowing the existing government by force. But Karl felt the German people were content. They had money in their pockets and food on the table. No need to take notice of Herr Hitler and his brown-shirted bully boys.

Karl was doing very well indeed. He had increased his distribution empire to include companies from Sweden and Norway. He had bought additional premises in Solihull, near Birmingham. He had been advised to buy shares and invest in some very solid stocks, but Karl went another way and invested in gold bullion, diamonds and property. He was able to attract the best people to work for him, as he paid such an attractive salary. He immediately replaced Grace as his secretary after they were married. On her obvious insistence the replacement was the very formal, middle-aged, bespectacled, Albert Briggs.

Once again Karl had married someone English, and having lived in England since before 1900, he considered he would not have a problem becoming a naturalised British subject now, so he once again applied for naturalisation. The application was rejected. He had forged links with countless successful businesses and now had friends involved in the management of manufacturing industries in England. He may have had an accent and he did of course still speak German fluently, but he regarded himself as British and found this inability to achieve the status he wanted very frustrating and puzzling.

"Lou, dinner will be about an hour," Grace called through to Karl from the kitchen. Despite his attempts to get her to call him Karl she had grown fond of calling him Lou and after a while he had grown used to it. Besides, virtually everyone he did business with called him Louis and his company name was officially H Louis Luddolph.

Karl looked up from his paper. "Thank you, my dear. By the way, did you see the result of the recent elections in Germany?" He knew this was unlikely.

Grace came through to the lounge. "Sorry, did you say something?"

"I was just remarking on the results of the elections in Germany. That odious little man with the stupid moustache that runs the Nazi Party won less than three per cent of the vote and only has twelve seats in the Reichstag, that's Germany's parliament. Ever since they changed their voting system to one of proportional representation they have ended up with lots of parties having a small number of seats, so no one party has a majority. It makes it almost impossible to govern." Karl paused and looked up at Grace.

"I am listening, but it seems really complicated and shouldn't you be more concerned about matters here in England?" Grace suggested.

"I'm concerned about matters here too, but with so much business with Germany I have to keep up to date with developments there," Karl argued. "I actually think that since the implementation of the Dawes Plan from America, Germany is doing much better. They have an opportunity to make more reasonable and realistic payments as part of the war reparations and as a result the economy over there is doing really well."

"I was able to get a lovely leg of lamb for dinner." Grace deftly changed the subject back to more domestic matters. Since marrying Karl, she had become a very efficient and capable housewife, although deep down she still missed the cut and thrust of the busy office that Karl controlled.

"Splendid. And will Freya be joining the rest of us this evening?" Karl tentatively broached the subject of his cantankerous daughter, who despite all attempts by Grace to build a relationship, refused to soften her icy and caustic demeanour.

"I spoke to Iris and she said she would try and encourage her to venture down from her room, but she didn't feel confident," Grace replied.

"Well, I am going to go and sort this out!" And Karl rose from his chair, about to make for the stairs.

Grace moved across the room to block his exit. "Lou, please, leave it tonight. If she chooses to join us it would be lovely, but let's not spoil our evening together." Grace did her best to placate the anger she knew that the 'Freya' situation was causing in her husband.

"Well, I am going to have to sort this out soon or it will get worse," Karl said as he moved back towards his wife. He put his arms around her and kissed her. "Are you OK, my dear Grace? It's a lot to deal with, from living at home with your parents to suddenly inheriting my entire family, which sections of are proving to be quite a challenge."

"Lou, I'm fine. I can cope with Freya. She's just growing

up and testing boundaries. Iris is a super nanny and little James is adorable. But I also wanted to tell you something that I learned only yesterday." Grace smiled at Karl.

"Oh yes, do tell?"

"It's very simple. I went to see my doctor yesterday and he confirmed that I am expecting our child and it is due in May of next year."

For a split second Karl was frozen, then he looked into the eyes of this woman who had brought so much of the joy back into his life since the loss of Lily. "My darling Grace, that is simply wonderful news." He continued to hug and squeeze his wife.

"You're not angry? I know we didn't really discuss this and I was concerned that with your age it might not be what you wanted." Grace tried to tread carefully. Not entirely sure what Karl's reaction would be.

"Ha! I'm forty-three, not sixty-three. There's clearly life in the old dog yet!" and Karl laughed loudly and once again embraced his wife.

"I haven't told anyone else yet, you know," Grace said, looking directly at him.

Karl quickly caught on. "Ah! Freya! Yes, this could be a tricky one. Do you think I should tell her, or maybe it might be better coming from Iris?"

Grace didn't answer, as her attention was drawn to the attractive young teenager with her arms defiantly folded who stood in the doorway.

"Tell me what?" Freya asked.

London
May 1930

Karl sat in the ornate waiting area. He took in the fine panelled interior of the room, with the high ceilings and elaborate chandeliers hanging from them. There was a familiar clerical smell to the room. He sat in a row of chairs arranged along one wall; there were two other people also waiting and Karl acknowledged them as he caught their eye.

Once again, he had applied for naturalisation. The most recent attempt was spurred on by the birth of his third child in May 1929. Grace had given him another son, who they had christened David. They had also sold the house in Edgware and moved back up to Solihull to be closer to his newest business acquisitions. Grace had fallen in love with a large house in Dove House Lane that backed onto Olton golf course. She had just started to take golf lessons and encouraged Karl to join her in an activity that they could both enjoy. Grace had also suggested that it might be the optimum time to try once again to gain his British citizenship. By now, Karl was such a prominent businessman that he had referees on his application that included the mayor of Leicester and others of equal social standing.

When the envelope from the Home Office duly arrived, Karl had dismissed it as yet another rejection, but this time the letter had invited him to attend the ministerial offices in London to discuss his application. A little surprised and curious, Karl now found himself waiting to be seen.

195

A very smartly dressed man came through one of the doors. Karl thought him to be about forty to fifty years of age, much the same as himself. He was of average height, with thinning light brown hair and a clipped moustache. "Mr. H Louis Luddolph?" the man enquired.

Karl stood. "Here." He spoke clearly and brought his feet together smartly.

"Mr. Luddolph, please follow me," and the man indicated for Karl to follow him through the door.

Karl walked into another ornately decorated room, this one dominated by a large, highly polished wooden table. On the opposite side of the table to him were another two smartly dressed men of indeterminate age. His escort held out an arm. "Do please take a seat," and Karl sat in the empty chair. The escort introduced the room. "Good afternoon, Mr. Luddolph. My name is Desmond Morton and I work for an associated government department. These two gentlemen also work for me within this department." The two gentlemen looked up at Karl and smiled at him simultaneously. Mr. Morton continued.

"We are not from the Home Office and we are not here to discuss your application to become a British subject, we have another matter we would like to put to you." And with that Mr. Morton sat.

Karl was struck dumb, his mind rapidly wondering what transgression he may have committed to incur the attention of these serious-looking men.

The man on the left opposite him cleared his throat.

"We have concerns about the security of our own country and find ourselves looking across Europe. In particular at the very fragile state of affairs that currently exists in Germany." The man spoke with a very clipped proper upper-class English accent. Karl was intrigued, as he was well aware of the situation in his country of birth.

The other man opposite spoke. "My colleague and I work

for the security services and both report to Mr. Morton here. He, in turn, reports to various persons within the Cabinet of the government and one or two currently not, if you understand?" Karl nodded as the man continued. "We are finding the information we can gather is quite limited and we are trying to build a network of people who, through perfectly legitimate means, can keep a close eye on German affairs without raising suspicion, and then report back to us with their findings." The man paused.

"I see, and are you suggesting that I be one of these people?" Karl asked.

Mr. Morton spoke: "Mr. Luddolph, we are just discussing the possibility that your own situation does play rather well into our sphere of intelligence. You see, as a German subject, fluent in their language, with a network of companies throughout the country, you are able to move legitimately across Germany, furthering your British-based distribution business. You must admit that you have all the attributes that would assist our intelligence gathering aim."

"And my application to become a naturalised British subject would possibly get in the way of this?" Karl began to see the picture before him.

"My dear fellow, we would of course be only too pleased to grant you the status you so rightly deserve. However, in the interests of national security, could we extend a tentative offer to rubber stamp your status, so to speak, but perhaps delay it until such time as your assistance to us has come to an end?"

"I see, so I work for you, but still operate as a German subject?"

"You've got it, sir! Make your journeys through Germany all the more authentic, what?" one of the men opposite added.

"But – and I say this with the utmost respect – I don't know any of you gentlemen. What guarantees do I have that you will honour our bargain if I agree to assist you?" Karl asked.

Without a word, Desmond Morton rose from his seat and walked to a door behind the two men seated opposite Karl. He knocked loudly on it, then returned to his seat. After a pause of no more than a few seconds the door opened and in walked a very familiar figure, surrounded by a thick cloud of cigar smoke. "Mr. Luddolph, or may I call you Louis?" There was the familiar voice with the confident tone, despite the slight lisp. "You know me, sir! And these gentlemen all report directly to me. I give you my word that your status and citizenship are guaranteed if you could accommodate us in our endeavour. What do you say, sir?'

Karl had risen to his feet as he recognised the figure before him. "Sir, I, well, I would be honoured to assist."

"Splendid, good man," and he held out his hand to Karl. Karl extended his own hand and found himself shaking hands with the Right Honourable Winston Churchill, MP. "These men will take care of you!" And with that he was gone from the room, leaving Karl staring open-mouthed at the closing door.

Mr. Morton returned to his seat. "Mr. Luddolph, Mr. Churchill is currently without a Cabinet position and consequently has come to rely on the information that can be gleaned from the men in this room, assisted by men such as yourself. We do not have a time frame in mind and we are quite keen to provide you with some training in such matters as self-defence and covert surveillance. When is your next scheduled visit to the factories in Germany you do business with?"

"Well, I have a visit planned next month. I was going to take my family and visit some old friends in Bavaria, make the business trip an excuse to give my family a chance to see Germany. Although my wife would argue that it's the other way around," Karl smiled.

"Well, that is splendid. Just keep your eyes and ears open

and then when you return, someone will be in touch to discuss your visit. How does that sound?"

"How will you know I have returned? Should I contact you?" Karl asked.

"My dear fellow, leave the details with us, we will be in touch." One of the two men opposite rose, indicating that the meeting was at an end.

"I didn't catch either of your names," Karl said to the two men now standing opposite him. "Mr. Morton introduced himself but I don't know what to call you."

"You are entirely correct, sir. We didn't give our names," and the slightly shorter of the men walked quietly from the room.

"I will be your direct contact," the other man opposite said. "You may refer to me as Colonel Z." And with that he too left the room.

Karl looked across to where Desmond Morton was standing behind his chair.

"If you would care to follow me? And one final word please. This matter is of the utmost secrecy, not even the closest members of your household are to be made aware of the events detailed at today's meeting. The country is at a crossroads and it's very future may well depend on the information that people such as yourself are able to obtain for us. I cannot emphasise more strongly the need for absolute confidentiality. You understand I'm sure?" Morton gave his warning in a decidedly polite but cold way.

"I, err, yes of course, I understand completely," Karl replied nervously, as Morton ushered him out.

"Good luck to you, Luddolph, and enjoy your trip." And with that he was gone, leaving Karl back in the ornate waiting room.

Lake Constance, Friedrichshafen
July 1930

Karl looked down the long table and caught the eye of his eldest child. She was an enigma to him. Since the start of this trip, she had been sullen and petulant. Now, since their arrival at Ziggy's house on the shores of Lake Constance, she was charming, polite and the antithesis of her previous incarnation.

"Grace, what has happened to my daughter since we arrived here?" Karl leant across and whispered to his wife. "Have you spoken to her?"

"For a man as observant as you are, you sometimes miss things staring you in the face. Your daughter, my dear Lou, has become a young lady of singular beauty and her eyes have been turned by the handsome features of our host's son, Lothar."

"I'm astounded. You mean the effect of Lothar has been to create an entirely new personality for Freya? It's been ages since I saw a glimmer of a smile from her and now we are reminded that she even has teeth!" Karl laughed.

"What's so amusing, Karl?" Ziggy Jurgens looked up from the long table situated on the patio overlooking the beautiful Bavarian lake.

"It would appear, and I am relying on Grace for my intelligence, that my daughter has become rather enamoured with your son, my dear friend," Karl explained.

"Oh! My serious young son. He has no time for women in his life! He spends his entire time engaged with this youth movement, dressing up in these brown-shirted uniforms, attending meetings and lectures in Munich. He doesn't know what he's thinking."

"I have to say, I'm surprised that you would allow such behaviour," Karl said.

"I have tried, but Hitler supporters are even in the schools now, indoctrinating their students with their warped take on society. He has become a firm believer in Herr Hitler's policies. You must have seen the difference in Germany as you travelled?"

"I am appalled by the way he's taking advantage of the unemployed and vulnerable to further his divisive agenda. What about from your perspective as a rising business leader?" Karl asked.

"Well, you can't fault his devious approach. He's got the financial elite believing that Germany is at risk from the communists and the Jews. He has this real problem with the Jews, seemingly blaming them for Germany's current fragile economic situation."

"It's understandable to be angry with people who have done wrong or who do not support Germany," Karl said slowly. "And I suppose to be against people who try and monopolise power in any walk of life. But what I fail to understand is being against a man because of his birth. How can a man help how he was born?"

"But you are an educated and thoughtful man who has already seen the effects war can have on us and would seek to avoid another confrontation," Ziggy explained. "For an unemployed German worker, Hitler points out someone to blame for their lot in life. He offers them the prospect of unifying the country which, as you know, currently consists of an amalgam of political parties coalescing to run the country. He plays to his strengths of whipping a crowd into a frenzy, promising a better future after our uncertain recent past."

'You make him sound faintly messianic," Karl retorted.

"And that's just it. To the impressionable masses and immature youth of Germany, he has gained in popularity exponentially."

"So, what is your view in the long term, my dear friend?" Karl asked.

"All the time that the other political parties manoeuvre and form ever briefer coalitions, Herr Hitler is able to gradually indoctrinate the people of Germany. I see him using his 'Brownshirts' to force people to follow his ideology and support him. We seem to have elections every few months as the partnerships at the Reichstag splinter apart," Ziggy explained.

"So where do you think all this leads?" As Karl spoke he did not see Otto Nadler come up behind him and was startled when he placed an enormous hand on his shoulder.

"Karl Luddolph, if I may interrupt? Ladies, if you will excuse us, but I wish to borrow your husbands for a short while," and with that both Karl and Ziggy rose from their seats and followed Otto into the house, leaving Grace and Petra with the children.

Karl sat opposite Otto and looked hard at his former chief navel instructor. He took in the broad powerful shoulders and thick neck and the huge bulk of his friend. He still looked incredibly fit and indestructible and yet Karl estimated that he must be well into his sixties by now.

"I couldn't help but overhear your conversation about the future of our country. You know that our factory floor now has a good many members of the Nazi Party within it. Hitler has spread his message of unity and solidarity against the people who oppressed Germany after the war. He speaks so passionately about who he sees as to blame for our poor economic situation within Europe and the rest of the world. Clearly, he is anti-communist, which we would all agree is the right way to be, but then he rails against the Jews and flies off into a wild rage talking of creating a country of racially superior people, where the Jews and other minority elements would be removed from our land." Otto paused for his words to sink in.

"How do you feel about this, Otto?' Karl said.

"I have spent my life in the service of Germany, I have been the most fervent supporter of my country. But if I have got this correct, in the eyes of Hitler I am a sub-class of human being, for whom there is no place in Germany." Otto looked up at his two friends.

"What on earth are you talking about, Otto?" Ziggy demanded.

"It's quite straightforward. My father was German and when he was a young man, he fell in love with a Ukrainian woman who came to work in Germany. It was of no consequence at the time, but she was a Jew. In the eyes of Hitler and his doctrine within the Nazi Party, that makes me, as her son, part of a weaker underclass with no right to be considered part of his new Germany."

"This is too far-fetched! You've spent most of your life in service to the German navy, there's no way anyone is ever going to consider that you are less than one hundred per cent German," Ziggy scoffed.

"What are your thoughts, Karl?" Otto looked across the table.

"I'm not as well versed in the policies and detail of the Nazi Party. Are they not still a minority within your government? Do you seriously see Hitler as a viable leader in the future? Where does the mass support come from?"

"Here I completely agree with Otto," Ziggy replied. "Hitler has made enormous progress in a very short space of time. He has taken advantage of the depression across the world and the economic uncertainty. He is gaining support within the working classes and he simultaneously persuades and frightens the financial elite and industrial owners that without him, the country will inevitably fall under more communist influence. Mark my words, I see him gaining seats within the Reichstag every time they hold elections, which seems to be three times a year at present."

As Karl sat on the ferry from Hamburg, with his family around him, he thought about the opinions and concerns of his two close friends. He added these thoughts to what he had seen in the various cities he had visited on his tour. Germany looked to be on a knife edge. The government seemed incapable of governing, there were so many different small parties vying for power, and all the while a certain Adolf Hitler was using his passionate oratorical skill and powerful uniformed guards to gain traction within the Reichstag. As Karl weighed what he had seen and heard, he felt an ominous inevitability that his country of birth would once again make a poor choice at a crucial moment that could have devastating consequences. He wondered what his handlers, Colonel Z and those shadowy others, would make of his report when he got back to England.

Kent, England
July 1932

The tranquil, rolling hills of Kent, just outside the little village of Westerham, were a sufficient contrast for Karl to relax and enjoy the pleasant countryside. He had arrived at the home of Desmond Morton, having been driven from King's Cross station in London in the company of his handler Colonel Z. They had chatted about his latest visit to Germany as they were driven south into the country.

"That's very interesting about your brother moving to the Krupps works at Essen," Colonel Z commented on this revelation.

"It was a surprise to me. I thought he had settled into a position in Dortmund, at one of the breweries there. He never mentioned any intent to become involved with steel production," Karl answered.

"Well, I think that is to our advantage, a legitimate way inside the Krupps empire." Z was smiling as he spoke.

"May I enquire why you asked me to wear walking attire today?" Karl asked.

"Desmond has several dogs and a walk in the countryside with them attracts so little attention," Z responded.

"I see. Well, I don't mind a walk," Karl said.

"How is your golf coming along?" Z changed the subject.

"I, err, I didn't know you knew about my taking up golf."

"My dear chap, we keep an eye on everything. We have

205

to be aware of everyone you and your family come into contact with just on the off chance that our opposite numbers in Germany see you as a potential asset for them; which would actually be quite a good thing." Z almost whispered the last bit to himself.

"So what else do you know about my family?" Karl was curious as to the extent of the surveillance his family were under.

Z laughed, next to him in the rear of the car. "Well, let me see! Your wife Grace has a lower handicap than you." Z laughed again. "Your daughter Freya has moved out and is now employed as a nanny for a family in Angmering, in Sussex. I understand that things between you and your daughter have been difficult since you married your former secretary Grace?"

"I really don't see any relevance to any of this." Karl was becoming faintly angry with the intrusion into his personal life.

"My dear chap, please, this is all standard background stuff so that we don't get blindsided if approaches are made to those close to you. I'm glad to see your son James has settled into his school and you have applied for a place for him at several good public schools in September, and of course David is clearly the apple of your wife's eye, just as it should be."

Karl didn't say anything. He just sat in the car and quietly cooled his anger as they continued through the south London streets.

"Good morning, Louis." Karl looked across the semi-circular driveway as he got out of the car towards the approaching Desmond Morton and the surrounding collection of dogs.

"Good morning, sir." Karl shook the civil servant's hand.

"Thought we would head straight out into the woods behind us and visit a neighbour where I believe we are invited for lunch," Morton explained.

"That's fine with me."

Together they walked towards the wooded area to the rear of the drive.

"Is Colonel Z not joining us?" Karl asked as he watched the car he had arrived in disappear with his mysterious handler still inside.

"He has work elsewhere, but have no fear, we will enjoy a walk and a splendid lunch, then I will have a car here later to return you in good time for your train back to Birmingham." Morton regarded him keenly. "So how have you been? How was Germany on your last visit? It certainly must be a most curious place at present."

"I'm not sure curious really covers it. There seems to be more violence on the streets. The government has been trying to ban the SA and SS as they are frightened of Hitler trying to use force to overthrow them," Karl said.

"He won't need to, judging by the results of the latest elections. And he was able to negotiate with Chancellor Papen for a reinstatement of his Brownshirts. Have you seen the latest poll results of yesterday's federal elections?" Morton asked as they continued through the leafy avenue of trees.

"I have not seen those results yet, no, sir," Karl replied.

"Well, let me tell you. The Nazi Party obtained over thirty-seven per cent of the popular vote, which is close to twenty per cent more than at the last elections. They managed to win 230 seats of the 608 seats in the Reichstag, making them the largest party. Events are moving so quickly that it is hard to keep up, hence the need to increase your trips back to Germany so that we have eyes and ears on the ground, so to speak."

"Oh! I have a trip next month to Sweden, but wasn't due back in Germany until November," Karl explained.

"Yes, we know. We can work out a strategy to get you back into some key areas for us in the next few months. Excellent news about your brother Max, by the way," Morton added.

Karl didn't answer as they crossed a small minor road and entered another area of woodland which opened onto a smaller private driveway. This in turn gave way to an area of well-tended lawn, with a view of a beautiful brick-built mansion.

"My dear fellow, may I welcome you to Chartwell? Mr. Churchill thought it would be suitably discreet to meet here and asked that you join him for lunch." Morton held out his arm and Karl found himself looking at the beautiful country house of Winston Churchill.

Karl once again found himself shaking hands with the famous member of parliament for Epping. The lunch was taken on a terrace and as Karl sat with Morton and Winston Churchill, he could only marvel at the way his life had led from the deck of an Imperial German navy battleship, via an internment camp, to sitting having lunch with one of the more prominent members of the House of Commons of Great Britain.

Karl found Churchill to be affable and engaging. Deftly he changed from topic to topic with a keen grasp of each situation and a robust opinion on most of them. He also showed a very real interest in Karl and what had led him to this luncheon table. Karl spoke freely about his time in the German navy during his national service. He explained how both he and his elder brother had tried in vain to emigrate to the USA, but when these efforts were thwarted, he described internment and the way his good friend Joseph Pilates had kept both mind and body together during the ordeal. He touched on the loss of his first wife whilst giving birth to his son James.

He found Churchill to be a surprisingly good listener and empathetic to his personal loss. He was fascinated by how Karl had used the Austin Motor company as a springboard to branch out and create a very successful industrial distribution business across Great Britain and beyond. This very neatly brought the conversation back to Karl's role in determining what was happening in Germany at first hand. Churchill had made it clear that he was currently 'out of office', as he put it, and how the information that Karl provided, via the shadowy Z and Morton, was essential to his understanding of events and keeping a close eye on things. This was so he could counter any issues raised in parliament from a more knowledgeable position. Karl felt that the man opposite him, puffing on another huge cigar, was treading water by being out of a Cabinet position, but he could see a steely determination in his eyes.

As Karl sat on the sunny terrace, he studied Churchill more closely. Karl was almost forty-seven years of age; he did not know it, but Churchill was in his late fifties and the sheer energy he exuded as he held court around the table was both staggering and inspiring. The three of them stood and toasted the King with champagne bringing lunch to a conclusion. Karl shook Churchill's hand as they bid farewell with an invitation to return at the soonest opportunity after his next visit to Germany.

Desmond Morton collected his dogs from one of the maids at Chartwell and they walked back through the shaded woods to Morton's own home. As they approached the drive once more Karl could see a car was waiting, its engine running.

"Ah! Splendid, Winston got someone to phone a car for you and it's already here."

"Thank you for such a wonderful afternoon, sir," Karl said, remembering his manners just in time.

"My dear chap, you have your instructions from Winston. Go back to Germany and visit your brother Max. Find out more about the Krupps plant and his role there. We also have one or two things that might be of use to you on your next trip. Colonel Z will explain all when you next see him. Now all that remains is for me to wish you a safe trip back to the Midlands." And with that Morton opened the rear door of the black motor vehicle and watched as Karl took a seat. Morton closed the door and Karl waved briefly as the car drove him away from Westerham and back to London and his train connection.

Karl had the rear of the car to himself and it afforded an opportunity to contemplate what his role was beginning to become. He was effectively now spying for the British government on the country of his birth. Still classed as a German citizen, he was about to embark on yet another journey to the industrial heart of Germany and, using the cover of his legitimate business interests, find out just what was going on in the factories over there. It occurred to him that there had been a good deal of violence on the streets of Germany on his last visit, and reports were that the situation was still every bit as volatile. It may be that Karl was heading into something that could be construed as dangerous. He pondered this prospect, mindful of his age, his lack of training and any experience in this field.

His planned trip would also include another trip to see Ziggy and his family. As he thought about his good friends' family he found himself thinking about his daughter Freya. She had found herself a position as a nanny almost the day she had turned eighteen and he was unable to dissuade her from leaving home to take up the role. All these thoughts of danger had made Karl think of his family and what might happen to them, should something befall him. He decided then and there that he would go down to Angmering and try and reconcile with his daughter, not wishing to be at odds with her, should the worst happen. He also resolved to try and meet with his parents in Leicester and his younger brother Willy, who lived close by. What he was going to tell them would need some work; but he decided that he wanted to at least have a chance to see them before his departure across the channel.

Essen
21ˢᵗ August 1934

"Max, I don't understand what has happened to you?" Karl sat opposite his brother in Max's small dining room. The family pleasantries had come to an end with Max's wife Elsa taking the remnants of their dinner back into the kitchen, leaving Karl and his elder brother to talk.

"I'm fed up with Germany being subjugated by the rest of Europe, limiting our economic growth. I said to Elsa that we need stability and that's just what has happened since Hitler became chancellor last year." Max seemed very clear about the matter. "You know he's just declared the results of the referendum to merge the roles of chancellor and president and received over eighty-eight per cent approval to do so? You see, he has the backing of the vast majority to be our Führer," Max finished proudly.

"Ha! How free was the vote, I wonder? I saw those Nazi thugs outside the polling booths, some were even seen marching people by force to the polling stations to vote. I heard rumours that a large quantity of polling cards were already marked 'yes'. Can you not see what is happening to Germany again?"

"The trouble with you, Karl, is that you don't understand how difficult it has been here for the last few years. At least under Hitler we are united in building Germany back to being a global power again."

"But he's passed so many laws recently that has made it impossible to stop him. There seems to be no constitutional way to remove him from office. Don't you see? He is now a dictator, running a one-party state." Karl was becoming angry. "Without him, we would have been overrun by the communists. We have had our eyes opened to those that are not worthy to be called Germans and who have always profited from the misfortune of others and are a cancer within the population of Germany." Max too was becoming heated.

"Oh! Finally, we see the truth of it. This race nonsense about the Jews has been concocted by Hitler as an excuse to blame someone, anyone really, for the failings within our country. All he's succeeded in doing is unifying the working class and giving them a focal point for their anger and bitterness. What of his Socialist values? Will he be removing all those industrial elites and other landowning aristocracy to even up the class divide? I see no evidence of it. The way he's rewarding and supporting your boss at Krupps proves my point." Karl tried to remain calm as he continued. "Hitler took Germany out of the League of Nations in October of last year and also from the world disarmament conference. Do you have any idea what his objectives are?"

"He wants to recover all the territory that we gave away after the war. He wants the Saar region, which is populated by Germans anyway, back within Germany. He wants the Sudetenland back from Czechoslovakia again, mainly populated by Germans. That's what he means by *Lebensraum*."

"Do you think he will stop there? At some stage, the rest of Europe will stand up to him," Karl said, trying to make Max understand.

"I don't see it. Europe is weak. Take that tin-pot empire you call home. Your leadership has no stomach for another war. They talk of conciliation at every turn and I suspect they're more likely to make alliances and treaties with Hitler than to try and forcibly stop him."

"You don't think that this will eventually lead to another bloody, and pointless war?" Karl pleaded with growing despair. "It may well come to it and this time Germany will be ready. We will increase our armed forces and armaments. I, for one, will not spend another war imprisoned by a foreign government. I intend to do everything I can to secure a prosperous and powerful Germany that will become the central power of Europe in the future." Max had stood up to reinforce his point. Karl stood too. "And what of Klaus? Are you willing to lose him in another conflict to satisfy the ego of that absurd little man in the Reichstag?" Max's only son, Klaus, had just turned thirteen.

"He will do his duty and if that should include serving as a soldier for his country, then he will do so. He believes whole-heartedly in the policy of our Führer and supports him one hundred per cent."

"I know, I've seen him in his Nazi uniform, remember? Does none of this bother you? Don't you feel even a little bit brainwashed and pressured into these feelings and beliefs?" Karl was running out of steam as he posed his questions.

"The Jews are the cause of this need for strong, powerful leadership. They are an underclass that do not deserve to be afforded the same values as the rest of us 'proper' Germans." Finally Max was displaying the virulent anti-semitic views of his Führer for the first time to his younger brother.

Karl sat back down and stared at the table. He had not wanted to believe it but it was clear: his elder brother was a committed Nazi, not a follower, but an actual Nazi, in a position of power within the industrial heart of Germany working high up within the management structure of the Krupps works.

After several seconds, Karl stood. "Max, I am sad to say that I do not support your view and that I can see only harm and cruelty thriving in the regime that Hitler has created. Please extend my thanks to Elsa for such an excellent dinner. I will not be staying the night. I will pack my things and leave immediately. Good night to you." And with that Karl left the dining table and made his way swiftly upstairs, not waiting for a response from Max. A short time later, he descended the stairs carrying his one suitcase. Max was waiting for him in the hall.

"Karl, if I went too far, then I'm sorry. We cannot let this come between us."

"Max, I'm sorry to say that it has come between us. We are so far apart in everything. You are black to my white, you are right to my left. I fear this may be a more final goodbye than either of us really know. I pray you come to see the error you are making. Goodbye, Max." With that Karl walked out into the still night air, not looking back at his brother as he got into his car and started the engine. Just as he was driving off Max strode forward, as if he wanted to say something more. Karl simply drove away, staring straight ahead at the road in front of him, not looking back.

Karl drove south through the night. He kept to the speed limits and did his best to keep to the minor routes for fear of encountering one of the groups of brown-shirted Nazis, who now seemed to be everywhere. His original intention had been to visit one of the machine tool factories near Berlin, but after the altercation with Max he had decided to head straight down to Bavaria. He had a new contract with the Zahn Group, which was where Ziggy and Otto were now working full-time. He had discovered that the Zahn Group were manufacturing a much more robust and effective differential to prevent wheel spin, used mainly for off-road motor vehicle racing. Karl was aware that several other companies actually locked their differentials in an effort to avoid this spin, but since this practice was now outlawed in motor sport as it caused excessive wear to tyres, Karl was keen to bring the German company's new solution to Great Britain. He was aiming once again to be the sole distributor for the new product. He was not sure if the Zahn Group had been able to complete the new system but in light of the attitude and thoughts of his elder brother, he had decided that a long overdue visit to see Ziggy and his family would be well worth the drive.

By 6 a.m. the following morning Karl had reached Überlingen on the shores of Lake Constance. He felt a palpable relief as he saw the lake in the early morning sunshine. *Only another half an hour or so*, he thought as he drove along the road parallel with the shoreline towards Ziggy's house on the outskirts of Friedrichshafen.

"You look tired, my old friend," Ziggy commented as he showed Karl into the entrance hall of his palatial home.

"It's been a long night. Thank you for being here. I just need some friendly faces right now. What is happening to Germany?" Karl said.

"My friend, we are living in precarious times. There are eyes and ears everywhere. We have passed from a monarchy through a fractured, ill-thought-out democracy to what we have now, which is a totalitarian state run by a dictator."

Petra came forward having seen Karl and hugged him warmly.

"Karl! Come, you must rest. Ziggy, take Karl's things and show him to his room. Let the poor man get some sleep. We can talk after lunch. It's so good to see you, Karl."

When Karl came downstairs a little after lunchtime he found himself staring at the most beautiful copy of Petra in miniature.

"Karl, you do not recognise Emma?" Ziggy stood behind his daughter, his hands on her shoulders.

"I would not have believed the change in you, my dear."

Karl recovered from his shock at how much Emma had grown and knelt down as she ran forward.

"Uncle Karl, I am so happy to see you." She had a beautiful, melodic voice and the same blonde-haired blue-eyed beauty of her mother.

"Emma, you are the spitting image of your mother, you know." Karl kissed Emma on the cheek.

"Come and have something to eat. Petra has some food for you in the dining room." Ziggy ushered Karl through and sat Karl down at the head of the table. Petra brought in a steaming bowl of soup with several slices of rye bread and put it down in front of him.

"Here you are, Karl, you must be starving."

"You are all looking well," Karl remarked. "Where is Lothar? He must be nearly twenty by now?"

Karl was about to start eating but as he looked up, he caught a look of fear and consternation pass between Petra and Ziggy.

"What is it?" he asked in some concern.

"He's gone, gone to Munich to join up with that rabble in charge," Ziggy explained.

"My God, it's like a disease! I've driven through the night, away from my brother Max in Essen, on hearing that he too is one of them now. What in God's name is happening here?"

"Lothar had no chance," Ziggy said quietly. "His school teacher was a rabid Nazi and totally indoctrinated him. We tried to talk to him, to make him understand that the teacher was spouting propagandist rubbish, but he shouted us down. By the time he had graduated from the Hitler Youth to be a fully-fledged Nazi, he was gone from us, in both mind and body."

"Where is he?" Karl asked.

"He moved to Munich about eight months ago," Petra said. "I understand from some friends at the university that he was seen in the uniform of an SS soldier. They were harassing and mocking some Jewish students who had been told to leave the university."

"My dear Petra, I am so sorry." Karl stood and moved to Petra and hugged her.

"We're doing what we can to protect Emma, but we have received notification that she must join the female equivalent of the Hitler Youth now that she's turned twelve. We're powerless to stop this inevitability." Ziggy sat down. Karl watched as for the first time his dear friend openly sobbed in front of him.

"Let's call it an adventure, shall we, Emma? A chance to see the country I now call home. You can even learn English while you stay with us. How does that sound?" Karl spoke to the beautiful young lady sitting in the passenger seat of his car as he drove north towards his ferry connection.

"But why do I have to come on my own? Couldn't my parents have come too? We could have made it a family holiday." Emma was almost tearful, reminded of the finality of the farewell she had received from her parents as she drove away from them.

"How much do you understand about the situation in Germany at the moment, Emma?" Karl asked.

"I don't know really. It seems like all my friends are excited about the organised clubs and camps that we have all been invited to. My teacher says it will help us to be more German and be fitter and stronger as we grow up."

Karl could only listen to the mind of his friend's daughter as she made clear the level of indoctrination that now seemed to permeate every facet of German society. After two days of talking with Ziggy and Petra they had between them hatched this plan to save Emma from descending into one of Hitler's youth movements. Karl had agreed that he would take her with him back to Great Britain where he would seek to protect her for the foreseeable future.

"Where do you live in England, Uncle Karl?" Emma changed topic with the deftness of youth.

"I live in a small town called Solihull, which is near to Birmingham, a big city right in the middle of England. We live on the edge of a golf course and have a large back garden that backs onto it," Karl explained.

"Where will I sleep?"

"You can have Freya's room. She has moved out to take up a position as a nanny. I'm sure she won't mind. Don't worry, I'm sure you will settle in. James is just a little bit younger than you and he is just about to start at a new boarding school in September. Is that something that would appeal to you?" He looked at her anxiously.

"Oh, Uncle Karl, I don't know. It's so much to take in. Is David at home too?"

"He is, my dear, being looked after by my sister-in-law, Iris. You will love Iris, everyone loves Iris. Let's not forget your Aunt Grace will be delighted to see you again too."

The journey back to Great Britain was uneventful save for a few minor hiccups when presenting Emma's German passport at immigration control at Folkestone. Karl made a quick phone call to Desmond Morton's office and after a brief word with him, passed the handset to the border official. The man visibly stiffened as he listened, then very politely replaced the handset in its cradle and immediately stamped Emma and Karl's passports and wished them a safe a speedy onward journey. Karl had been able to send a telegram from Germany explaining the additional guest he would be bringing and Grace, as he knew she would, had prepared Freya's room for Emma and had made the most extravagant English cream tea for her to enjoy upon her arrival.

Karl left Emma in the very capable hands of Grace and Iris the following morning as he hastily contacted Z to arrange another debriefing and once more got on the train to London.

Z was in the front passenger seat of the car, with the other man Karl had seen at the Home Office now sitting in the back. Karl took the empty seat in the back.

"Good morning, Louis," began the stranger. "Bit irregular, but I thought I would be in on your latest news from Europe. Also thought it about time you knew who you are working for. My name is Colonel Stewart Menzies and I am the deputy director of MI6, working under Sir Hugh Sinclair. Between us we are in the process of setting up a new secret intelligence service. That, my dear Louis, is who you are effectively working for."

Karl gave an account of the nature of things as he saw them in Germany while was being driven south in the company of these two intelligence operatives. He then repeated the conversation once again around the luncheon table at Chartwell to a thoughtful and quite obviously frustrated Churchill. This time Churchill was keen to hear Karl's thoughts on how the situation in Germany might develop. Menzies and Morton, around the table, gave their own take on Karl's information and between them they felt they had a clear and concise grasp of things.

Karl had mentioned how he had taken his good friend Ziggy's daughter from her home in Bavaria and brought her home with him. Morton had clearly been busy and presented Karl with an extended visa and effectively diplomatic status for Emma, which, while she would never require it, gave her immunity from pretty much everything.

"So, Louis, when can you go back?" Churchill asked suddenly as he ignited yet another cigar, after the large lunch.

"Well, I hadn't really thought. The factory contracts I have are all newly signed and complete. It's going to be difficult to access Krupps with my brother as he is, but not insurmountable. I was thinking that I could legitimately go back for contract renewals in 1936 and perhaps use the Olympics

Games in Berlin as another excuse to be in Germany?" Karl offered.

"What do you think, Stewart?" Churchill asked the intelligence deputy.

"Well, we have several other operatives out there, keeping us up to date. It might be more authentic for Louis to be in England for a while. Plus, Louis, your additional guest at home might benefit from having a German speaker to talk to while she learns English?" Menzies commented.

"Splendid idea. So, Louis, plan to return to Germany for the Berlin Games and until then work hard at home. Now, Desmond, is there more champagne for us?" Churchill asked his friend.

Karl returned to Solihull determined to concentrate on his own life and that of his family. There had been a slight realignment of responsibilities within the household since the arrival of Emma. Grace now concentrated on getting David ready for school each morning. James was now boarding, so Iris switched her responsibilities to caring for Emma. The language barrier was initially tough for both of them, but Karl was now on hand to spend an hour most days to help with Emma's grasp of certainly the spoken word and a rudimentary ability to write in English. Karl always marvelled at how Iris was able to devote so much of her life to the care of his children without seemingly having any life of her own. For her part she had never had any inclination to venture out into a world beyond that she had known in all the years she had spent in Karl's house. The one man who had made her doubt her singular life was Karl's former senior naval training NCO, Otto Nadler. He was the one person she had met that she would have given everything up for!

Karl worked hard at his various office premises and distribution warehouses around Birmingham. He had several clandestine meetings with Colonel Z as 1935 drew to a close and they planned his extensive visit to Germany for the following year. He had also been able to meet Churchill on several other occasions on visits to London. Dining with the gregarious politician was always a monumental affair and Karl had to be on his guard to avoid trying to keep up with the great man's appetite. Churchill remarked on the ever-increasing threat from Germany as they discussed the vote earlier that year of overwhelming support by people of the Saarland to reunite with Germany. In March the German Wehrmacht was increased to over 600,000, on Hitler's direct instruction. This was a clear breach of the limitations placed on Germany by the Treaty of Versailles. Churchill was aghast at the way his colleagues in parliament condemned this escalation but did nothing to stop it.

Karl was aware that the information he had been supplying about what was being done in the factories of Germany was missing from the conversation. Without Churchill directly suggesting it, it became clear that it was imperative to have Karl back in Germany to see the level of military expansion and, more importantly, the speed of this increase. Karl had watched earlier that year as Churchill had been returned to parliament with an increased majority in the general election. Stanley Baldwin had replaced Ramsay MacDonald as prime minister, but there was still no room in the Cabinet for Churchill. Karl felt that it was such a waste of the talents of this direct and vital man, to leave him on the sidelines, when he could have had such an effect on the important decisions that must surely come soon?

As Karl left London just before Christmas of 1935 he mulled over the decision he had made to bring forward his trip to Germany by six months and commence the tour in early January 1936. It would mean curtailing the very pleasant and meaningful time he had been able to spend with his family. He decided that he would make the Christmas holiday a special time and organised a full house of extended family to spend time with him. Grace had only met Karl's parents on one previous occasion and was delighted to have them spend the holiday with them. Albert was particularly pleased to meet Emma and admired the trouble she took to greet him in English.

Freya returned home and Karl believed that there was a definite softening of the atmosphere between his daughter and Grace. He was more than a little surprised that Freya was only too happy to be given a guest room and not insist on evicting Emma from her own former bedroom. On the contrary, Freya immediately bonded with Emma. She was warm and kind to her two younger brothers and stole everyone's heart with her style and beauty.

Grace mentioned that she had offered to help with the cooking and was on hand to help Grace to clean and tidy the house.

Karl watched his daughter from afar; he knew her mind and wondered what plan she possibly had that included currying favour with his wife and generally being the most amenable and excellent company. Whatever the cause, Karl was not going to derail the change in his daughter by questioning her. *I'm sure it will all become clear in the end*, he thought.

When his younger brother Willy came to visit on Boxing Day bringing his wife and family to join the gathering, Karl felt it the right time to make everyone aware of his impending visit to Germany. There was a mixed reaction. Grace had an idea it was coming and expressed a sadness, but understood the need to renew industrial contracts. Karl's father was concerned as to the safety of visiting Germany at that time. Karl did his best to reassure him. "After all, the Olympics are being held there next year," he said.

His sons were both sad to be having to spend more time without their father. David was particularly crestfallen, having got used to enjoying his father telling him stories in bed most evenings.

Emma was desperate to come with him, to return home to her parents; but Karl said that the time was not yet right.

Finally, he waited to hear what Freya had to say on the matter.

"I would very much like to come too. My employers are moving to South Africa and I have an extended period of leave. Can I come please, Dad?" Freya politely enquired.

"Well, you see, I have so many people to see and will be in the car much of the time. I'm sure you would be bored, my dear."

"I'm sure I will get used to it, and I can drive myself now. I could share some of the driving," Freya answered logically.

"Well, I don't know." Karl looked to his wife for support. "Grace, what do you think?"

"I think it's a splendid idea. I take it you'll visit Emma's parents to give them an idea of how well she's settling in, while you're there?" Grace suggested rather than asked.

"Well, I, well I suppose I'll always find time for Ziggy and Petra," Karl said, thinking out loud.

"...and Lothar too," Freya added quickly.

"Aha! It all becomes much clearer now, my darling daughter!" And for Karl, the penny finally dropped.

Hotel Esplanade, Berlin
21st January 1936

"According to the waiter, Kaiser Wilhelm used to stay here," Freya whispered to Karl as she sat opposite him in the sumptuous dining salon of the grand Berlin hotel.

Karl looked up from his breakfast plate. "I never actually met him, but I was in Norway for the coronation celebrations of their new king and the Kaiser was there. He once cancelled a visit to my ship during the Kiel Regatta. We were inspected by King Edward VII that day," Karl recalled.

At that moment the very smartly dressed waiter brought that morning's edition of the *Times* newspaper. Karl thanked him and unfolded the broadsheet.

"The King is dead," Karl read. "George V died peacefully in his bed yesterday. His eldest son will be crowned King Edward VIII."

"Oh! Daddy, I know it's sad, but Edward is such a dashingly handsome man. Will this change our plans?"

"He worries me, my dear daughter. He is not a serious man and I do not believe he understands world events, plus he is currently seeing an American divorcée. As to our plans, I don't think we need to change anything. I'm sorry for the number of factory visits I must make, but how about when we travel to Leipzig, we stop in Apolda and I will show you where I used to live as a young boy?" Karl suggested.

"Yes, I would like that. Thank you for agreeing to take me

with you." Freya poured another coffee from the ornate silver pot and took in the elaborate surroundings of the dining room. What she failed to notice were the two very serious-looking men in the corner behind her. Outwardly they looked like a couple of guests, possibly businessmen, but they were actually part of a newly formed *Geheime Staatspolizei*, now usually abbreviated to Gestapo. This secret police force had been created by Hermann Göring in 1933. By 1936 it was under the command of the much more ruthless Heinrich Himmler, also head of the SS (the *Schutzstaffel* paramilitary wing of the Nazi Party). These two sinister-looking men were there at the express order of Himmler to keep a close eye on the activities of Louis Luddolph and his factory visits. It was believed that information was being passed to the British government by this busy industrialist.

As Karl and Freya rose from their breakfast table and walked from the large dining space the secret policemen waited for a few seconds. One followed them out into the reception area while the other took up a position outside the hotel, able to see the vehicle that he knew was the one being used by Luddolph.

About forty-five minutes later Karl and Freya emerged from the hotel, a liveried bellboy carrying their luggage behind them. The bags were loaded and Karl, as was his custom, handed the man some Deutschmarks and got into the passenger side of the vehicle leaving the driving duties to Freya, which had been one of the reasons he had decided to take her on his trip.

"So, we head southwest out of the city and you will hopefully see signs for Leipzig," Karl instructed his daughter.

"What is in Leipzig, Daddy?" Freya asked.

"A trade fair starts there today and I'm hopeful that some of the other machine tool industries will be in attendance, as well as Jerwag," Karl explained. "Perhaps I can gain some new business and get to talk to all the exhibitors, get their take on new developments."

Freya manoeuvred the car out into the busy Potsdamer Platz and drove away from the hotel. One of the men from breakfast rushed out of the hotel and together with his waiting colleague they got into their own vehicle and followed.

The following car kept a good distance between themselves and the target vehicle. Using other traffic to conceal their presence they were able to maintain line of sight and observed their target head south out of the capital and along the main road towards Leipzig. They were still keeping a close watch as the target vehicle pulled into the large area set aside for visitors at the annual Leipzig trade fair. They parked far enough away but were still able to watch both Luddolph and the young lady exit their vehicle and head inside the fair. They followed on foot.

The trade fair was a huge success. Business certainly seemed to be booming in Germany. There was a conscious optimism about the future, although Karl sensed a certain quiet trepidation about the man they had elected as chancellor, who had since then assumed and merged the presidency, becoming the stand-alone Führer. Karl noticed the increased uniformed presence within the trade hall and the numerous times that Freya and he had to show their identification and travelling papers at the checkpoints and just randomly as they moved about.

Karl first became aware of the possibility that they were being watched as he escorted Freya from the trade fair and they were walking back to their vehicle. He had decided to leave early, wanting to make the journey south to Munich to be able to arrive there in good time. Karl estimated that it was roughly two hundred and fifty miles to Munich, which travelling via Nuremberg he estimated would take him between four and five hours. As he opened the passenger door of the car for Freya, he caught a glimpse of a man walking swiftly from the trade fair entrance hall. The man was gesticulating towards another motor vehicle. Karl got behind the wheel of his own vehicle and drove from the parking area and out onto the road heading south. He saw another car exit the parking area behind him and slot into a gap in the traffic two cars behind. He decided to employ one of the tactics suggested by Colonel Z to check for the possibility of interest in his movements. He made a quite unnecessary stop at a roadside restaurant near to Eisenberg.

"Why are we stopping, Dad?" Freya asked as they pulled into the lot in front of the café.

"It may be nothing, but I have a feeling someone is following us," Karl said levelly.

"Oh! Have we done anything wrong?"

"Not as such, but I have been taking perhaps a closer interest in the Ruhr factories than I normally would, visiting the shop floor and viewing the production lines. If they are aware of that, it may cause some issues," Karl explained.

"Are you spying, Dad?" Freya asked abruptly.

"Erh! Well, not really, but I am paying attention to what is going on here in Germany." Karl tried to limit what he told Freya, mindful of his agreement with Z not to let anyone know of his true reason for being in Germany.

"Bloody hell, Dad, this is exciting!" Freya giggled as she took in this news.

"Young lady, it is very serious. I have no idea what these people are capable of, we must tread very carefully. Now see if you can spot a dark sedan with two people pull in here in the next few minutes."

Between them they waited nervously, looking through the rear window of their vehicle back down the slip road. Sure enough, after a few minutes a car slowly crept into the parking area by the restaurant and the two occupants within stayed put.

"OK, let's get a coffee, use the facilities and press on. At least now we know. I hope there is a public telephone in there?" Karl indicated for Freya to get out of the vehicle.

"I'll get us some coffee. Who are you going to call, Dad?" Freya pushed open the door of the small café.

"Over there, look." Karl pointed to a wooden phone booth in the corner of the dimly lit coffee bar. "Get the coffees. I'm going to call Ziggy and, failing that, Otto," and with that Karl walked over to the telephone booth, while Freya practised her basic German and ordered two coffees from the bar.

By the time Karl emerged from the booth, Freya was sitting at a table by the wall with two steaming coffee cups in front of her.

Karl sat opposite her and took a quick look around the room. There were several other couples eating or drinking. Worryingly there were four brown-shirted Nazi troopers sitting, talking loudly. Thankfully they paid no heed to Karl and Freya. Karl spoke quietly in English. "I could not speak to Ziggy, but Petra answered and said that he and Otto are in Munich today. They are trying to find Lothar, as he has not been home in months. She has said that Ziggy always calls her at 6 p.m. When he does, she will get him to meet us by the town hall clock tower in Marienplatz at 7 p.m. Then we can decide what to do."

"Lothar is missing?" Freya leant forward at the mention of his name.

"I don't think he's missing. I think he is well and truly within the grip of the Nazis. They've indoctrinated him with their vile rhetoric and he's totally under their spell. Ziggy and Otto want to find him and see if they can convince him to return home." Karl watched the group of brown shirts carefully while he spoke.

A man wearing a long fawn raincoat with the collar up and with a dark felt trilby hat on his head entered the café.

He surveyed the area slowly and walked straight up to Karl and Freya.

"Your papers please?" he ordered curtly.

Karl and Freya produced their passports and other travelling permits, required now in Germany, and handed them to the man.

As he examined the documents, Karl noticed that the attention of the four brown-shirted youths across from them was now fully focused on him and Freya.

"Where are you travelling to?" Karl noticed that the 'please' was missing from this next question.

"We are heading to Munich and from there to one of my business contacts in Friedrichshafen. I have many business deals with some of the excellent German machine tool industries," Karl replied in his perfect German to the officious man in the raincoat.

"You made a number of unscheduled visits to factories in the north, without proper permits or authority. You are both to come with me now." The man did not return any of the papers to Karl or Freya. He turned his back on them and moved to the door.

Karl and Freya stood slowly and put their coats on. As Karl put his arm through his coat sleeve he moved closer to Freya. "When we get outside, run to the car," he whispered. "It's unlocked. Get into the driver's side and get the engine started. Don't look back at me, just do it." They followed the man outside, unaware that the Hitler Youth were following them too.

As Karl and Freya emerged, Karl produced a small Beretta Model 1915 from inside his jacket and fired two shots, hitting the tall raincoated man in the back. As he did so, Freya was running for the car. Karl moved swiftly after her as shouts rang out from the Hitler Youth, and he jumped into the passenger seat. A man emerged from the dark sedan and took up a firing stance as Freya roared away. Karl heard some shots, then the glass window behind him shattered, as Freya turned the corner, out of range, taking them back to the main road heading south.

"Bloody hell, Dad! What are you doing?" Freya screamed as she pressed her right foot as far down on the accelerator pedal as she could.

"Easy, girl, slow down a little and take the next exit. I think we may need to keep to the back roads," Karl said soothingly.

Freya eased the speed a little and after a mile or so, took an exit off the main road and into the German hinterland.

Freya had slowed to a more sedate pace as she negotiated the smaller roads, with Karl calling the directions as they came across junctions and crossroads. They meandered their way south, close to the existing eastern border of Germany. They passed through Regensburg to the southeast of Nuremberg. They had had to stop for fuel at a remote filling station on the edge of a small village called Moosburg. Karl began to recognise the countryside as they drew closer to the northern suburbs of Munich. As they got further into the city, Karl directed his daughter to head south but keep to the east of the signs for the centre. When they reached an area known to Karl called Steinhausen, he told Freya to slow the vehicle and look for somewhere with lots of parked vehicles where they could leave the car.

"Why are we leaving the car?"

"The shattered side window will draw attention to it and no doubt the man that shot back at us will have issued a description of both of us, and the car. We'll go the rest of the way on foot." Karl looked at his watch. "It's dark now, just after 5 p.m. If Petra manages to get word to Ziggy and Otto, then we can hopefully meet them at 7 p.m. in Marienplatz."

"What about our bags, Dad?" Freya suddenly asked.

"Well, we will have to leave the suitcases. Pack your smaller soft bag with everything of value that you can and anything that may be useful. We have no documents now, so we need to avoid any places where we might be checked. We will have to hide somewhere in Marienplatz until we spot Ziggy and the unmistakable figure of Otto," Karl suggested.

For once Freya understood the seriousness of their position and simply did as she was asked and redistributed her belongings into a small leather holdall she had been using as a sort of handbag on their day trips out and about. Karl thought it best to try and alter their appearance in some way.

"Can you change your top and maybe your coat, my dear? Perhaps you can rearrange your hair, put it up? Or better still, have you got that brown hat I saw you wear on the ferry over here?"

They had been walking for about half an hour when they crossed the River Isar over the Kabelsteg footbridge and onto the embankment road, Steinsdorfstrasse.

"How much further is it, Dad?" Freya was clearly tired and frightened by their situation.

"Less than half a mile, I reckon. We have plenty of time. We can rest here, there doesn't seem to be anyone about." Karl stopped in a quiet backstreet just behind the main thoroughfare. Freya removed her bag that she had been carrying like a rucksack. Karl had a similar bag, but carried it in his left hand. Karl looked at his watch and thought out loud. "It's just after six, so we have about an hour before our rendezvous. If we leave here in about fifteen minutes or so, I reckon we will get to the town hall by 6.45. If we find somewhere to watch from, then hopefully we just need to wait for Ziggy and Otto to turn up."

"That's if Petra speaks with them. What if he doesn't phone her?" Freya momentarily allowed her fears and concerns to manifest themselves as she spoke.

"I understand, my dear. Don't worry, I have a plan should it be necessary, but until we know for sure, let's put our faith in our friends turning up, eh?" Karl tried to calm his daughter as they leaned against a tree in the leafy side street, close to the centre of Munich.

"What time is it now?" Freya asked for the third or fourth time since they had taken up position in a building archway across the square from the town hall building in Marienplatz.

"It's about a minute after the last time you asked," Karl mumbled to himself, aware that Freya probably heard too.

"I can't see the clock tower from here, that's all." Freya's customary petulance made a brief appearance as she replied, then she caught herself. "Sorry, Dad, I'm just scared."

"I know, I'm scared too and it's two minutes to seven, not long now," he added.

As he finished reassuring his daughter he once again looked out across the square towards the ornate town hall and was rewarded with the sight of the immense figure of Otto striding across the plaza towards the municipal building with Ziggy beside him. Karl watched them pause at the entrance and then turn and look out over the square.

"They're here, Freya." Karl grabbed his daughter by the hand and led her from their hiding place out into the square and towards his friends.

Ziggy half turned in Karl's direction and his eyes lit up when he saw both Karl and his daughter walking quickly towards them.

Suddenly, as both Ziggy and Otto moved to greet them, a detachment of six brown-shirted Nazis ran from the town hall building and surrounded them.

Everyone froze as the leader of the group stepped towards Karl. "You are the British businessman Louis Luddolph. You are to be detained on suspicion of activities against the German state and to be questioned about injuring a security officer outside of Leipzig earlier today. You are to come with me now, the rest of you can go."

"Hello, Lothar, it's been a long time." Freya spoke quietly, but confidently, looking straight into the eyes of one of the Nazis standing behind the leader.

Ziggy had been slower to recognise his own son wearing the evil brown uniform, but he now also looked into the eyes of his son. "Hello, my boy. What are you doing with these people?"

The captain of the squad swung his head round to look at Lothar Jurgens. "You know these people, Jurgens?"

"This is my father and some of his friends, Hauptmann," Lothar replied nervously. "There must be some mistake. I have known this man and his daughter for years."

"Well, Luddolph is to be detained on direct orders from Reichsführer Himmler himself, now take him," and the man ordered his squad to arrest Karl.

Before the squad had moved two steps, Otto had grabbed the front two soldiers and crashed their heads together, knocking them unconscious, and was just picking up a third when he stopped and saw Karl pointing a gun at the captain of the guard, Lothar and the one remaining soldier still vertical. Otto dropped the soldier he was holding, who scurried away behind his leader.

"We are leaving now," Karl said calmly as he continued to point his gun at the captain of the small group of Nazis. "Nobody else needs to get hurt. Otto, will you please grab Lothar? Ziggy, if you can please look after Freya." Otto took a firm hold of Lothar who was visibly shaken by the events, then the small collection of friends and family hastened from the square, the sound of whistles and shouts audible behind them.

"I take it you have a car somewhere, Ziggy?" Karl gasped as the five ran down a side street.

"Next street on the left," Ziggy shouted back.

Karl and Freya got into the back, Otto bundled Lothar in next to Freya as he got behind the wheel and Ziggy took the front passenger seat.

"Everyone in? Good, let's get out of here." And with that, Otto floored the accelerator pedal and they roared away from the centre of Munich.

Karl kept a constant watch through the rear window of the vehicle as they headed through Munich's suburbs, heading southwest towards Friedrichshafen.

"No sign of anyone giving chase," he informed the rest of the occupants, as Otto continued at a good pace along the quiet road.

Lothar was by now more or less over the shock of seeing his father's good friend pointing a gun at his captain. "They will have radioed ahead. They have such good communications they'll know where you're heading. They know where you live, Father, and have been watching Mother because of her links to the university in Munich and her support of the student body arguing against what the Nazis stand for." The information came out in a rush, as if Lothar was keen to purge himself of everything he knew.

"My boy, I'm glad that you have come to your senses." Ziggy turned to look at his uniformed son in the back of the car.

"Hello, Lothar. It's good to see you again," Freya said quietly, and smiled at Lothar.

"Freya, I've dreamt of the day I would see you again. I just wish it were under better circumstances." Lothar looked down at the beautiful young woman next to him.

"May I suggest we formulate a plan to get to Petra, then we probably need to get out of Germany," Otto said as he negotiated the highway.

"Who would have been watching your mother, Lothar?" Karl enquired.

"Gestapo. I was only aware of it because I overheard my captain discussing it with the regional Gauleiter for Bavaria. They are worried about resistance groups forming and building a following that will usurp their authority," Lothar explained.

"How many would be watching?"

"There would most likely be two pairs, alternating their watch," Lothar replied.

"Right," Otto decided, "we get as close as we can then proceed on foot. We split into two teams. I will go with Lothar, and Ziggy, Karl and Freya can take an alternative route to Ziggy's house. We will wait until 11 p.m. and then make our move. That is subject to what we find once we reach our vantage points."

"What weapons do we have apart from Karl's automatic?" Ziggy asked.

"I have my war service pistol, it's an old Beholla, with seven rounds." Otto held up the gun as he drove.

"I have five rounds left in the Beretta and I also have this." Karl reached into his coat and produced an evil-looking knuckleduster knife, with about a 5-inch blade.

"Goodness, Dad! Where did you get all this stuff?" Freya looked wide-eyed at the knife.

"Err! Let's just say that several men in London have been supporting my trips to Germany these past few years." Karl said lightly.

"I have my Hitler Youth knife." Lothar pulled the blade out from the scabbard on his belt.

"I've just thought, Lothar is in his uniform. The chances are his presence with us will not have been noted yet, and even if it has been, they will suspect that he was taken under duress. That might work to our advantage," Otto said, thinking out loud.

Otto parked their vehicle three streets from Ziggy's home. It was a little after 10 p.m. They all quietly climbed out and

Otto and Lothar went one way and the other three went in the opposite direction. They had agreed to get close enough to observe the house then at 11 p.m. Lothar would go in first, in an attempt to draw out any observers.

After twenty minutes or so, Ziggy, Karl and Freya found an area of scrub and woodland that overlooked the rear of Ziggy's house and concealed themselves as they waited for the lights of the house to appear – their signal to move.

Otto and Lothar spotted a car parked with two occupants sitting in it. One had a lit cigarette and the smoke was escaping from the open passenger window.

They found a low wall behind which they could hide, but still observe both the house and the suspicious car.

Time passed and the two groups both began to feel the cold of the night air. At 11 p.m. Lothar rose from his position and walked purposefully up to the front gate of his house. As he got within a few yards of the gate, both occupants of the car got out and blocked his path.

Otto observed them question Lothar about his identity and relax their posture as Lothar produced his correct papers. Otto had noticed one of the men had a gun in his right hand. Otto crept forward and as he took one of the men in a headlock he pointed his gun at the other. "Drop the gun – NOW!"

In an instant the man holding the gun took in this giant holding his colleague fully off the ground around the neck and saw a small gun being pointed at his stomach. He dropped his own gun which Lothar immediately picked up and pointed at him too.

Otto dropped the other man, like a sack of potatoes, and he stayed on the floor gasping for air. "Lothar, search that one for a gun," Otto ordered.

Lothar bent down and pulled another small firearm from the coat pocket of the Gestapo officer.

"Inside, both of you." Otto prodded the man standing as

Lothar held a gun on the other. He rose slowly to his feet and they all walked up to the entrance of the house.

Lothar knocked on the door and stepped back. After a short while, lights appeared in the hallway and the door opened.

"Lothar, Otto, what's happening? Who are these men?"' Petra stood there, pulling her robe around herself.

"My dear Petra, may we come in? Can I ask you to get dressed and go and pack a few things, as quickly as you can, now please?" Otto gently pushed Petra inside and grabbed the two Gestapo and made them sit on a bench in the hall. Petra, sensing the urgency of the instruction, ran back upstairs to follow Otto's instructions. Lothar ran through to the rear of the house and turned all the lights on.

Within five minutes Ziggy, Karl and Freya arrived at the patio doors and Lothar let them in. Ziggy ran through to the hall, noticing two men trussed up like chickens with Otto glaring menacingly at them, as he bounded up the stairs to be reunited with his wife.

Lothar followed his father into the hall. "Perhaps a change of clothes, young man?" Otto suggested to the Nazi-uniformed lad before him. Lothar looked down at his clothes and then at Otto, before he too ran upstairs.

Otto continued to restrain the two Gestapo with some cloth gags he fashioned from a couple of dusters he found, and then finished his task by tying their legs together with their own boot laces and then to each other with some fishing line he found on a rod in a cupboard.

Ziggy returned to the ground floor with Petra and Lothar, carrying two small bags and they all reunited with Karl, Freya and Otto, who were sitting drinking water at the dining room table.

"What now?" Karl asked.

"I think we have limited options. We can't stay in Germany and I think we need to leave fairly quickly. I'm sure more men have been despatched here after the events in Munich tonight," Otto suggested.

"The port and ferry terminal at Friedrichshafen will be watched and there are no ferries at night anyway," Ziggy offered.

Otto stood and held his finger to his lips then whispered. "We will head south to Langenargen and try and steal a boat. In the meantime, listen and support what I say verbally all right?" The others around the table nodded.

Then in a clear but not too obvious way Otto said, "We will head north to Immenstaad and try and get on a boat. From there head across the Lake to Kreuzlingen, is everybody OK with that?"

"How will we get there?' Ziggy quickly caught on to Otto's ruse.

"Take the Gestapo car and abandon it in Immenstaad," Otto replied.

With that the six stood and made their way into the hallway, where the two Gestapo were now lying on the floor.

Otto went over and with his back to the others gently cut off their air supply in turn.

"Otto, you didn't....? Petra began to ask, as he returned.

"No, no, no, my dear. Just put them to sleep for a little while. We need them to send any other forces the wrong way."

"Is everyone ready?" Ziggy asked. Nods of approval in reply indicated it was time to go.

Unbeknown to the group, two other Gestapo agents had arrived and on finding their colleagues' car abandoned, had taken up a watching brief at the opposite end of the street. This was not before they had made a quick journey to the local police station and communicated to their superiors that two agents were missing and reinforcements should be despatched. In the meantime, they mobilised a cadre of six armed police, who were in as much fear of the Gestapo men as any of the general public would have been. The Gestapo positioned the police van and its six occupants at the junction with the main street and the small collection of side streets that fed onto it, one of which was where Ziggy's house was situated. They instructed the leader of the police to wait until they saw them appear and to follow them wherever that may be. The two then quietly returned to a position where they could watch the empty car of the two missing men.

"Take the Gestapo car," Otto said, as he waved some keys in the air and hustled the group over to a black sedan parked almost opposite Ziggy's house. Otto didn't see another car hidden in the shadows. Somehow, they all clambered into the sedan and Otto started the engine and moved off down the street. As he made a turn onto the more major road, Ziggy exclaimed, "Bloody hell, there's a police van! Floor it, Otto!"

Freya, sitting on Karl's lap, saw people inside the van as she looked through the rear window. "Go, Otto, there are police inside," she said tensely. Otto accelerated the sedan and it screeched around the corner and away. Within ten seconds or so, the other Gestapo car appeared and the driver leant out of its open window and bellowed, "Follow us! They have stolen that car and are all fugitives." He then roared away in the same direction as the first car. The police van rumbled out of its parked position and followed.

"Headlights behind," Petra said, as she too looked out of the rear window of the car.

"Faster, Otto," Ziggy encouraged his great friend and mentor.

"How far to this place where there are boats?" Karl asked Ziggy.

"It's about eight to ten miles, should be there in ten to fifteen minutes; or sooner if Otto could drive a little bit faster!" Ziggy looked across at the furrowed brow of his friend now wrestling with the steering wheel as they negotiated a tight right-hand bend.

Otto fought to control the vehicle as he pressed his right foot further down on the accelerator pedal.

"The lights are further away but still coming and I think I can see a second set now too," Freya shouted.

"Everyone, keep calm," Otto ordered. "Another five minutes and I can turn into one of the side roads that takes us to the coast. See if we can spot anything we can use to get across the lake."

As they approached another sharp bend, Otto slowed and took a side road towards a small habitation called Eriskirch.

"I think I can find a back way down to the small harbour at Langenargen," he explained as he roared down the empty smaller road through some streets full of houses, then out into another area of trees and farmland. Otto had also turned off their lights as he used the night sky to vaguely give him some visibility. Very soon they were among the outskirts of another suburban sprawl of houses. Otto continued at a good pace, negotiating the various back streets as they drove further into the town.

"This is Langenargen. I'm going to make for Schloss Montfort," Otto explained. "We can abandon this car in the wooded gardens just inland of the castle. From there we can walk to the small harbour where we should be able to get a boat."

"We will need to move quickly so we leave the luggage we brought and just take ourselves," Karl instructed them.

"OK, the wooded garden is just ahead, everyone ready?" Otto steered the car up onto the grass verge and then in between some trees, before coming to a stop inside a small thicket of bushes.

"Let's go," Ziggy said as he assisted everyone out of the rear of the car.

They made their way across the rest of the garden and found a concrete embankment path that led away from the

Schloss and towards some houses.

"I can see some masts," Freya said as they all walked quickly along the path.

Within a few minutes they had discovered a small enclosed harbour crammed full of sailing yachts and other craft.

"Find one near to the end of a pontoon and see if we can get inside and start its engine," Ziggy said.

As Lothar lifted the cabin lid of a small single-masted yacht, a shot rang out in the still night air. "I've have found one," he shouted, and within a few seconds was joined by the others. Otto cried, "Get on board, I think we have company," as a second shot splintered the wood on the deck of the boat next to Karl.

Karl literally threw Freya below then followed her down into the dark cabin and found the control panel. After assessing the controls, he started the small motor and popped his head up on deck.

"We're good. Get the moorings, Ziggy." Lothar, his dad and Otto started untying the line at the front.

"Where's Petra?" Karl shouted as several shots rang out and the boat took more hits.

"Lothar! Did you see your mother?" Ziggy cried out as he jumped off the boat back onto the pontoon.

Lothar, busy with the rear line, shouted, "She was with us as we turned onto this platform, I'm sure."

Otto had heard the cry and looked carefully back up to the wall where the shots were coming from. Suddenly he spied a bundle on the ramp down to the pontoon. Without a word he raced along the wooden struts, attracting fire, and at one point he went down. Ziggy was following him and he too had to dive for cover as shots continued to ring out. Karl took aim with his small Beretta and tried to provide a degree of cover as his two great friends clambered along the wooden pontoon towards the figure lying by the ramp.

Otto reached Petra and immediately saw the blood coming from her mouth. With no apparent effort he lifted her and turned to shield her body as he walked back towards the boat. Ziggy ran up and took the small firearm from Otto and began to fire back at the wall. Shots were now coming from several directions and Karl saw both Ziggy and Otto take at least one or more hits. Otto hefted Petra aboard and Lothar lowered her below where Freya laid her on a bunk. Otto then lifted the now weakened Ziggy aboard before he too climbed onto the small boat, which now began drifting away from the pontoon.

Karl grabbed the steering wheel, pushed a lever away from him, and the boat began to move slowly out towards the harbour entrance. Karl was out of bullets and could do nothing but hunker down in the rear of the boat as more shots found their target and shattered and splintered the wood all around him. One found his left hand as he shifted his position. He cried out, but was able to steer the craft through the harbour entrance and out onto Lake Constance. Once beyond the wall, the shots slowed and then stopped, as the boat motored slowly out of range and began to cross the dark, tranquil lake.

Lake Constance, Switzerland
January 1936

"Try and stop the bleeding, apply direct pressure to the wound and dress it with whatever you can find," Karl ordered from the top of the steps leading down to the small cabin. He looked around the little space. There appeared to be blood everywhere. Dark smears on the interior fittings looked dull red in the dim glow of the cabin lights. Lothar was attending to his mother, who was clearly unconscious, with blood around her mouth and nose. Freya was trying to staunch a wound to Ziggy's abdomen and had already bandaged his arm with what looked like a dish cloth. Otto had shrugged off his jacket and his light-coloured shirt was stained dark red with his own blood.

"How are you, Otto?" Karl asked nervously.

"I turned my back to try and protect Petra, so most of the damage is probably there. I felt at least three strikes to my back and my left leg is bleeding behind my knee," Karl's huge friend replied stoically.

"Can I do anything?" Karl felt totally inadequate as he asked.

"Just get us across the lake to safety," Otto replied.

Karl returned to the cockpit at the rear of the boat and continued to steer a course due south. He pulled a pristine white handkerchief from his trouser pocket and wrapped it around his injured hand. Below, Lothar wiped away the blood from his mother's beautiful face and staunched his tears on his sleeve as he tended to her.

"Is she breathing?" Freya looked across at this well-built, blond-haired vision as he crumbled and wept over the lifeless body of his mother.

Freya rose and felt for a pulse at Petra's wrist. Finding nothing she tried further up her arm and then her neck. There was nothing. Freya leant forward and put her ear to Petra's mouth: again nothing, no breathing, no pulse. Then Freya saw the double entry wounds on her chest. Fighting back the tears, she turned to Lothar and put her hand on his shoulder. "Lothar, she's gone," she said quietly but calmly. "Please, I need you to help me if we are to save your father."

He looked up at Freya standing above him, then back at the still, pale face of his mother. He very deliberately kissed his mother on the lips and rose to look at the bloodied body of his father, being tended to by Otto.

"Where is he hit?" Lothar whispered.

"The wound to the arm is superficial, I think it went right through. But he was hit in the stomach, must have been as he was running with me to rescue Petra. I can't stop the bleeding." Otto spoke more gently than Freya would have thought possible for such a big man.

Ziggy suddenly opened his eyes and smiled up at his son and his best friend's daughter. "Now isn't that a match made in heaven?" And he smiled as he saw his great companion Otto tending to his wounded stomach.

"Why so glum? Where's Petra?" Ziggy watched the faces of the three of them as he asked the question.

"She's gone, Dad. She lost too much blood," Lothar said, his voice breaking.

Ziggy seemed to shrink at the news and a sudden paleness came over him.

At that moment Karl once more looked down into the

cabin. Sensing something, he lowered himself down the short ladder and came and stood above Ziggy.

"Karl, will you take care of Emma? Help Lothar find a new direction, my good friend?" Ziggy's voice was fainter now. "I am proud of you today, son, more than you could possibly know. Make your life worth something, my boy," and he offered his hand to his firstborn, who slowly took it.

"Karl, Otto. You are the best friends a man could wish for. Live as we have lived and continue to fight for a better Germany." Ziggy's words were now slow and almost inaudible.

"Ah! Freya." Ziggy caught sight of Karl's daughter at the edge of his vision. "Your father loves you more than he will ever tell you. Make him proud, my dear girl."

Freya leant forward to hear the words as Ziggy took his last breath on the small bunk in a boat on the waters of Lake Constance.

The service was a simple affair, conducted by the local priest from Arbon, Switzerland. Both Ziggy and Petra were cremated and their urns were carried in the luggage the group had been provided with by the British embassy in Bern. After numerous phone calls back and forth, a wide-eyed Foreign and Commonwealth official had been sufficiently rebuked by numerous people including the head of the newly formed MI6, a mysterious colonel (who never gave his name) and Winston Churchill, no less. The correct and proper travel papers were prepared so that the four survivors from the boat could be flown back to England within twenty-four hours.

Karl had even had an opportunity to speak to Grace. He kept the details vague, but assured her that both he and Freya were fine and that he would be bringing both Lothar and Otto to stay until other arrangements could be made. He also shared the devastating news of the loss of both Ziggy and Petra, but declined to speak further on the matter on the telephone.

Chartwell
February 1936

"How's the hand?" Churchill looked at the bandaged left hand of this man who had risked and lost so much in Germany.

"They removed my little finger and half my ring finger, sir, but it is healing well and I am led to believe I will have full use of the rest of the hand in time," Karl explained.

"Menzies has told me about the loss of your friends, my dear chap. I am so deeply sorry. Please convey my condolences to their children who I believe are currently living with you." Churchill changed to business in an instant. "I have read your report. You paint a grim picture of the situation. Do you feel there is no way to stop Hitler? No way that we can deal with him?"

"Sir, he has surrounded himself with sycophants and men as ruthless as he. He wants it all and will stop at nothing to get his way. He will not be bargained with, he will not negotiate nor compromise. In my opinion he is looking for a fight, and judging from my visit he will soon have the resources with which to conduct and possibly win it."

"We are distracted by our new king and the furore over his divorced partner. We have taken our eye off the problem of Herr Hitler and his Nazis."

Karl listened to Churchill's words, probably one of the first men to hear the way Churchill, with his distinctive slight lisp, pronounced the word Nazi (to rhyme with khazi!).

"What are your thoughts, Luddolph?" Churchill asked directly.

"We must prepare for war, sir. We must build up our armed forces. We must build an air force to rival that which Hitler's deputy Göring is creating. We must be ready to intervene if Hitler steps one foot beyond the current border of his country," Karl replied simply.

"I believe you are right, my dear fellow. The trouble is, apart from the distraction of the King's mistress, those currently in power would seek to do anything to avoid a confrontation," Churchill responded. "They do not want to go through another war and that is blinding them to the risk from that lunatic in the Reichstag. Well, in the meantime, I want you to return to your factories and warehouses and begin to convert them to be able to manufacture munitions and possibly aircraft. Take advice and support from Morton here."

"I will do so immediately, sir." Karl rose to leave.

"Not so fast, Luddolph. Morton has something for you that he was able to obtain from the Home Office. I can only apologise for the length of time it has taken, but I can think of no man more deserving of it." Churchill gave the table to Desmond Morton, as Karl sat back down.

Morton opened his brown leather satchel-like briefcase and brought out a selection of buff-coloured folders and envelopes.

"My dear chap, it is with the humble thanks of a grateful nation that I can finally officially announce that you are now and will henceforth always be a British citizen." He then passed over a small blue booklet to Karl. Karl opened it to the picture page and stared back at himself and smiled as he finally gripped his own British passport.

"I took the liberty of providing all documentation for the children of your friends who tragically lost their lives during your escape and also of your good friend, one Otto Nadler," Morton added as he passed a large envelope across to Karl.

"Sadly, I think your cover in Germany is blown," Churchill added, "and that means that Menzies here can no longer use you in the field, so to speak. But I understand that we may have a use for you. Is that right, Stewart?" He turned to the quiet Stewart Menzies, head of the newly formed MI6.

"I think we can find a role for Luddolph, at least in teaching German to our other agents in the short term, and possibly a more varied role as the need may arise." Menzies said.

"What do you say, Louis?" Churchill looked across at Karl.

It was the first time that Churchill had used Karl's more British first name and the significance was not lost on him. "Sir, I will attend to my various premises and make them available for the manufacture of whatever the government may wish. I would be delighted to assist in whatever way I can be of service." Karl was still shocked to finally have become a British subject after nearly thirty years of trying.

Churchill rose from his seat and raised a glass of champagne. "To Louis Luddolph and his brave friends who gave their lives in the service of our great country." Everyone stood and drank from their glasses.

"Please, Louis, do not be a stranger. I fear we have difficult times ahead. I will need sound advice and counsel in the coming years, should I find myself once more in a position of some influence within government." Churchill sat once more and busied himself with lighting a large cigar.

Karl sat back down and watched this great man as he puffed on the ignited tobacco. *How can they not require this vital, intelligent man to be part of the leadership of this country?* Karl thought. *Surely, it's only a matter of time...*

Solihull
October 1938

"How is your English coming along?" Karl looked up from the dinner table into the eyes of his dearest friend's son.

"I have a good deal to understand, but I have a good teacher," Lothar answered in English, while smiling at the woman sitting next to Karl, his daughter Freya.

"Daddy, he is doing so well and his knowledge of everything at your factories is excellent." Lothar had learnt a lot working for her father at one of his biggest factories.

"He will soon be as good as me!" A small voice at the end of the table exercised her own grasp of the English language.

"Emma is such a good student. Even after Iris moved out and I continued with her studies." Grace tapped the small hand of the girl seated next to her.

"Some of us, as more mature students, needed the expertise more than you, my beautiful young girl," Otto Nadler boomed, and looked into the eyes of the lady sitting next to him, Iris Pope, sister of Karl's first wife Lily.

"I'm sorry James could not be here this weekend, but that school of his is very strict in their term-time exeats," Karl said.

"He will be home for Christmas, my dear," Grace said, trying to provide a more optimistic answer for her husband.

"May I ask if you are fully recovered, sir?" asked another small voice nervously from between Lothar and Emma, looking at the large bulk of Otto Nadler.

249

"David, you do not ask such things," Karl admonished him.

"No, that's all right, Karl. Well, young man, I was hit three times, and once in the back of my leg, just below my knee. It means I need this fine silver-topped cane that your father gave me. The other bullets struck my back. They were of such low velocity that they were lodged in the muscles in my back and luckily for me didn't hit any vital organs." Otto had forgotten he was talking to a nine-year-old.

"What does velocity mean please, Uncle Otto?" David innocently asked.

"Ha! It means that I was very lucky. The bullets were so small and travelling at such low speed, that when they hit me they didn't have the force to go too far below the skin. You understand?" Otto smiled as he answered.

"That, coupled with the fact that you have the skin of a rhinoceros, you old devil," Karl added playfully.

Those around the table laughed, except Iris, who could only stare in adoration at the enormous figure sitting next to her.

"Iris, have you become more settled in our old house, since we moved up here?" Grace was keen to reassure Iris since she and Karl had gifted their old house to her when they moved to this new, larger property in Dove House Lane.

"It has taken a while to realise that it's ours; but we love the place. I suppose I have lived there so long, it will take time to get used to it." Iris spoke quietly, looking into the eyes of her great bear of a husband Otto.

"We're just so happy we can help you both. Karl and I have so much to thank you both for. I see you as the link between the different generations of family in Louis' life," Grace said.

"Iris, we are all so happy for you. Although your choice of husband took a few of us by surprise. He is, of course, the finest of men and the greatest of friends." Karl smiled at Iris, making her go crimson with embarrassment.

"Hear, hear!" Lothar chimed in. "Uncle Otto was my father's greatest friend and confidant. I am sure he would be delighted that you have finally found the right woman to tame you." He smiled as he finished.

"Enough! All of you! You are embarrassing Iris." Otto banged his plate-sized palm on the table as he spoke.

"No dear, they are trying to embarrass you." Iris timed her response to perfection as everybody laughed at her retort.

Karl stood at the end of the table in his newly furnished dining room. As he did so, he glanced around at the faces of those seated and then gave a quick look towards the two urns given pride of place on the sideboard opposite the large patio doors that led to the substantial garden. "I would like to propose a toast, if you could all be upstanding. With the eyes of our dear friends Ziggy and Petra watching on, no doubt, I wish to toast the happiness and devotion that we see in my great mentor Otto and his beautiful wife, Iris. So, to Otto and Iris," and he raised his glass, as did the rest of the dinner table, before they all sat back down.

Otto, sensing the occasion, stood and spoke. "I thank you, Karl or Louis. No, I think I will stick with Karl," and those around the table laughed. "I have you to thank for our salvation in England. For acquiring British papers and citizenship for us through your mysterious contacts. Young Lothar and Emma have been welcomed into your family and I feel confident that they have a future, now they are away from Germany in its current state. As a newly accredited British subject, I would like to propose a toast to our new king. Ladies and gentlemen, if you will once again stand please." The entire table once again rose to their feet.

"To King George," and Otto raised his glass.

"To the King!" the room responded in unison and drank to the health of the young king, who had inherited the crown from his elder brother after the abdication.

"Sir, I have something that I wish to ask." Lothar stood nervously in Karl's study.

Karl stood opposite this fine-looking young man, who was as good-looking as his father had been. Karl found himself thinking back to a time long ago, when he and Ziggy had been standing on a beautiful summer's afternoon on the grassy area below the lighthouse on Plymouth Hoe, both dressed in their Imperial German naval uniforms. Karl recalled how dashing and handsome Ziggy looked and now here he was staring at the same classically handsome features of his son, Lothar.

"Yes, my boy, what is it?" Karl smiled inwardly having been briefed by Grace, via Freya, about the subject of Lothar's question. He decided to have some fun and make it as awkward as possible for him.

"Well, sir, as you know, well, I have been, well, that is to say, we have become quite close friends now and I..." Lothar stumbled through his words.

"Come on, man, spit it out," Karl said, continuing to torment the young man.

"Sir, I want to ask you, what I mean to say is, well, I was hoping that..."

"Come on, man. Just take a deep breath and out with it."

"Sir, I wish to ask your permission for Freya's hand in marriage."

"WHAT!?" Karl shouted loudly, having immense fun at the expense of his great friend's young son.

The door to the study burst open and Freya charged into the room.

"He is the man I want to marry and it's too late, Daddy, I have already said yes! I am old enough to make my own decisions and this was just Lothar's idea anyway, to do things properly. I don't care if you refuse. To be frank, your indignation frustr..." Freya looked up at her father as she continued her rant, stopping mid-word when she saw the wide smile on her father's face and he started to laugh.

"Dad?" Freya said nervously.

"My dear Lothar. It would appear that my daughter has decided that your polite enquiry with me is not really necessary, as she has already said yes. I, on the other hand, am honoured that you wished to formally ask for my permission to marry my headstrong, wilful, impudent daughter. Are you sure you are making the right decision?" Karl was now laughing loudly, as Grace, Iris and Otto joined them in the study.

"Everyone! It gives me the most enormous pride and pleasure to announce that this fine young man, my best friend's son Lothar, has asked my daughter, the irascible Freya, to marry him. She has apparently said yes and I just wish to add my blessing to what I am sure is a perfect match. I am sure your father would have been so proud of you," and Karl shook Lothar's hand.

Freya, unable to contain herself, rushed forward and hugged her father.

"Now she hugs me...!" Karl said as his daughter squeezed the breath out of him.

Chartwell
October 1938

"That bloody unnecessary business with the abdication meant we took our eye off Germany, just long enough for Herr Hitler to carry on with his rearmament programme with impunity. We were caught up in the struggle to maintain our monarchy, rather than focusing on a much more real and sinister threat from Europe and the Nazis." Churchill finished with his customary favoured pronunciation of the word Nazi, causing Karl to smile as he looked across the table at this vital and brilliant man, who seemed to have gained some vigour and a sense of purpose since the last time he had seen him.

"Louis, what do you see as his next gambit?" Churchill suddenly turned his gaze across to Karl, who was here to meet with Churchill through a direct invitation from Desmond Morton.

"Well, he will take the Sudetenland, and within weeks I imagine he will probably take the rest of Czechoslovakia. Then he will look to the east, to the edge of the old Prussian empire, which means that I suspect he will look to move on Poland." Karl summarised what the rest of the table assumed would be the case too.

"You see! You are not a Chamberlain man then, Louis? You don't think that this jumped-up corporal will be satisfied and stick to the agreement hammered out at Munich?" Churchill queried.

"No, sir! You remember I saw this man speak at a beer hall in Munich. He has an ability to speak in public and bring an audience to his side within a minute or so. It was an almost magical thing to witness. When you look into his eyes, you see that he has a distant and chilling stare. He will not be stopped by agreements and treaties. The man has decided to wage war if necessary to get Europe under his yolk, and this country needs to prepare for that," Karl concluded.

"You see, Desmond? Louis can see it, you and Menzies over there can see it. How is it our esteemed prime minister cannot see it? Things are afoot in parliament. Loyalties are changing by the day. The opposition is fed up with this 'appeasement' strategy. Desmond, I need you back in London to keep an eye on everything and gauge the mood of the house. I have a feeling Neville may well have a short time left and Halifax is lurking in the shadows. But he doesn't have the stomach for it either!" Churchill suddenly turned his attention back to Karl. "Louis, I understand that you have booked passage to America on the *Queen Mary*, leaving on 12th November?"

"Yes, sir." Karl was astounded by Churchill's information. He had only booked tickets on the new liner the week before.

"I need you to do something for me. I am concerned that with the threat of war extremely likely, as you readily concur, we need to seek the assistance of our American cousins. I want you to go to Washington and meet with President Roosevelt. I am going to need to build a good friendship with this man if we are going to be able to seek very real military aid from America. Without their intervention, I do not see Great Britain being able to hold off the newly created might of the German air force for very long." Churchill paused to take a drink from his wine glass.

"Yes, sir. Who will arrange for me to meet with the American president?"

"Desmond will arrange for you to meet him at the Omni

Shoreham Hotel. A room has already been booked in your name and Roosevelt is attending an event there. He will find a window in his schedule to meet with you in your room, I believe," Churchill explained.

"Of course. What is it you want me to say?" Karl gulped at the magnitude of the task ahead of him.

"Desmond will fill you in, in due course. Now tell me about this new ship and who you are going to be travelling with?" Churchill, as was his way, swiftly swung the conversation on to the next thing on his mind, seemingly having sorted the business part of the lunch.

Southampton Docks
12th November 1938

Karl once again settled into the sumptuous armchair in his first-class stateroom. He had acquired an information bundle as he boarded the new flagship of the Cunard-White Star Line, RMS *Queen Mary*. As he sat there, he remembered the occasion a time long ago when he had sat in a small library in Wilhelmshaven in Germany with his dashingly handsome friend Ziggy, as they collated information about their new ship, during his time as a recruit in the German navy.

God, I miss you, Ziggy, Karl thought as he opened the literature about this new and opulent vessel.

He shook himself back to the present and began to read. As ever, the numbers fascinated Karl as he read about the twenty-four Yarrow-style boilers that powered the four Parsons single-reduction geared steam turbines, producing 150,000 Kw of power to the four shafts. This gave her a top speed of 28.5 knots; ample to win back the Blue Riband for the swiftest crossing of the Atlantic from the French ship *Normandie*.★

He had stayed in his cabin to ostensibly read the information about the ship but he also wanted a little bit of time alone, thinking back to his days at sea with his Ziggy. This was where Grace, Freya and Lothar found him, asleep in the armchair, the bundle of papers scattered on the carpeted floor around him.

257

"Lou, are you all right, my dear?" Grace, as ever, with the gentlest touch on Karl's arm, woke him and looked into his clear blue eyes.

"Hello, my dear Grace. I just dozed off," Karl exclaimed.

"That's perfectly all right. Freya, help pick up your father's papers please." It might have previously been cause for histrionics from Freya; but since her return from Germany, she had come to see the love between her father and his second wife, just as she too fell in love with Lothar. She saw the significance of the moment and as she bent to pick up the sheets of paper, she placed her hand gently on top of Grace's and simply said, "Leave it to me, Grace."

The four days on board the *Queen Mary* passed as a pleasant break for Karl. He found time to get to know his future son-in-law better. He saw some of the bold confidence exhibited by Ziggy when Lothar was introduced to the seemingly endless succession of fellow passengers who were on board. He witnessed the way his daughter radiated her love for the son of his great, lifelong friend. Though he spent most of the crossing hunched over the desk in his stateroom study, he found time to experience one of the liner's two indoor swimming pools. He took advantage of the newly acquired telephone connectivity to speak urgently with Charles, his office manager, about chasing some contract renewal papers from a company in Sweden while he was away. They dressed for dinner and dined in the wonderful Grand Salon, three storeys high, supported by great columns, with fantastic artwork and wood panelling that had been sourced from across the extent of the British Empire. Karl became fascinated by one wall of the salon that had a huge map of their route across the Atlantic, with a small motorised version of the ship that moved to indicate their position.

Grace was a vision each evening when she appeared in a new and wondrous dress that she had kept hidden from Karl until the voyage. After dinner, they would lose Freya and

Lothar, who had found that in the evenings the Verandah Grill turned into the Starlight Club, where they could dance the night away together. Karl and Grace ventured in one evening, but Karl decided that it was just a little too lively for him and despite his entreaties for Grace to stay and enjoy the atmosphere, she devotedly returned to the more sedate and peaceful first-class smoking room.

"It was such a short meeting that I can hardly remember him," Grace commented as they discussed the invitation Karl had received to stay with Joseph Pilates in New York.

"I suppose so. You know he told me that he met his wife Clara on that very trip to America. It was a turning point for him, you know. She gave him the support and confidence to create his first studio in New York." Karl recalled Joseph's exercise and breathing regime that he had benefitted from all those years ago on the Isle of Man as a prisoner.

"Are we really staying at the Waldorf Astoria, Lou?" Grace said, checking their itinerary.

"Yes, my dear, three rooms for our brief stay. I thought Freya and Lothar could stay in New York while I go to Washington. You are welcome to stay too, if you would rather?" Karl had told her that he needed to go to the American capital, but not about the nature of his visit.

"Oh Lou, I'm looking forward to travelling by train to Washington, plus I will just be in the way of Freya and Lothar. It will be nice for them to have some time in America on their own."

"Then that's settled. We're only there for the one night and I will explain the reason for our visit when we get there," Karl replied.

Grace knew better than to question her husband further on the subject of the brief visit to the American capital and, as was her way, switched the conversation to the selection of another brandy for her husband.

As Freya sat back down in the corner of the dimly lit restaurant-cum-nightclub she watched her fiancé standing with his back to her at the bar. She studied his confident stance and his broad shoulders within the stylish dinner suit he wore. She had fallen in love with this handsome man when she had first set eyes on him, when she was just a girl. To her delight, the feelings had been mutual. But she had been unsure about their future. She knew that she would have the financial support of her father, but this might be awkward for Lothar. He was after all a proud man who would not take kindly to being kept by his wife.

"Your martini, madam." Lothar appeared in front of her holding a glass in each hand.

"Perfect timing, Loti. Sit down. Let's just enjoy the others dancing. Are you all right?" Freya had been asking specifically about that evening, but Lothar perhaps answered in a more profound way.

"I am finding my way, my darling. I'm still coming to terms with the sudden loss of my parents and the foolish way I was indoctrinated and led down the fascist path of the Nazi regime." Lothar paused as Freya took his hand in hers.

"I'm ashamed of my behaviour and the pain it caused my family. Events have moved so swiftly that I have not really had a chance to take it all in. My salvation has been my love for you, my dear Freya." And Lothar leant forward and kissed Freya gently on the lips.

"Oh Lothar! I only meant how are you tonight, but I'm so happy that you can share your thoughts with me," Freya smiled.

"Ah! Well, at least I have got it off my chest! I think that is the expression you English use?" And he smiled back at his beautiful companion. "But this trip has given me the opportunity to think about our future. We're both young without any ties. I am a German living in a foreign country, one that has very generously given me status as a British subject. But my origins, much like your father's, could cause problems in the coming years." Again, Lothar paused while he watched Freya's reaction.

"Go on, Loti, tell me what's on your mind." Freya stroked his hand as she listened.

"I think we are in a position to try a fresh start. I can think of no better place to begin our lives together than in America. Obviously, we can discuss it at length, but I just wanted to share my thoughts with you now." Lothar stopped and looked again into the eyes of his wife-to-be.

Freya smiled back and after a brief pause, she kissed Lothar and hugged him.

*The *Queen Mary* would hold this record until 1952, when *the* SS *United States* superseded her.

New York
November 1938

"How are your rooms?" Karl studied the young couple closely, keen to see if there were any conspiratorial looks between the two of them as he had been at pains to provide two separate rooms. Karl was, and would remain, a traditional conservative member of society and believed in appropriate behaviour before marriage.

"Yes, thank you, Father, we were able to resist temptation and stayed in our respective rooms. Thank you for checking." Freya quickly closed down the conversation, smiling at Lothar sitting next to her at the ornately laid breakfast table in the Waldorf Astoria dining room.

Grace, too, picked up on the atmosphere Karl had created with his question and selected a safer topic. "What time are we going to meet with Joseph, dear?"

"He's invited us to meet him at his studio with Clara at eleven o'clock. He said we should look for a ballet school when we get to Eighth Avenue, which uses the same premises as he does."

"Sir, thank you for allowing Freya and myself to accompany you. Freya was explaining to me that you met Mr. Pilates while you were both interned on the Isle of Man, during the war?" Lothar looked across at Karl.

"Lothar, do please call me Louis or Lou; I think we can dispense with the sir. Yes, I met Joseph at a camp in Lancaster

262

and we were both transferred to the Isle of Man in 1915. I do not believe I would be here today if it were not for the creation of the techniques that Joseph developed and that we all tried to follow during our years of incarceration." Karl looked vaguely emotional as he told the story of his time as a prisoner.

"You met him, Grace, didn't you?" said Freya. "On the ship that was taking him to America?"

"I did indeed. Your father was in Ireland with me, visiting premises near Dublin and we drove down to the port at Queensferry and went on board and had tea with Joseph while the ship was moored there briefly. I only met him for that short time but he was a whirlwind of energy and ambition."

"Did you meet Clara?"

"I didn't, but I know she was a passenger on the same ship and that during the voyage they met and fell in love and have been together ever since," Grace explained.

"Oh! That is so romantic don't you think, Daddy?" Freya was never able to miss a chance to have fun with her father.

"What! I saw him on that ship, he had his eyes everywhere. I suspect he was quite keen on Grace, if I recall, judging by the attention he was giving you, my dear." Karl looked up from his breakfast.

"Nonsense! But he was a fine-looking man," Grace said quietly, leaning forward towards Freya and smiling.

Freya laughed. "I very much look forward to meeting him later."

Joseph had maintained his rigorous fitness and exercise regime, ably assisted by his beautiful wife Clara. He rushed forward as Karl, Grace, Freya and Lothar entered his first-floor studio. "Karl. My dear friend!" And he caught Karl in a powerful bear hug before releasing him and hugging Grace in similar fashion.

"Now who is this vision?" Joseph looked hard at Freya.

"This is my daughter, Freya, and her fiancé Lothar."

Joseph took Freya's hand and kissed it gently and then shook Lothar's hand. "It is a great pleasure to meet you. Your father missed you so much while he was with me on the island. When he eventually received a picture of you, as a baby, it became his most prized possession. I don't think a day went by when he would not be sat on his bed, in those damp and cold wooden huts, with that picture clasped in his hands. You are every bit the beautiful young lady that I would have expected," Joseph said gallantly.

"Thank you. My father never really talks about his time away from my mother during the war. It is lovely for you to have remembered for him." Freya leant forward and kissed Joseph.

"Now please come and meet Clara and some of my other students. Lothar, you look like someone who might enjoy some of the exercises I teach." Joseph was immediately appraising the fine physicality of the young man before him.

"Sir, I might find it difficult in this suit," Lothar smiled.

"Ha! we have a whole range of lost property and spare clothing and footwear we can provide you with." Joseph was quite insistent.

"Go on, young man," Karl said warmly. "I think it would be good for you to experience Joseph's methods."

"Oh yes! Go on, Loti." Freya squealed with delight as she pushed Lothar forward into the studio.

A very attractive lady in loose-fitting clothing came forward from a group in the corner of the studio.

"May I present my wife, Clara? She is the one who has got me to where we are today, within the dancing community of New York," Joseph said.

Grace moved forward and embraced Clara. "We are so delighted to meet you."

"Likewise, my dear Grace. I have heard so much about Karl, but almost nothing about you. This must be Freya?" Clara moved forward and hugged Karl's daughter and then looked at the young man holding Freya's hand.

"Clara, this is my fiancé Lothar and he would very much like to take one of your classes this morning," Freya said smiling.

"One of our top students, Ernst, is going to take a class. Joseph, take this fine young gentleman to the changing rooms and find him something more appropriate to wear," Clara said. "Now while they are exercising, why don't the rest of us have a seat and Freya can tell me all about her fine fiancé and Grace can tell me all about her life with Karl." Clara ushered them to an area of chairs at the edge of the dance floor. She watched Karl follow her husband and Lothar to get changed. "So, Grace, how did you meet Karl?"

"Well, it was a job interview to be his secretary…"

The next day Karl and Grace left Freya and Lothar at the hotel and took a taxi to Penn Station, a grand building with hundreds of columns supporting the roof.

Grace and Karl quickly found the correct platform and a very efficient guard assisted them with their luggage and settled them into their first-class compartment.

The train departed on time and a little over four and a half hours later pulled into the vast Union Station in Washington DC.

Karl, as was his way, tipped everyone who came to their aid as they made the journey to the north of the city and arrived at the hotel.

The recently built Omni Shoreham Hotel was situated one block over from the junction between Connecticut Avenue and Calvert Street. It had been built in 1930 and was regarded as one of the finest hotels in the city. In March 1933 it had hosted the first inaugural ball of Franklin D Roosevelt. Its relatively recent construction ensured that it had been equipped with a ramp and elevator to accommodate the needs of the wheelchair-bound president.

Karl took in the open-plan interior as he and Grace walked through the spacious entrance lobby. They were greeted by a very smartly dressed lady who came from behind the long reception desk to welcome them.

"Good afternoon, sir. My name is Maddie and I would like to welcome you to the Omni Shoreham. May I please take your name?"

Karl was instantly impressed with the quiet courtesy and politeness of the receptionist. "Good afternoon, I am Louis Luddolph and this is my wife Grace," he replied.

"We have been expecting you, sir, and a suite is prepared for you on the seventh floor. If you would care to follow me, I will have someone attend to your luggage," and she led them to the shiny elevator doors. Karl and Grace gingerly stepped into the carpeted interior and gripped each other's hands as the doors slid closed and the elevator rose swiftly to their designated floor.

Maddie led the way down a wide corridor to a door at the end. She opened the door and allowed Grace and Karl to enter before she joined them in the lounge of what was a luxurious suite. "I trust this will be acceptable, sir?" she asked.

"My dear young lady, this is beautiful. I thank you for your efficiency and politeness." And Karl subtly handed the lady a folded bank note, as she bid them good day.

Within a minute there was a knock at the door. Karl opened it and a bellboy brought in their luggage and took it through to the dressing area and then returned to the lounge. Karl once again handed him a folded banknote as he made to exit the suite.

"Why are you so generous, Lou?" Grace always found it less natural to tip the various staff who attended to their needs whenever they travelled anywhere.

"I'm not altogether sure that I was that generous to be honest. I haven't quite worked out the exchange rate and have been handing them a note with a picture of Lincoln on it.

Looking at one now, I see it's only $5, so it may be that I have been rather mean!" Karl smiled and sat down on a very comfortable-looking sofa and picked up a copy of that day's *Washington Post* newspaper.

"What time is your meeting?" Grace now knew why Karl was in Washington DC. It had become clear to Karl that since the desperate events that had occurred back in Germany, he would let Grace know everything that was being asked of him by Churchill and others within the British establishment. He had spoken to Desmond Morton about divulging his clandestine activities and Morton, having done some thorough vetting of Grace, had agreed it was probably best to let her know the truth of his involvement with officers within government. Grace, for her part, never spoke to anyone about her husband's involvement for the rest of her life.

"I have been informed that the meeting will take place after dinner tonight. We are to dine in the main hotel ballroom and then return to our suite by 11 p.m. Shortly after our return, we will be visited by the President when I can convey the message from Churchill," Karl explained.

"Then I have time for a deep and relaxing bath before dinner," Grace decided, looking at her husband who was by now engrossed in the pages of the broadsheet newspaper.

Dinner was wonderful, with American hospitality at its best. Grace had selected a stylish, but demure burgundy gown, pinning her hair up to accentuate her slender neck. She was wearing a large diamond necklace, with matching earrings, Karl's anniversary gift to her. By the time Karl was gently sipping a large brandy, the clock had reached 10.45 p.m. Grace quietly cleared her throat to remind him that they ought to be heading back to their suite.

As they entered their rooms, Karl took hold of Grace's hand. "I neglected to say how beautiful you look this evening, my dear," and he kissed her.

"Should I make myself scarce in the other room?" Grace enquired.

"No, I am sure the President of the United States would like to meet you and, after all, you have been comprehensively vetted now too." Karl smiled warmly at his wife.

"Well, if you're sure then I would be delighted," Grace replied.

Karl heard a sharp knock on the door and opened it to be faced by a stern, tall, well-built man, probably in his early thirties, who introduced himself as Mr. Stevens, the head of the President's security detail. Karl took a step back to allow Mr. Stevens and another security official to enter and search their suite. After this had been completed a familiar figure in a wheelchair entered and offered his hand. "Franklin Roosevelt. It's a pleasure to meet you. I understand that you are a close and trusted confidant of Winston Churchill?" Karl tentatively shook the President's hand and allowed him to wheel himself into the centre of the lounge.

"Sir, may I introduce my wife, Grace?" and the President shook Grace's hand as she stood before him.

"It's a pleasure to meet you too, young lady. Now please both of you, do sit down; this meeting is not happening, so we better make it quick." And the President indicated for Karl and Grace to sit together on the sofa.

Karl began. "Sir, Mr. Churchill believes, as do I, that Great Britain is in a grave position. The appeasement policy of our government will do nothing more than slow Germany's expansion. It is only a matter of time before Hitler turns his attentions beyond Czechoslovakia. Britain is not equipped, as yet, to defend itself against the newly generated military might of Germany. I have been asked if the United States will be in a position to provide support and material aid, when the time comes." Karl paused.

"I have admired Winston for some time now. I think

he is misunderstood within your government and I firmly believe you will need his sharp mind and tactical acumen in the years ahead. I have a great deal of opposition within both Congress and the Senate. There are calls to maintain our neutrality and not to plunge ourselves into an unnecessary war with Germany. That being said, I have had some success in winning support for supporting Great Britain and other European nations. Hitler lost a great deal of his standing with his annexation of Austria and the dreadful scenes witnessed on Kristallnacht. I have to balance my position, but I wish to create a dialogue with Mr. Churchill and as such I have a letter for you to take to him." Roosevelt held up his hand and Mr. Stevens moved forward and took the letter from the President, which he in turn handed to Karl.

"Sir, Mr. Churchill is also keen to develop an understanding between our two countries and has drafted a letter too." Karl pulled an envelope from within his jacket and handed it to President Roosevelt.

"Do I detect a German accent, Mr. Luddolph?" the President smiled as he asked.

"Indeed, sir. I was born near Leipzig but grew up in England. My journey to this point in my life has not been without one or two challenges," Karl candidly replied.

"I can only imagine," Roosevelt offered. "I must leave you now. This meeting, as I intimated earlier, did not take place. But please reassure Winston that I will read his letter and I look forward to speaking with him soon. I understand you are due to return to New York and then on the *Queen Mary* back to England in the next few days?" President Roosevelt asked.

"You are well informed, sir. We depart for England the day after tomorrow," Karl explained.

"Then I bid you farewell and wish you safe passage back to England. Please make it clear to all those who you speak to that I will ensure that the United States does not sit idly by for much longer. Mrs Luddolph, my dear lady, I am sorry not to have had a chance to know you both better." And with that, he turned his chair and was wheeled from the room followed by the steadfast Mr. Stevens and the rest of his security detail.

"Did you get to see any of the sites in Washington, Dad?" Freya asked as they enjoyed a fine dinner on their last night in New York.

"Unfortunately, our visit was too quick. I needed to meet with a business contact to try and negotiate a new client base here in the United States. We just enjoyed a lovely evening at an excellent hotel there."

"Sir, if I may? Freya and I have a proposal that we wish to put to you," said Lothar nervously.

"Oh, yes, well come on then, let's hear it," Karl replied perhaps more sternly than he wished.

Lothar cleared his throat and spoke. "I thoroughly enjoyed meeting your friend Joseph Pilates and his wife was impressed with my understanding and implementation of their exercise philosophy." Lothar paused.

"Yes, we were all impressed with the way you threw your-self into the class," Grace said, smiling at Lothar.

"Mr. Pilates and Clara spoke at length with me while you were away and are keen to expand the studio they run. I have thought long and hard about my position in Great Britain. Like yourself, sir, I find myself living in a foreign country that I fear will soon be at war with the country of my birth. My view is that I will always find it more than challenging to make a life for myself in England and I have concluded that I need to make something of myself in a new and fresh environment."

"I see. Would this mean that you are intending to stay here in America?" Karl guessed the way that Lothar's determination was going.

"Don't interrupt, Daddy! I want to stay with Lothar and think he is making a wise choice, please don't try and dissuade us." Freya face reddened as she made her feelings clear.

"My dear Freya, please. Allow me to speak. I admire you both. You are the apple of my eye, the physical embodiment of your wonderful mother. I support you in everything you do. Please, I am not angry or in any way against this suggestion. My brother and I were in a similar position many years ago. At that time, the authorities saw fit not to grant our wish to emigrate here. I can think of nothing more fitting for my daughter and her fine partner to make a new life for themselves here, if that is what they choose." Karl looked up at his daughter to see the tears on her cheeks.

"I am delighted for you both," Grace put in. "Lou and I will both miss you, but I feel that you are making a good decision."

"I think that some champagne is called for!" Karl recovered himself and ordered a bottle from the attentive waiter. "Now, both of you can stay here for as long as it takes you to find a place of your own. I will happily fund such an endeavour and increase your allowance, Freya." Karl immediately became more businesslike again.

"Sir, I cannot accept such generosity. I'm sure we can manage," Lothar protested.

"Nonsense, my boy! I will call it a loan anyway. I have every confidence that you will make a success of whatever you set your mind to." Karl laughed, causing the rest of the table to join in. "Oh, and I will continue to pay for two rooms here, so please do me the courtesy of using them both," Karl added, as they drank the champagne.

"DAD!" Freya scolded her father playfully.

Solihull
3rd September 1939

"Churchill was ultimately frustrated by President Roosevelt's lack of action following the exchange of letters. I know he has become increasingly angry at the way our prime minister is continually trying to appease Hitler. Now we are at the very brink, waiting to hear if Germany will listen to our demands and act on them," Karl sat and stood and variously paced around the lounge of their home.

"Would you like some tea, my dear?" Grace, as ever, was the cornerstone of Karl's life and her judgement about how to measure and manage her husband's moods was finely tuned.

"Oh! Yes, thank you, Grace. Can you switch on the radio? I believe an announcement is imminent." Karl stood and watched as his wife turned a switch on the large wooden cabinet that housed their radio and then disappeared into the kitchen.

Karl adjusted the volume and turned the dial to reduce the static and crackling through the speaker. He looked at his watch: 11.10 a.m. "Grace, come on, I'm expecting the broadcast to start," Karl shouted through to his wife.

Grace reappeared carrying a cup of tea for her husband and they both sat down on a three-seater sofa, facing the ornate mahogany radio cabinet.

"And now, here is the Prime Minister."

"I am speaking to you from the Cabinet room of 10

Downing Street. This morning the British ambassador in Berlin handed the German government a final note stating that unless we heard from them by eleven o'clock that they were prepared at once to withdraw their troops from Poland, a state of war would exist between us. I have to tell you now that no such undertaking has been received, and that consequently this country is at war with Germany.... We have a clear conscience, we have done all that any country could do to establish peace, but a situation in which no word given by Germany's ruler could be trusted, and no people or country could feel itself safe, has become intolerable. ... Now, may God bless you all and may He defend the right. For it is the evil things that we shall be fighting against, brute force, bad faith, injustice, oppression and persecution. And against them I am certain that the right will prevail."

"Twice in my lifetime, I don't quite believe it," Karl murmured as they took in the Prime Minister's message.

"What happens now?" Grace was equally dumbfounded by the news.

"Well, they have to get this country on a more serious war footing immediately. Chamberlain and his government have hardly done anything of note to strengthen our position."

"What about Mr. Churchill?" Grace was quick to see how this might affect her husband's secret government contact and friend.

"They will have to bring him back into the Cabinet. He has guessed correctly at every move Hitler has made. He made himself as well informed as he could have been and I would suggest that they need him now."

"Do you think Mr. Churchill will want to see you?" Grace asked quietly.

"I would not be at all surprised. It affects us all, Grace. James is old enough for conscription and it will undoubtedly affect David's schooling. My business will be hit by a loss of all my European contacts, but I have made provision for that. We will also have to make our resources available for the war effort."

"You must speak with Freya and Lothar. They will be worried about us all." Grace thought of Karl's daughter, now happily married to Lothar and living in New York.

Solihull
4th June 1940

Karl spent the latter part of 1939 at home in Solihull, consolidating his business interests and adapting some of the factories he controlled to the production of military equipment and ammunition, under licence from the government. Winston Churchill, now the prime minister, had come to the Midlands and visited a number of manufacturing premises, including Karl's, to bolster support and encourage a feeling of national pride in stepping up production levels. During a private meeting with Churchill, it was clear that the weight of office was focusing his mind and he encouraged Karl to open more premises to increase production still further, during the quiet period that had overtaken the warring sides since September of 1939.

At home in Karl's back garden, a Home Office-designed Anderson shelter had arrived and together the still physically imposing Otto Nadler, his eldest son, James, and to a lesser extent his youngest child, David, buried the shelter in the ground and used the majority of the spoil from the hole created to cover its corrugated iron roof and sides. Karl was a little confused as to why no drainage system or soak away device had been provided with the shelter. Mindful of the damp conditions experienced in Great Britain, Karl improvised a system of both ceramic and rubber pipes that led away to another trench he dug at the very bottom of his land and filled with loose shingle, to leach the water away from the bottom of the bomb shelter. The fact that Karl's house backed onto a golf course reassured everyone that in the event of any sustained attack, the golf course would provide an alternative place of safety should remaining in the shelter become untenable.

James had returned from school ready to take up a place at Bristol University, studying geology. Having just turned eighteen he was also keen to enlist at the earliest opportunity. He faced his father across the dinner table where both Grace and David were mere onlookers at the conversation between the two.

"But I can easily get your enlistment deferred. You can stay here working at one of my factories or commence work on your degree in October. Why this sudden rush to want to go off to war?" Karl was angry, but was doing everything he could to sound supportive and to try to offer alternatives.

"I want to serve my country. I understand your reservations, but I have to follow my heart. You went off and did your national service when you were my age."

"That's different. It was compulsory service and we were not at war with anybody at that time," Karl countered.

"But you were living here in Leicester, you didn't have to go and serve Germany. You chose to go. I think that in the same way I am aware that I do not have to go, but I want to," James explained.

"So, who are you going to join? Most of the British soldiers we still have are recently returned from the fiasco at Dunkirk, who will you join up with?"

"I've decided upon the Cheshire Regiment. Several of my mates from school are going to join them too."

"It sounds like you've already acted upon your decision and that this is not really a debate, just you keeping us informed," Karl said more quietly.

"Dad, I am going to do this. I just want your blessing

before I join up at the end of the week. I do understand your concerns and appreciate all that you could do to keep me here with you." James looked around the table at his stepmother and younger brother as he spoke.

"Then, if I may, dear, I wish you all the good fortune in the world and above all I pray that you will be kept safe and come back to us soon," Grace said quietly.

"Then I too accept, reluctantly, your decision to enlist. If there is anything I can do then please do not hesitate to ask. Come here, my boy," and Karl stood and beckoned James over to the top of the table where he embraced his son and kissed his cheek. "Please, come back to us," he whispered in his ear.

So, James went off to war to fight for the British. The son of a German immigrant who had himself been interned for the duration of the Great War, now volunteered to fight against the Germans in this conflict. Deep within the fear of losing his son, Karl also felt an enormous sense of pride in his actions. David watched the events around him unfold. He was still at school, about to start his secondary education. His father may have been home more than he had ever been previously, but the fact was that he missed his elder sister Freya and her fiancé Lothar. Now James was going to join up and Emma was living with Iris and Otto. He suddenly felt a great surge of loneliness as he walked through the normally vibrant house. Where once had been constant chatter and laughter, was now an atmosphere of emptiness and quiet. David decided that he would be better off at the boarding school his father had selected for him in the country and resolved to make sure he passed the entrance exam.

And so, the country once more went to war. As the wonderful summer of 1940 drew on, so the reality of the situation began to be understood by the British public. Churchill seemed to be forever on the radio giving rallying and, what would go down in history as, legendary speeches to the House of Commons. Karl was still visited by Colonel Z at his place of work and, on occasion, spirited away to meet with Churchill in his wartime lair below Downing Street.

Karl was shocked by the transformation in Churchill. He was looking so much older, but seemed to have limitless energy and a desire to know every snippet of information so he could make better-informed decisions. He spoke to Karl about the need to galvanise the public and make them ready for the fight to come. He wanted to use Karl's knowledge of Germany to help educate a new secret force he was setting up, known colloquially as 'Churchill's secret army', or sometimes 'The Ministry of Ungentlemanly Warfare'. Karl found himself assisting at a number of secret locations in and around Buckinghamshire, Hertfordshire and Essex, usually at commandeered stately homes. One soldier recruit suggested that the initials SOE (Special Operations Executive) might actually stand for 'Stately 'omes of England'. Karl spent time explaining the geography of the country of his birth. He delivered a rudimentary language course of essential German, being able to add regional variations and slang to what was the standard course in German.

When not engaged in these more covert enterprises, Karl was busy assisting with the improvements to several production lines within the network of factories he now controlled. As the real war began, the area experienced its first air raid by the German Luftwaffe. Initially concentrated on the southern England radar stations, further raids progressed to London and then any areas of perceived industry and military production and significance. Karl and Grace became close 'air raid' friends with their direct neighbours in Dove House Lane, often sharing the well-drained and comfortable shelter in Karl's garden.

Grace, for her part, spent long days working as one of the very few female shop floor supervisors at one of the armament centres in the Midlands. Her quiet, sympathetic but determined demeanour helping to maximise production amongst the almost entirely female workforce. With David now staying with Karl's younger brother Willy in Mountsorrel, just to the north of Leicester, Karl felt he had more time to devote to both his overseeing of wartime production and to the assisting with the training for the hastily created SOE.

A brief telegram from James was all that Karl and Grace had to warn them that their son had now shipped out to North Africa with the 1st Battalion of the Cheshire Regiment, and they were on standby in Egypt. Communication with Freya was more or less as limited. They received a letter from her to say how little the war in Europe was affecting the people of America, with the policy of isolation still clearly holding sway despite what Karl knew to be Roosevelt's desire to assist Great Britain and other European countries. Grace was heartened by the warm tone in the letters towards her. She had never really felt true warmth and love from Freya and understood where it came from. But now there seemed within the neatly written pages a genuine, caring love for Grace, as if she now accepted her as a confidante and partner for her father. Lothar was settling well into their American life and still studying under Joseph and Clara Pilates in their studio.

The golf course behind their house had been closed that summer so, without this hobby, Karl and Grace drove up to Cannock Chase to take long walks through the outstanding countryside and developed a keen interest in visiting similar areas, such as the Peak District. Karl was mindful of his own mortality and at fifty-five he was determined to stay as young and fit as he could for as long as possible, assisted by his much younger wife, still only in her mid-thirties. Karl turned to his garden, creating a large vegetable plot close to the newly installed bomb shelter. He also grew flowers and shrubs to make the space more appealing to the eye. When on one occasion Iris had visited with Otto and Emma in tow, the former naval instructor had remarked on what a revelation to see Karl tending what was now a beautiful garden. Karl studied his great friend and now neighbour. He estimated that the chief was in his early seventies. He was still a powerfully built man with prodigious strength, but Karl saw that he moved more slowly than he once had and there was a stiffness to his walk. He was clearly very well looked after by his sister-in-law Iris, but it saddened Karl when he saw the mortality of the once seemingly superhuman Otto Nadler.

This feeling would not go away and led Karl to think about his own situation. As much as he felt he was doing his bit for the war effort, there was a nagging feeling within him. He was a man caught out by the passage of time. He had been destined for a life of military service, or so he thought. A chance encounter ashore had encouraged him, through the love of Lily, to return to England at the end of his national service. A culmination of fate and circumstances had brought him to be interned during the entire Great War. Now here he was, finally, a British subject, a son already enlisted and preparing to fight for King and Country in North Africa, but he was now too old for enlistment himself. He was a middle-aged man of his time, caught between two warring countries now experiencing another world conflict, but destined not to fire a shot. He felt an enormous sense of helplessness creep over him and pondered this feeling as he sat in his garden.

"Where were you, Lou? You have a faraway look in your eye that I very rarely see." Grace, perceptive as ever, had been watching her husband as he sat there deep in thought.

"It's nothing." Karl shook himself. "Just remembering something from the past."

Grace carried on watching; she had seen this same look once or twice and it worried her.

"Is it time for tea, Grace?"

Grace smiled and stood up. She bent forward and kissed Karl as he sat there. "I will go and make us some now."

Karl found the next few years to be a struggle. His mind was still as active as it ever had been, but the lack of focused activity frustrated him. He felt that everyone around him was fulfilling a more useful role. His daughter had sought his assistance with her and Lothar's situation in America. With their entry into the war in 1941, the United Sates authorities were starting to ask questions about Lothar Jurgen's status in the country. This gave Karl a brief opportunity to feel vital and important as he sought some government assistance from Desmond Morton. Desmond used his influence to ensure that Freya and Lothar were hastily granted American citizenship and that additionally, Lothar was excluded from the draft and also from the prospect of his own internment.

Karl's specialist duties assisting SOE became less frequent and visits to Churchill tailed off as the war raged across the world. He had very little knowledge of the whereabouts of his son James. He knew he had fought right through the North Africa campaign and then been despatched with his battalion to Malta as part of the defence of the island. Letters tended to arrive such a long time after they had been written, that Karl wondered if his son had moved on to some new theatre of war by the time he was reading of his exploits in Africa and on the small Mediterranean island.

As the tide of the war began to turn against Germany, so Karl began to return to his more optimistic and determined self. He wrote and received long letters from his youngest son, David, now happily attending a school in the Leicester area. It gave Karl an opportunity to develop a closeness he had never really had with his younger brother Willy and his family. He knew Willy ran a successful barber's shop and after some persuasion he was delighted when Willy accepted his gift of much-needed funds to expand and update the business. They may have been brothers, but they had never been close. The opportunity to get to know his younger brother was tempered with sadness over the loss of all contact with his elder brother Max. Information regarding Max's situation in Essen was unknown. Karl had tried to use Colonel Z and Stuart Menzies to see if there was any knowledge of him, but such a request was not deemed a priority and they politely declared that they were unable to assist.

By the time Karl received notification that James was now in Holland, the allied forces had landed in Normandy and were moving swiftly across Northern France. The seemingly endless years of conflict that Karl felt he had lived through might actually be coming to an end. Karl celebrated quietly in his garden on VE day, with just a few close friends and neighbours joining them. David had returned home, the years away having turned him into a fine-looking young man of sixteen. Several months passed before James was returned to them also, with a collection of stories to enthral them with. Karl was justly proud of his son, but found it difficult to express it to him. Grace wondered if he might be jealous of his son, who had actually been to war. Karl never expressed an opinion, he just found it difficult to show his feelings in a public way.

One thing that returned to both their lives was a chance to take up golf once again. Grace was still the better player, but Karl applied himself to the challenge and became a reasonable club golfer. He met and became friends with a good number of his fellow members and they quickly formed a small society that got together every Friday. Since the end of the war, Karl had been able to appoint some new managers to take on some of his responsibilities. Grace was pleased that as he celebrated his sixtieth birthday he was beginning to think about taking a more peripheral position within his business empire. He still trusted the drive and vigour of both John Pope and Charles Ebden and was now keen to spend more time with his wife on the golf course and tending his garden. He also broached the subject of retirement for the first time with Grace.

Fulton, Missouri
5th March 1946

"It's black tie tonight, my dear, so wear that beautiful full-length gown I saw you pack," Karl suggested to his wife as they sat in the back of a huge limousine on their way to the hotel.

"Has Mr. Churchill cleared this with the American security people? This does all feel a little bit last minute." Grace sounded rather nervous.

"I spoke with his aide, who said that Winston had discovered we were in New York visiting Freya and asked if we would be able to join him this evening for dinner at Westminster College and that we were to be guests at his speech at the college this afternoon.

"What is President Truman's wife called?" Grace asked.

"Bess. You don't need to be nervous, you look as radiant as ever, my love." Karl stared at his wife, who was now in her early forties.

"Do you have any idea what Mr. Churchill is going to say?"

"I suspect the state of the world since the end of the war and the way that Russia is behaving towards the countries that neighbour it," Karl guessed.

Grace sat next to Karl within the auditorium of the college. They were three rows back from the raised platform of the stage. The dean of the College had introduced the guest speakers one by one, leaving the former British Prime Minister until the end. Churchill rose slowly from his chair and gripped the lectern and surveyed the assembled audience. His familiar low, tremulous voice with the slight lisp began. He delivered a fascinating take on the new order of things since the end of the war. The message was clearly a warning to the western world of the perceived threat from Stalinist Russia, as Churchill saw things.

"From Stettin in the Baltic to Trieste in the Adriatic, an *iron curtain* has descended across the continent. Behind that line lie all the capitals of the ancient states of Central and Eastern Europe – Warsaw, Berlin, Prague, Vienna, Budapest, Belgrade, Bucharest and Sofia. All these famous cities and the populations around them lie in what I must call the Soviet sphere, and are all subject, in one form or another, not only to Soviet influence but to a very high and in some cases increasing measure of control from Moscow..."

He went on to strongly criticise the Soviet Union's exclusive and secretive policies and formation of a state police. He commented on the distrust that was felt by the allied nations towards the Soviet Union after the war. He warned that regions under their control were now expanding their leverage and power without any restriction. He added that in order to put a stop to this ongoing phenomenon, the continued and commanding force and strong unity between the UK and US was necessary.

The speech was warmly received by the audience, but Karl was left with a feeling of trepidation from Churchill's message. The dinner was a quiet affair in the dean's private quarters. Despite the gloom of the message he had delivered, Churchill was charm personified and held court around the small table and kept the group enthralled with tales of his adventurous life. Karl found himself staring in rapt fascination at the man. He saw so much of himself in this plain-spoken, but charismatic former leader.

"Sir, if I may." Karl looked into the rheumy eyes of Churchill. "You truly believe that the Russians pose a threat to our future?"

"History has an ability to repeat itself," Churchill replied. "You and I have both born witness to Germany's past sixty years. Russia, under this Stalinist regime, will follow the same path and we will need all the might of our American allies to balance what will become a stand-off between those countries who possess nuclear weapons."

"And, sir, if I may ask. What of you now? Will you continue as the opposition leader?" Karl was embarrassed by his own question.

"I continue to serve, as long as they will have me. It's all I know, my boy. What of you, Louis? What does the future hold for a businessman such as yourself?" Churchill, quick as a flash, turned the spotlight on Karl.

"Oh! Well, I am seeking to give my managers more control of the day-to-day operations and Grace and I want to spend more time enjoying our time together. That sounds almost selfish compared to the work you continue to do," Karl said quietly.

"Nonsense! You have served throughout your life. You served your country of birth as a well-respected and decorated naval rating. You overcame the harshness of internment, but then took control of your life and built a successful business, that in turn enabled you to be of great service to your adopted country of residence. Your heroic exit from Germany was not without cost to you personally, but still you answered the call and continued to serve. I wanted you here tonight as a chance to actually thank you for your steadfast support of me and Great Britain. Nothing can ever be official. You will have to content yourself with just these few paltry platitudes from me. Our paths may cross again, but I was concerned that I had not had the decency to actually thank you, Louis, just in case they don't." Churchill leant forward and reached out his hand, which Karl took and the two men smiled at each other.

Solihull
August 1948

Karl had begun to organise the packing himself, but then as the magnitude of the undertaking confronted him, he decided to delegate the project to a professional company of removers. He was finally doing what Grace had suggested and retiring from his Midlands-based business empire, leaving the operation in the capable hands of his first wife's brother, John Pope. They were leaving their palatial house in Dove House Lane and moving to a more modest bungalow on the south coast. Grace had grown fond of the area on a couple of visits there and now she had finally been able to persuade Karl to move. The proximity of a new golf club to experience had played its part, as had a private section of beach that was reached through the back garden and then down a residents' only footpath and steps to golden sand.

The move to this enchanting smaller property was going to be for just Karl and Grace. James had virtually finished his degree and had an offer of employment from a mining company in Johannesburg. David had finished school and was just embarking on a job within one of Karl's companies as an office clerk, keen to learn from Karl's great friend John Pope. Iris and Otto had sadly said goodbye to Emma when she took advantage of an invitation from Lothar and Freya to visit them, as they began the next chapter of their lives in California.

About a week after settling into their new home, Karl and Grace were receiving mail forwarded by the post office from their previous address in Solihull. Karl spied an official-looking envelope addressed to David. Thinking it might be important he opened it to find that David had been called up for his national service and was to report to the Royal Artillery Barracks in Woolwich, London on 16th January 1949.

Karl read and re-read the letter several times. He sat in his armchair in his new sitting room, mulling over the irony of his son now having to serve within the British military. It was where Grace found him, when she came through with some curtain material for him to inspect.

"What is it, Lou?" She looked deep into her husband's eyes.

"Your son has been called up for national service. David is to report to a barracks in Woolwich in January. it's just unbelievable! After what this family has given over the years and what lengths I have gone to for the right to be called a British subject, my son now qualifies to eighteen months' compulsory service."

"Does he know?" Grace asked.

"I doubt it. The letter was forwarded from Dove House Lane. He's due to visit us at the weekend."

"Well, you never know, it could be the making of him." Grace clung to a positive outlook about the news, but inside she was not so sure.

"It was to be expected, Father. Several of my school friends have also received letters and at least two of them are going to be attending Woolwich barracks on the same day as me."

Karl looked at his youngest child across the dining table and smiled. "You are not at all worried about this, David? The change to a career within the engineering world? This could upset the path I had in mind for you." Karl rubbed his chin.

"I understand. But maybe this is an opportunity, rather than an impediment to me. I had to helplessly watch James go off to war and serve our country with distinction. What shows more dedication to the country you now call home than serving within its armed forces? I'm keen to face this and put one hundred per cent of myself into making the best of my time within the Royal Artillery Regiment."

Karl looked at his son with a new sense of pride and contentment. His boy reminded him of his own thoughts at that age. Wanting to serve his country of birth. Karl remembered his time in the Imperial German navy and smiled when he thought back to his first meeting with Ziggy on the train from Hamburg to Wilhelmshaven all those years ago.

"Then you go with my blessing and my full support. I will keep a position for you with John Pope, but if you choose a different path then I will understand and support you down that road too." Karl stood and ushered his son to him and they hugged. "Now go and help your mother with the dishes. I suspect your impending military career may not be quite such a joy for her."

Highcliffe-on-Sea
February 1952

"The King has died! My God, he was only fifty-seven. His daughter is now to become the Queen. She is only, what, twenty-five?" Karl was reading aloud from his newspaper, sitting in the beautiful garden of their idyllic house on the south coast of England, situated about eight miles from the town of Bournemouth.

"Are you going to get somebody to cut that hedge, dear? It's out of control, you said you would get it done." The unruly hedge ran around the entire boundary of their sizable garden.

"Leave it to me, Grace, I'll do it," Karl replied soothingly.

"I don't want you to do it. I want you to employ someone to do it, please."

Karl muttered something quietly and returned to his newspaper as Grace took their tea things back indoors.

After finishing the crossword, he put the paper down and contemplated the knotted mass of foliage that was his twelve-foot-high beech hedge. *I can trim that*, he thought to himself. A quick glance to see if he could see where Grace might be and he disappeared into his large workshop-cum-shed and brought out a large wooden stepladder and placed it up against the hedge at the top edge of his garden, right at the back of the garage. He then returned to the shed and selected a large pair of garden shears. Thinking no more about the scale of his enterprise, he scaled the rickety ladder, carrying the rusty shears to one rung from the top, and proceeded to slash and cut away at the offending foliage. As he progressed, he was forced to lean as far as his centre of gravity would allow. He then climbed down the ladder, moved it along and climbed back up to continue. On the third such manoeuvre he saw a particular frond of foliage from the hedge and decided he could just reach it. As he leant out from the ladder, there was an audible creak from the wooden rungs. He pressed on. All of sudden, the ladder tilted, throwing Karl off his perch, and he crashed into an arrangement of flower pots, smashing his head on an earthenware display of fuchsias.

Karl opened his eyes slowly and took in the bright artificial light and the strong antiseptic smell that emanated from his surroundings. As his eyes grew more accustomed to the light he could make out that he was in a small but comfortable room. There was a large window to his left and an armchair in the corner within which sat a very concerned-looking Grace.

"Oh! Lou, how are you feeling? I don't know what you thought you were doing. I told you we should get someone in to cut that hedge. How are you feeling?"

"Where am I? And how long have I been here?" Karl replied.

"You are in Boscombe Hospital and you've been unconscious for a little over twenty-four hours. I'll go and find someone," and with that Grace rose and left the private room.

Karl lifted his right hand to his head and felt a swathe of bandages wrapped around his skull. He also felt some pain in his left leg. He lifted the sheets and saw that his left thigh was also wrapped in a large bandage. The door opened and a tall thin man who Karl estimated to be in his fifties, wearing a white coat, strode in followed by Grace.

"Ah! Mr. Luddolph, it's good to see you awake. I am the consultant surgeon Mr. Ferguson. Let me explain your situation. You took a fall from a step ladder in your garden. In addition to banging your head, causing a concussion, you managed to impale yourself on your shears. You have a nasty tear to the muscle of your left thigh, which is quite deep and has required a number of stitches. We are also concerned about the risk of infection and as a consequence we are going to keep you in for a few days to monitor you."

"Well, that all seems a little unnecessary. Just give me a stick until this stiffness goes away and I'll be fine." Karl was keen to be gone from the hospital.

"We'll see, Mr. Luddolph. I have to be satisfied that the antibiotics have worked and you are free from any infection in that wound. For the moment you are going to stay here." Dr. Ferguson paused. "Is there anything else?"

"No, Doctor, thank you for your opinion." Karl surrendered to his situation and lay his head back down on the pillow.

The consultant smiled down at his patient and left the room.

"I've brought you some magazines and a copy of today's newspaper, dear." Grace bustled forward and lay the literature on the bedside table, next to a jug of water and a bunch of flowers in a vase.

"Thank you, my dear, but please don't fuss. I will be out of here in a couple of days, please let's not make an issue of this." Karl was a little embarrassed about the cause of his predicament and keen to gloss over the incident swiftly.

Grace smiled down at her husband, uncharacteristically subdued. "I understand, dear. Perhaps I can now employ someone to tend to the hedge." She looked hard at Karl and smiled her sweetest smile, causing Karl to break into laughter, and Grace laughed with him.

During the next ten days Karl began to feel strange; his temperature ranged greatly, he was sweating profusely, then shivering with cold. Nurses came and went and changed his bedding and checked his temperature. Dr. Ferguson came and went, checking the wound in his thigh and making a series of tutting noises as he examined Karl. On the eleventh day Karl was so weak he could hardly lift his head off the pillow and his voice had become a faint croak. He could make out the wide-eyed fear in the face of his wife as she fed water to him through a straw.

On one occasion when his wound was being examined before re-dressing he had seen that it was heavily swollen and there were livid red lines above and below the area of the stitches, where the skin was now a dark blue, almost black colour.

Karl was finding it a fight to keep his eyes open on the twelfth day and the room appeared to be changing shape around him as he began to slip out of consciousness. His last vision was of his wife looking over him as he finally gave up the fight and closed his eyes.

The haze of blurred lights slowly came into focus as Karl stared at the ceiling of his hospital room. He attempted to lift his head, but had to content himself with turning it slowly to the side. Out of the corner of his eye, he caught sight of Grace. He could see she had been crying; there was a wetness to her cheeks and her eyes were red and puffy. He tried to speak, but couldn't form the words in his dry throat. He tried again. "Grace?" All he could manage was a slight whisper.

"Oh! Lou, you're back with us." Grace attempted to compose herself and be strong for her husband. "The doctor is here with me; your leg had become seriously infected and they had to operate on you yesterday afternoon…"

"Mr. Luddolph." Dr. Ferguson interrupted his wife as he stood at the end of the bed and moved closer, so that he was in Karl's eye line and looked straight at him. "Mr. Luddolph, you have to understand that we were not able to halt the infection and despite attempting to cut away the infected area, we could not contain the spread. Without the procedure yesterday, I fear we would have lost you. It gives me no pleasure to say this, but all we could do to save your life was to amputate your left leg halfway up your thigh."

There was a silence as Karl rolled his head back to one side to see his wife once more. He contemplated the information he had been given as he looked at the tearful anguish on her face. "Grace, Grace!" he whispered. "You know me well enough to know that I accept this news. If the alternative was to die, then the good doctor here has given me at least a little longer with you."

"Oh! Karl, I really did think I had lost you." Grace moved forward and embraced her stricken husband.

"Not yet, my dear. Now, Dr. Ferguson." Karl turned his attention to the consultant. "What are my options going forward? Have you left me with a sufficient stump to attach some sort of artificial leg?"

"Mr. Luddolph, I would expect to leave you to take in the magnitude of this surgery and talk of such things in the weeks ahead." The surgeon was stunned by the pragmatism of his patient.

"No time to waste in here. I want to enjoy whatever the rest of my life may have to offer. I will adapt to losing a leg and try and live as normal a life as possible. What I now expect from you is a discussion of what we can do to achieve this as quickly as possible please," Karl said politely.

"All right, sir. We will start by letting the stump heal and ensure it is strong enough to take a prosthetic leg. Once we can attach a leg, then we will literally teach you to walk again and understand the power you have left in your stump, to propel yourself around," the surgeon explained.

"How long will this take?" Karl asked.

"Usually three to six months, but I can see you are going to be an impatient patient, so I expect that that time could be a bit shorter." The doctor smiled.

"Too right, and I take it I have to be incarcerated in here for the duration?"

"Well, once we get the stump nicely healed and strong, we can release you into the hands of our rehabilitation centre in the New Forest, where they will teach you how to walk unaided, or at least with minimal use of a stick," the surgeon offered.

"No stick, thank you! I can't play golf or drive a car if I need a stick, eh Doctor?" Karl smiled up at his surgeon.

Grace had to take the full force and ferocity of Karl's impatience as he waited in the hospital bed for his wound to heal sufficiently. She had to contact the family and ask that they refrain from visiting, on the express orders of her husband.

"The last thing I want is a hoard of family and friends standing around my bed, trying to look sympathetic, as I recover. Please make them understand that I will be back home in good time and that I will be back to my old self within months. I heard you whispering to a nurse about Freya flying over to see us from America. Please, Grace, stop her. As much as it would fill me with delight to see my daughter, now is not the time and certainly not the place."

"As you wish, my dear." Grace nodded and then made mental calculations as to just how many relatives and friends she was now going to have to contact to stop them coming.

Once Karl was moved to the rehabilitation centre, he took full control of his recovery. He harangued and argued with the staff at every turn. He forced them to allow him to practise much longer than any of the other amputees. He found the use of the prosthetic leg both difficult and painful. His stump became raw and bled most days, but he never let up. He learned how to stand from a chair unaided. He was able to walk forward and perform turns to the left and right. He was able to sit down again. Grace made a mental note of the need to reinforce their armchairs at home, the way Karl now crashed into a sitting position. He never stopped questioning the staff. He asked about driving and realised that he would have to adapt a vehicle to hand controls for changing gear. Grace brought a driver from his golf bag and he spent an afternoon practising his swing. He soon understood that his stance would have to change, to ensure his balance and weight distribution kept him upright. After two or three hours, with Grace constantly worrying that he was pushing himself too hard, he reckoned he could strike a ball satisfactorily.

Karl returned home a little over four months from when his leg had been amputated, a new record according to the staff at the rehabilitation centre. Karl walked unaided from the taxi into his house in Highcliffe. Grace had learnt to give her husband space and not to fuss around him. There had been many occasions during the lessons with his new leg that he had fallen and banged his head, arms and shoulders – just about every part of him in his determination to master walking again. Grace, for her part, had removed some items of furniture from their home to provide more space and fewer obstacles for Karl to crash into. She had arranged the garden furniture on the terrace so that Karl could sit out in the garden on his first afternoon at home since the accident. She kept her distance as Karl negotiated the French windows from the lounge out onto their terrace. He sat down heavily in a deep outdoor armchair and wiped his brow.

"Would you care for some tea, dear?" Grace suggested.

"That would be perfect, thank you," Karl said, and she disappeared back indoors.

Karl looked out into his garden and contemplated the scene. *That bloody hedge still needs cutting*, he thought as he surveyed the unruly foliage border.

Rothesay Drive, Highcliffe-on-Sea
July 1955

"When will he be back, Grace?" Freya asked her stepmother.

"He is playing in a fourball at the golf club and the others in the four know to get him back here for 3 p.m., so we have a couple of hours to get the place ready," Grace smiled back at Freya.

"This really is a beautiful place you've found," Freya remarked, looking out at the splendour of the large well-tended garden.

"You know, I thought after his leg, he would have been keen to employ a gardener, but he won't have it. He insists on doing all the planting and cutting and tending to the array of plants he's brought into the garden. He still works too hard and every so often I catch him trying to climb that ladder. Last week he finally relented and let me arrange for someone to come and tidy the hedge around the garden. It's the first time he's allowed anyone else to work here." Grace was proud of her small victory.

"Mummy, can I have something to drink please?" A strikingly blond, young child of about seven had marched into the kitchen, where Grace and Freya were talking.

"Oh! Yes, Karl, you must ask your Grandma Grace." Freya looked towards her stepmother.

"What would you like, young man?" Grace asked the confident little boy who was a miniature replica of his father Lothar.

"May I have some water, please?"

Grace smiled and filled a glass with chilled water from a jug in the fridge and handed it to the youngster. "There you are, Karl," and the boy smiled.

"Thank you, Grandma," and with that he was gone.

"He is a fine boy and so tanned. I take it you're thriving in Los Angeles since you moved there?" Grace asked Freya.

"Oh, you must come and see us. The weather is glorious and Lothar is doing such a wonderful job with the new studio. We are just beginning to attract some of the famous people, keen to try anything new really. Joseph was so kind to take on Lothar and to allow him to develop a new studio on the west coast."

"Hello, has anyone seen Grace?" came a voice from the garden.

Grace and Freya rushed through the lounge and out into the garden from the terrace to see a smartly dressed and very tanned man standing on the grass, holding hands with a stunningly attractive girl.

"James, oh James, it's wonderful to see you," and Freya rushed forward to embrace her younger brother.

"Freya, Grace, I would like you to meet my wife, Alice. She's from Cape Town and this is the first time she has left South Africa."

"I'm delighted to meet you, Grace," and Alice stepped forward and handed Grace a small but elegantly beautiful bunch of flowers.

"Alice, how did my boring brother manage to catch you?" Freya laughed and punched her brother's arm.

"He was the most charming man I have ever met and took forever to ask me out." Alice laughed too as she embraced both Freya and Grace.

"Grace, this is the most wonderful idea. Who else is coming?" Freya asked eagerly.

"Well, David has promised to be here. He's driving from Larkhill near Salisbury. It will be the first time anyone will have seen their first child and only the second time I've met his wife Anne," Grace indicated. "It is wonderful they are now so close."

"Anyone else we know?"

"I hope Otto is able to travel. He is quite weak now and rarely ventures out according to Iris, but when she mentioned the party to him he said he wanted to be here."

Suddenly a tall, fit-looking man with a shock of blond hair bounded up to the group, with his son, Karl, in tow. "Good afternoon, I have just seen my sister arriving with her fiancé. I will go and fetch her," and he just as promptly disappeared.

"Emma too! Grace, you really have outdone yourself. What about Dad's brothers?" Freya continued to enquire.

"You know that Max was killed in the war, but his son, Maximillian, did answer my letter and he said he would try. His mother is too weak to travel. Willy has been in regular contact since I mentioned the idea and I expect him anytime now, bringing as many of his own family as he said he could muster." Grace laughed. "There is one other special guest, but it's a surprise and I think I will just keep it that way." She smiled briefly. "Now I must get the rest of the food prepared. Would anyone care to help?" she added knowingly.

"Lead the way, my dear mother," and Freya took Grace by the arm.

"That is the first time you have ever called me Mother," Grace whispered quietly.

"And I assure you it will not be the last," Freya replied as they walked back into the house.

Karl wouldn't have minded another drink in the golf club bar before returning home, but his fellow golfers had all made various excuses. Even George Withers, his lift for the day, had suggested that he needed to get home so Karl accepted the decision and adjusted his prosthetic leg as he got into the front of his friend's car.

"You make that look remarkably easy," George commented as he watched Karl sit in the passenger seat.

"It took some getting used to, but like golf, with time and practice, you get the hang of it," Karl smiled at his friend.

"Don't we know it? Your handicap needs some consideration by the secretary, the way you fleeced us all today," George said laughing.

"It aches from time to time and I do rub the stump raw from trying to do too much, but not a word to Grace please or I will be confined to the garden." Karl looked seriously at George as he reversed the car out of the parking space and drove out onto the Lymington Road.

"Very kind of you to run me home, George. I still can't find a car capable of being converted to either hand controls or one with an automatic way of changing gear. I'm sure I will find one soon, but in the meantime, thank you, my friend."

"It's not a problem. You only live two minutes from the course and it's on my way home so it's my pleasure, Lou." George kept a straight face as he turned almost immediately into Rothesay Drive and then left in front of the old castle and down to where Karl lived.

Karl was now so used to being called Louis or Lou, that he almost never used or heard his real name.

Karl spotted several unfamiliar cars as he extricated himself from George's passenger seat. "Uh oh! Looks like we have visitors, George, but please come in and have a drink before you go," Karl offered.

"I would be delighted." George stood back as Karl negotiated the driveway, knowing better than to offer to assist.

Karl put his key in the door and opened it.

"Hello, Dad!" Karl stared straight into the eyes of his

beloved first wife Lily and momentarily lost his stability and had to grab onto the wall to steady himself.

"My God! Lily," was all he could mutter as his voice gave way and his emotions overtook him and tears began to stream down his face.

"Dad, oh Dad! It's me, Freya. We've come to surprise you for your birthday. Everyone is here, please, Dad, don't cry. Come and see who's in the garden. Willy is here, even Otto and Iris are here."

"It was the shock, my dear Freya, you look just like your mother and for a moment there I was back in Plymouth where we first met." Karl tried to recover himself as Freya led him through to the garden.

It was a whirlwind of emotion for Karl as he greeted his many friends and relatives. He had found it difficult to move around the garden, until Grace insisted that he sit down and then people could come to him. "You make me feel like a grand emperor, Grace," he whispered to his wife as she helped him into a chair at the edge of the patio.

Karl was overwhelmed by the abundance of good wishes and real love he felt from those gathered in his garden. He smiled as he caught sight of Otto, still using the stick Karl gave him all those years ago, and he shuffled amongst Karl's relatives, Iris in close attendance. He stood to embrace his younger brother, Willy, and was introduced to his entire family. A rather awkward-looking young man stood stiffly in front of Karl and after introducing himself as Max's son Maximillian, they had a wonderful conversation reminiscing about the young man's father and his Uncle Karl.

Karl was just watching Otto light his favourite pipe when Grace came up to him.

"I never thought he would come, but I've left him in the lounge before I bring him out into the garden," she said.

"Well, whoever it is, get him out here," Karl implored.

Suddenly a hush fell amongst the group of people gathered in the garden, as a hunched and bent figure walked slowly out onto the patio. He was in an unfamiliar light-coloured suit, but he was still unmistakeable all the same.

The people just stared in quiet surprise as he approached Karl, who was struggling to get to his feet.

"Sir, I, well, I am delighted to see you," Karl stumbled through his words.

"Sit down, Louis, it is I who am delighted to see you," and they shook hands.

Churchill looked frail, but the voice still had the same comfortable note to it.

"Ladies and gentlemen, I don't wish to interrupt proceedings, but I was keen to visit my good friend Louis here and wish him a very happy seventieth birthday. His wife Grace was kind enough to extend an invitation and as I am no longer confined with affairs of state, I simply had nothing more pressing to prevent me attending. As I drove into the road I caught sight of the old castle that bears the name of the town here. Did you know that Kaiser Wilhelm stayed there for a few weeks in 1907? I believe he was convalescing from some ailment that had befallen him. It was about this time that young Louis here had just finished his national service with the Imperial German navy. I believe you met the Kaiser, Louis?" Churchill smiled at Karl.

"I did indeed, sir, at a summer event in Norway."

"Well, it got me thinking, ladies and gentlemen. Louis never really took sides. He followed wherever his life took him. He often found himself at odds with his homeland, through no fault of his own, but simply through the vagaries of this century's political landscape. Despite all of the things he has had to endure, he never gave up, he never faltered in making a better life for his family and himself. One day Louis will tell you all of the friendship and support he gave me when

I needed allies more than ever. He is a modest and quiet man, but he has led an exemplary life to this point and it is my wish that he continues to do so for many years to come. Ladies and gentlemen, I would like to wish this fine and honourable man the happiest of birthdays. What do you say to that?" Churchill looked out into the garden.

Loud cheering and applause suddenly filled the garden as Churchill again shook Karl's hand.

"Will you stay, sir?" Karl asked.

"My dear chap, the last thing you want is for some past-it politician sullying your gathering. No, I will take my leave. You must come up to Chartwell, don't be a stranger," and with that Churchill turned and walked from the party, applause and cheering ringing in his ears.

The many well-wishers and guests now all descended on Karl, wanting to know all about the surprise appearance of Winston Churchill at his seventieth birthday. Karl shooed them away.

"Enough questions today, he is a friend and came to wish me a happy birthday, no more no less, now please can I enjoy my party?" Karl smiled. The gathered people reluctantly moved back and gradually the party continued, with food being brought out along with a good deal of wine and beer to drink.

Karl was able to retake his seat and watched as the guests all enjoyed the fine food and drink. No one noticed when Karl may have momentarily closed his eyes.

"Are you my grandfather?" Karl opened one eye, to see a blond-haired angelic-faced little boy staring at him.

"It's rude to stare. Has anyone ever told you that?" Karl quipped.

"My mother says that to me too," the little boy confided.

"Well, your mother is wise."

"I am nearly seven years old, Grandpa," the child offered.

"And I am ten times that age, young man," Karl laughed.

"My father says that you were great friends with his father. Is that true?" the boy asked.

"You father's father was called Ziggy and he was my best friend. We had many adventures at sea together when we were both in the navy," Karl told his grandson.

"I like the sea, we can see it from my bedroom window at home," the boy said.

"Well, would you like to come and see a sandy beach now?" Karl was suddenly keen to have some space.

"Oh, yes, Grandpa, is it far?" the boy asked.

"No, not far. There is a secret path by the castle that leads to it."

Karl stood slowly and had a quick look around, but no one seemed to notice.

"Come on then," and Karl held out his hand and they began to walk from the garden, Karl taking it steadily on the uneven path. A large old-fashioned pram was parked on the path in the shade. Karl leaned in to see the child asleep within.

"Do you know who this is, young man?" Karl asked his young companion.

"No, sir," the polite young child replied.

"This is my youngest son David's first child, his name Ralph. Shall we take him on our walk to the beach?" Karl thought that the pram would provide some welcome support for him over the path to the beach.

"Oh yes, Grandpa," Karl Jr. said.

"And where are you all off too?" Freya stood behind them, hands on her hips.

"I thought I would take them down to the beach. Could you tell Anne please? We won't be long." Karl smiled at his beautiful daughter.

Freya smiled back. Then quick as a flash she held up a small new-fangled camera.

"Smile then please!" and she took their picture. "Have a lovely walk. I'll let David and Anne know you have stolen their baby. Be good for your grandfather, Karl," and with that she was gone.

As they walked through the trees Karl turned to the young child.

"Did your mother ever tell you what my name was?" Karl asked.

"She told me that you are called Louis and almost everyone calls you Lou," the boy explained.

"Well, let me tell you a secret. My real name is Karl," and Karl smiled.

"That's my name too," the boy cried out excitedly.

Karl laughed too. "I know!"

It had taken almost three years of requests and form-filling, but it would appear that Graham was going to finally get some answers. As he walked along Burlington Avenue in Kew towards his destination he recalled how difficult it had been to get to this stage of his investigations. There had been a peremptory two-line email declining his query to have his grandfather's sealed records opened. They had been classified and were not to be opened until 2050.

He sought leave to appeal and after two years, permission was granted for the files to be unsealed, but Graham would have to attend in person as the files would not be uploaded to the National Archives website. Another year passed before Graham was in a position to apply to visit the Archives at Kew.

After some rigorous security checks and further form-filling, Graham arrived at the modern grey building that housed the National Archives, armed with his reader's ticket. Once inside, after completing more security checks he was finally ushered into the large, air-conditioned reading room. Some paper and a pencil were on his numbered desk. Having read the briefing pack before attending he picked up some foam wedges to protect the spines of any ancient books, some weighted cloth strings to hold pages open and finally a pair of pristine white cotton gloves. His application had requested three files: two from the Home Office and one from the Foreign and

Commonwealth Office. These files were placed in a storage locker just outside the reading room. He remembered as he opened the locker that he was only allowed to take one file at a time into the reading room.

Graham returned to his allocated desk and opened the first folder. It contained a musty-smelling ledger.

These are the originals, Graham thought as he looked at the neatly bound sheets of paper cataloguing in alphabetical order German immigrants who had been detained and interned from 1914. Graham was shocked by some of the caustic and dismissive notes on the front of some of the individual documents.

"Application to return home – denied – HB"

"Complaint about conditions at Knockaloe camp – This subject has complained before. Can we please sift out the frequent complainers – HB"

"Application to return to Germany with his family – Denied – They are interned for a reason! – HB"

This HB sounds a pretty officious bloke, Graham thought.

He turned to the L's: Luddolph. Karl L and Max A.

```
Detained and transferred to Lancaster Camp June
1915. Request to emigrate to the USA received.
```

Then a letter supporting the application from the US government.

A polite letter in reply denying the request from the Home Office.

So, he tried to leave. He tried to get to America with his brother. They denied him permission to leave and instead imprisoned him for the entire war. Graham shook his head as he made notes on the paper next to the old ledger.

The second folder also contained an old ledger. This one contained a series of people granted naturalisation certificates, all neatly stamped by the Home Office.

Graham gently turned the pages until he found the entry for Louis Luddolph. Certificate of Naturalisation granted, dated 1936.

1936! It took over thirty years living here before they gave him his citizenship. Graham was becoming angry as he began to realise the time it had taken for his grandfather to be recognised as British.

The final folder contained a buff-coloured cardboard file tied with a red ribbon. It was creased and faded, with numerous scribbled entries on the cover. Everything was of secondary notice to Graham, due to the large red stamp on the cover, marking the file as sealed until 2050.

Graham found it difficult to read the notes on the cover and gingerly opened the file. On the inside of the cover was a handwritten note:

```
To MI5. One for you. He might be what
you are looking for. AJ
```

On top of an assortment of papers was a typed letter:

```
Have seen your comment
We will take this file

Z
MI5
```

Graham sat back in his chair. "Bloody hell," he whispered quietly to himself.

After a short time, he adjusted his seat and continued to read the file...

Appendix

Prince Louis and Princess Victoria had been friends since childhood and were first cousins, once removed. They had four children. The eldest, Princess Alice, married Prince Andrew of Greece and Denmark in 1903 and one of their children was Prince Phillip, who went on to become Queen Elizabeth II's husband, the Duke of Edinburgh. Prince Louis of Battenberg was forced to resign, as anti-German sentiment began to proliferate in British society in the run-up to World War I. He anglicised his name to Mountbatten and lived out the war in private on the Isle of Wight. His youngest son, Louis, would go on to become the Right Honourable the Earl Mountbatten of Burma KG GCB OM GCSI GCIE GCVO DSO ADC PC FRS, the chief of the defence staff.

Acknowledgements

When I embarked on writing this, my second novel, it required a good deal of research and questions to a number of people. When I set out to write a story based on the life of one of my ancestors I was keen to find as much detail as possible. But when you are yourself fifty-seven and the subject of your research died when you were a baby, it becomes more difficult. Those who knew him directly, like his second wife and my own mother, have both sadly passed away. If you ever find yourself wanting to know information about the origins of your family, then I would recommend you begin to ask pertinent questions at a much younger age and secure various photographs and memorabilia, which may pay dividends when you want to put someone's life together.

As has been the case since the beginning of my writing, my wife Paula has been my rock and sounding board at every stage of the production and publication of my work. As I forge ahead with working on my next project it is always with the heartening knowledge that my wife is totally behind me and actively supporting my endeavours. To you, my love, there are no more words. You know the immense part you play in my embryonic writing journey.

The National Archives at Kew was a very useful and interesting starting point. My grandfather, Karl, was recorded in several files. The earliest and slightly peremptory entry was from the Home Office regarding his incarceration in a prisoner of war camp on the Isle of Man during the First World War.

The refusal by the Home Office to allow both my grandfather and his elder brother, Max, to travel to the United States was easy to see. The third and final file had originally been marked as sealed until 2050. An earlier request by myself had allowed the file to be viewed. It dealt mainly with my grandfather's attempts at gaining his British citizenship. A cryptic and mysteriously vague letter sent to MI5, and their equally brief reply, was atop the sheets of paper making up the file. The bulk of the file dealt with my grandfather's handwritten application for naturalisation, written in the 1930s. I marvelled at his tenacity to still be chasing this status, having first arrived on these shores in the 1890s and having married an English lady who bore him two children and was now married a second time to Grace, my grandmother.

Using a timeline, I was able to establish that Karl lost his first wife to illness in the 1920s and very quickly married his second wife. The naturalisation was the only tangible documentation available to me at the Archives. Another possibility was any records of his time interned on the Isle of Man. There were some brief entries at the Archive at Kew, clearly showing that after arrest both Karl and his brother were taken first to the camp created in Lancaster. It was then I stumbled across a charitable organisation that were trying to collate information about the huge number of prisoners held at Knockaloe on the Isle of Man. The majority of the records were destroyed and the physical evidence of the camp has long disappeared. But with the incredibly warm and heartening help of Alison Jones at the Knockaloe Charitable Trust I was able to place both my grandfather and his brother in the camp. I was also able to discover that their younger brother Willy was most likely at a camp elsewhere, possibly Alexandra Palace for a while. My great-grandfather, Albert, was also caught up in the detention and moved around various camps in the north of England. There was evidence showing his various illnesses treated at

Leeds Hospital and detention in Wakefield internment camp. The trust continues to do great work in uncovering this poorly documented area of British History.

While researching our family tree on one of the various sites available, I was lucky enough to come into contact with Amanda Gould. She turned out to be a great-granddaughter of the aforementioned Willy, Karl's younger brother. Thank you, Amanda, for your support and virtual friendship this past year.

My elder brother, Richard, was able to give me a glimpse at the nature of the man Karl in reality, a strict and domineering man, who was in charge wherever he was. He was also a quiet and reserved man, perhaps weary of the life he had lived.

Karl, or as everyone knew him, Louis or Lou, sadly died when I was only three. But he leaves us with our unique, slightly anglicised surname and also for me one of my middle names: Louis.

The idea of the story is very much the story of my grandfather's life. But I decided at an early stage to make the detail of the story a fiction. I created fictional characters to weave into the fabric of the family that existed. I also used real people of the time to blend into the fictional story along with the real family and those additionally created characters. I found the challenge to blend real events with fictional people and using real people in the narrative to be both enjoyable and educational. I learned a great deal about several periods of history I was not familiar with.

Very few real places used in the story still exist today. One that does is the old wagon works factory on the outskirts of Lancaster. A brief visit showed the central clock tower as familiar today as in the black and white photographs of Lancashire Regiment soldiers marching off to war in 1914. It felt both real and rewarding to stand in the footsteps of my grandfather.

Robert Graves did spend time as a guard at the Lancaster camp and his subsequent book, *Goodbye to All That*, did include some detail of the poor living conditions endured by the internees at the makeshift camp. More recorded media archives also went into detail about some of the lapses in discipline within the camp and at the time, unsavoury behaviour of locals, clearly desperate for money while their husbands were away fighting. This led to a premature closing of the camp. But by the time this happened the Knockaloe camp on the Isle of Man was open and I would suggest that the camp at Lancaster would have closed anyway.

I was lucky enough to find a friend in the form of Iain Franklin. He showed an interest in my first published work and as a consequence, I found he was receptive to having a read-through of this, my second story. Iain, I thank you for your time, understanding and willingness to become part of the process. I very much look forward to our continued relationship.

Stories of family are rarely an easy exercise and this one was no different. I realised that there is a responsibility that comes with the process. You want to get it right, but have so many blank spaces that need to be filled. To those in my family, I hope you will forgive my licence to produce a flowing story and the opportunity to add flesh to the skeleton of what we knew about Karl Louis.

So, thanks finally to Karl. For the life you led and the way you lived it. I never knew you; but I am proud as one of your grandchildren to have had the opportunity to write down some of what you went through.

Guy Robin
May 2023

About the Author

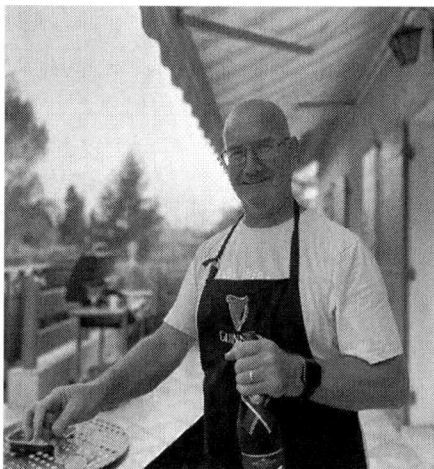

Guy grew up on the South coast of England, near Bournemouth. He lost his father when he was five and was brought up by his mother, who then secured his education at Reeds School in Surrey. At 21 he joined the Metropolitan Police Service, serving for 30 years in a variety of roles and departments, but regards his time at Battersea Police Station to have been his most enjoyable time in the Job!

Since retirement Guy had worked as a document collection and statement taking agent. He has been a driver for several driving agencies and private clients. Guy is married to Paula and after having lived in Sussex for many years they decided to embark on a new challenge in 2023. In July of that year they moved to a small village in the Dordogne, France.

The time is now spent between tending their large garden, supporting Paula's continued business interests and finding time for Guy to continue his writing.

Guy's interests are many and varied. He played hockey for many years for the Police and then for Crowborough Hockey club, where he met Paula. Guy enjoys the outdoors, particularly walking great distances across the South Downs and now the numerous bouclé's in France. He collects stamps and Scottish Malt whisky. He is a keen motorcyclist, and it is easy to now tear around the highways and byways of Europe. Guy has more work in the pipeline and he continues with his writing as a pleasurable and cathartic hobby.

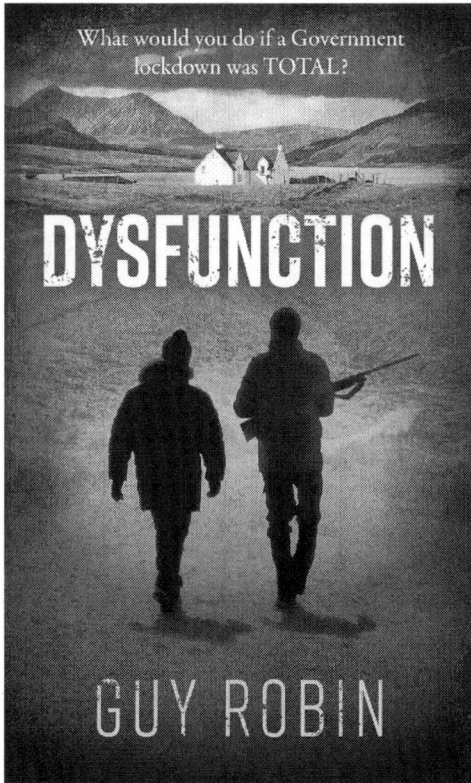

Printed in Great Britain
by Amazon